*This book is dedicated to
Jennifer, Charlotte and Ollie,
and all who helped Mayo along the way*

Andy

– Lessons Learned in Pursuit of Glory

Andy Moran

with Colin Sheridan

Andy – Lessons Learned in Pursuit of Glory

Andy Moran
with Colin Sheridan

Published in Ireland in 2021 by

Mayo Books Press
Castlebar, County Mayo

Edited by
Liam Horan

Design and layout by
SiobhanFoody.com

ISBN: 978-1-914596-01-8 (main edition)
ISBN: 978-1-914596-02-5 (limited edition)

CONTENTS

By Niamh Fitzpatrick

During my 30 years as a psychologist, I've learned much about the capacity of the human spirit. Key among those learnings is that we're capable of *so* much more than we believe. When the Mayo senior football manager, Stephen Rochford, approached me in the spring of 2017 with a view to working with his squad it was clear that he held his players in high regard. Without a flinch, he backed them. He had a solid belief in their footballing skill set. I was impressed by Stephen. I liked his thorough, detailed and considered approach. I thought he had an exciting football mind and an abundance of courage. And I admired his vision, so I said 'yes' to the role. Among other things, my job would be to help ensure that these players believed in themselves as much as he believed in them.

I love sport. I have a particular *grá* for Gaelic sports. Parish against parish, county against county. I love the rawness of it all. A game wrapped up in layers of history, tradition and passion. Generations of togetherness. The weekly ritual of families and communities pouring colourfully into the stands in support of sons and daughters of the locality, heart-swelling pride in their jersey. It feels tribal. I love the quiet joy expressed by players when they're selected for their county, the honour they feel at representing *their* people. Bittersweet feelings sometimes, because that joy can come with a weight of expectation, a pressure to do well, to not let anyone down. It's fair to say that my love of sport comes from the perspective of being captivated by the human experience of it all more than from being a diehard follower of any particular team.

So, it came to be therefore that when I first met Andy at one of my first sessions with the Mayo squad and I plucked him from the player group to help me with an exercise, I didn't recognise him. I had to ask him his name. In all honesty, I was probably the only person standing on Mayo soil who wouldn't have recognised Andy Moran! We didn't know anything about one another then but none of us in the room that day could have imagined the depths of the journey we would soon travel together in that summer of 2017. How we would be richly, authentically and profoundly impacted by our influence on one another in ways that go far beyond sport.

Because competitive sport isn't only about winning or losing. It's about facing your deep-down fears. Publicly and repeatedly. Am I good enough? Are we good enough? Can we carry the weight of expectation held by an army of the loudest, proudest and most fervent supporters ravenous for success after decades of deprivation? Can we empty the tanks, play without shackles, do *everything* we can possibly do – on every day that we're asked? Committing fully, pushing ourselves again and again, no hesitation, no reservation. Baring our souls, risking reputation and ego. Can we weather the inevitable barrage of criticism levelled at us by those observing our efforts? Can we have the courage to pick ourselves up and go again when we make errors on the field, big or small? Can we navigate our differences and work as one? Supporting, encouraging, forgiving mistakes and putting 'we' before 'me'? Can we consistently do those tedious, tiresome tasks which form the bedrock of optimum performance? Can we handle it if we put our whole selves on the line and yet still fail? Can we handle it if we succeed? When this is all over, will we be able to look ourselves in the mirror and live with the reflection looking back?

My work around the psychology of performance involves guiding a squad through all the above and more. Supporting and facilitating the individual and collective reach for optimum performance. My experience with Mayo in 2017 is that the entire squad pushed aside whatever scepticism they (undoubtedly) held and embraced the work we did. I admired these young men for they steadfastly refused to be defined by past losses and instead resolutely pursued their deep-seated drive to be the very best they could be and to see where that could take them.

On a personal level, I felt an immense gratitude to the people of Mayo for how they had helped my family that year during our time of need. My sister, Captain Dara Fitzpatrick, was one of four crew members who died when Irish Coast Guard helicopter Rescue 116 crashed off the Mayo coast early on the morning of 14 March 2017, while out on a mission. For my family, life as we knew it ended that day. In our darkest hours, the people of Mayo showed us immeasurable warmth, love and support. I will never forget that compassion and kindness. I wanted to give something back to the people of Mayo and it very much felt therefore that the Mayo footballers and I were meant to be together on this journey.

I pushed myself to my very limits and I asked of them the same. They responded unanimously and produced some powerful performances. I'm honoured to have been part of the backroom team for this group and that summer sits among my proudest work and is one of my all-time favourite personal life experiences. It felt special even at the time: I knew then that the work we were doing was changing us all forever.

Because this was more than sport. It was taking life by the scruff of the neck and *really* living. Not sitting in the shadows, playing it safe, accepting the role of gallant challengers, but daring to go for it, to really believe and to act in line with that belief. Not half-hearted 'we think we can, but we'll hope for the best' stuff, but real, deep-down belief that we were good enough to be the best of the best and to get the job done. Though we did not succeed in lifting the Sam Maguire Cup, having that collective courage as a group to trust one another and take the leap off the cliff in an attempt to soar brings a lifetime of satisfaction. On cold dark November days for the rest of our lives, each person involved that year could say that when it was asked, we did all we could. We left nothing behind. We dared with greatness. What more can you ask?

Andy played a pivotal part in this journey. On that first day, he didn't scoff or roll his eyes at the woman who stood on his turf and asked his name in front of his squad. Rather, he threw himself into the exercise I had selected him to do and he continued to throw himself into our work for 16 weeks until we played the final championship match in Croke Park in September. Walking the walk. Encouraging others to do the same by his word and his deed. Getting on board. Showing up. Being a team player in the truest sense of the word.

Whatever internal reservations he might have had, I found Andy to be open-minded right from the beginning. Now don't get me wrong, Andy Moran knows his own mind and he holds and expresses his opinions strongly! But some things are not mutually exclusive and as well as letting his feelings be known, he exhibited the admirable traits of interest, curiosity and the capacity to reflect. No better man to bring a challenge, he was also open to being challenged. He listened, engaged and committed fully to the process of what we were about as a squad. He gave to all of us, and he learned from all of us. Was he always like that as a player and as a person? I've only known him a few years, but I don't imagine so for none of us tend to be born so balanced. But Andy has grown and learned throughout life and by the time we met I think he had hit that sweet spot between experience and attitude. He was just ready to learn some more.

Andy showed particular courage in his approach to football that year. He was coming towards the end of his playing career so it would have been both easy and understandable if he had played it safe, content to simply be within the set-up, to make up the numbers. But Andy Moran doesn't do safe. Rather, he does ambition, excellence and possibility. In his latter days as a player, he had the audacity to demand more of himself than his body might have felt he had any right to ask. But he was justified in that approach, and he was right to back himself because he delivered to such a magnificent level that 2017 saw him named Footballer of the Year for the first time, aged 34. Now that's a measure of a man whose reflections and words are well worth reading.

In writing this foreword for Andy, I am conscious of the fact that his story does not stand alone but is entwined with the story of 40 others who togged out for Mayo that summer. Andy was one individual within the collective and, like everyone else involved, he got the balance just right. The individual needs the collective; the collective needs the individual. You need to be totally focused on yourself and on the team, contradictory though that may sound. That summer, everyone involved got this incredibly delicate balancing act just right too. As an experienced and highly decorated player, Andy set a great example and made an enormous contribution to the team while also improving himself as a footballer.

Andy, many congratulations and warmest wishes for the success of this book.

And reader, you're in for a treat.

– **Niamh Fitzpatrick**, *Psychologist*

Sport Teaches All of Us

FOR all the countless minutes, hours, days, months and years I have spent thinking about football, I have never considered one of them a waste of time. That is not to say I am obsessed – sport is certainly not *all* I think about – but it has guided me on how I live as a husband and father, a businessman, a friend and a fan.

I hope and expect that it will guide me too as a coach. The lessons I have learned from all the hours being around Gaelic football have influenced every aspect of my life. We may not have won an All-Ireland in my time, but far from there being any personal resentment or bitterness about that, I count myself extremely fortunate. Football has moulded me. The people I met in dressing rooms and dugouts influenced me more than I ever could've imagined when I started out. The experiences I played through, winning so often and losing so dramatically, are the reasons I am the way I am today, for better or worse.

Sport teaches all of us so much: how to work in a team, how to communicate and how to handle triumph and loss. We learn about taking responsibility and about duty to others. It promotes health and wellbeing. It teaches us the importance of fitness and diet. The list of how it improves our lives on even the most basic levels is endless. I often contemplate a simple question: what was the greatest lesson sport taught me? There are so many but understanding a life without privilege is perhaps the one that endures. I saw so many footballers more talented than me, and I saw them suffer the same way I did. The same way we all do: suffer in training, suffer for confidence and suffer in their personal lives. Sport gives nobody an easy ride, and yet, we all love it. The pain of a yo-yo test; the gut-wrenching anxiety of team selection – nobody is immune, from team captain to new kid on the block. Accepting and embracing the pain of it all has been the great leveller for me. The lessons it can teach young people are infinite.

That is, if they'll listen.

I didn't always listen. Rather, I often only heard what I wanted to hear. Feeling hard done by is a common trait in a teenager. That was me. If I wasn't selected or if I was taken off – in my mind, the fault never lay with me. It was with the coach, or it was with my teammates, or it was with the whole goddam world. For quite a while, as a kid evolving from boy to man, I felt only the privilege of playing sport, little of the hardship and none of the responsibility. That would all reveal itself through the people I was lucky enough to come to know, who mentored me and showed me the error of my ways. To have a coach or a teacher who talks to you with honesty in the proper manner can be life-changing, especially for a young adult. To that end, I got lucky more than once.

Being from Mayo, luck is something on which we can sometimes fixate: the luck of a bouncing ball, of a freak own goal or a bad injury or decision. Talk of luck – the bad kind mostly – can be heard all winter long on high stools and church pews but, when I reflect on my time playing, I think only of the good kind. How lucky was I to share dressing rooms with people like John O'Mahony, Karl Lacey and Cillian O'Connor? How lucky I was to play football for almost two decades for a team I love. How lucky am I that after all of it I still love the game?

Luck is only part of it, though. And this is not a book about luck. It's a book about people and the lessons I've learned. I have finished playing. I haven't finished learning.

I hope by telling my story through some of the people who inspired me, I can tap into what is so special about Mayo football. I never felt anything other than pride in pulling on the green and red jersey. No torture. No misery. Just pride. We should all count ourselves blessed that the journey we travel together is one that sets us apart as people. It's a journey I have loved reflecting on, and one that will continue long beyond the winning or the losing of a single game.

ONE

Key Influences

'Children are great imitators,
so give them something great to imitate.'

– Anonymous

BALLAGHADERREEN, my home, is a funny little town. The parish of Ballagh' crosses into Mayo and Sligo but the town itself lies four miles inside the county of Roscommon. We live in Roscommon, go to school in Roscommon, shop in Roscommon, yet we play all our football in Mayo, an anomaly as old as the GAA itself. This quirk of administrative fate did not just affect me in a footballing sense, it subconsciously afflicted my personality: I grew up seeing myself as something of an outsider both in the county of Roscommon where I lived and the county to which I pledged my footballing allegiance, Mayo. The dynamic had its invisible perks. As a teenager, it gave me a healthy chip on my shoulder – a cause to fight and a system to prove wrong. Conversely, it often made me, and many of my peers, lazy, as our imposter syndrome became an excuse, a crutch to lean on when we weren't being selected for county teams. In Roscommon we were viewed one way, in Mayo another. Always hard done by, we often felt ignored because of our outlier status. It never occurred to us it might be down to our lack of talent and effort. We were, in our own jaundiced minds, branded. This persecution complex was particularly fertile in the insecurity of our teenage

years: "why does no one take us seriously?" I now understand this is the common refrain of a vulnerable teenage
mind but, in my formative years, we conveniently had our
answer: we were from Ballaghaderreen.

If I were prone to indulging in self-pity, I wasn't licking
it from the ground. Like many parents, my mother and father would have done almost anything for me, and even
more, for a peaceful life. I say this now not as a criticism
but as a parent of two small children myself, reflecting in
genuine awe on how they did what they managed to do for
us. Part of that pursuit of peace was telling me I was the
best at everything. So, when I came home upset from a
game due to a coach who substituted me, a teammate who
ignored me or a referee who wronged me, my natural state
of injustice was fertilised by my parents' disbelief at my ap-
palling mistreatment. While united in their message, they
had different approaches. My Mam would regularly focus
on my coaches and teammates:

Why were you taken off and that other fella left on?
Sure, you're better than him!
You can't do anything if they don't pass you the ball!

My Dad was a little more strategic in his outlook:

Don't mind them. It's all politics.
Tell them to stick it up their arse.
You should be working, not wasting your whole day playing
football when they have no respect for you.

For a young kid already afflicted with a persecution complex, their words reaffirmed my growing cynicism towards
a world conspiring against me. To this day, much to my
shame, it's an internal battle I still fight.

How lucky I was then, that as a spoiled teenager, the
panacea for my affliction was right in front of me in the
guise of my teacher, coach and mentor John O'Mahony.

The irony is that Johno was one of us. He was from Ballagh' and so should have fully embraced and understood
the complexities of our tortured condition. Instead, he

loathed the outsider narrative. As young men, he challenged us constantly and in so doing taught me the greatest lesson of my young life: how to be accountable.

Nowadays, everybody in sporting circles knows John O'Mahony: as a teacher, TD, Senator, footballer, All-Ireland winning manager, husband and father of five children, he has lived a full and fascinating life. The role he played in mine had much humbler beginnings.

I started my second-level education in St Nathy's College in 1996. By then, Johno had already managed Mayo to an All-Ireland final in 1989, losing to Cork. Perhaps most remarkably, in 1994 he had led Leitrim to their first Connacht title since 1927, beating his native Mayo in the final. During my time in Nathy's, he brought Galway to three All-Ireland finals, winning two of them in 1998 and 2001, the first two wins of any county west of the River Shannon since 1966. Apart from Sean Boylan, he was the most recognisable and respected manager in the country. To us, he was our coach, teacher and clubmate.

As I reflect now, I am struck by the fact that, at a time when he enjoyed so much respect and success in the game he loved, he made so much time for us. This was best reflected in how much joy he took from our successes and, perhaps more profoundly, the disappointment he felt when we didn't fulfil our potential.

This is why a coach is so important, why John O'Mahony was so influential in my life. From Johno, I learned that honesty is the foundation of all good coaching. I learned this in a variety of ways, including those times I fell foul of him. The people closest to you more than likely won't be honest. Not because they are trying to hurt you. Often, it's the opposite: they love you and are trying to protect you. As I'm now learning myself, it's hard to be objective when it comes to your own.

That is the potential positive power of a coach. To have a mentor who talks to you with honesty in the proper manner can be life-changing for an individual of any age, but particularly for a teen. Johno's skill lay in the questions he asked. They always related to something he had already taught us:

*How was **your** preparation?*
***Your** job was to do this; why did that not happen?*
*Why do **you** not have the proper gear on?*
*You didn't get much ball; how was **your** movement?*
*Your kickouts didn't go well; how much practice did **you** do during the week?*
*Why were **you** late?*
*Yes, I took you off; what could **you** have done differently?*

The power was always in the question. He never found fault with something he hadn't taught you. But he always insisted on an honest self-assessment of your performance in front of him, a coach who knew infinitely more about the game then we ever could. At times, it was intimidating but with repetition, it had the desired effect: it forced you to be honest with yourself. It stopped you blaming others and made you think about what you could have done differently. If you were daft enough to bring up another player with Johno, you had lost.

As coaches, mentors and teachers, we have the responsibility to be honest with those who trust us to teach them. It's a two-way street, obviously young players need to be heard, too. As I learned from Johno, we are not just training young people to play. We are equipping them for life. Our influence may often be small but profoundly impactful.

As young people growing up in Ballaghaderreen, we were lucky to have many great people helping us develop as players and young adults. Among them were Hall of Fame handball coach John Gaffney, Frank Kelly and Brian Tansey from the GAA club, and my great friend Barry Solan, who currently works at Arsenal FC as strength and conditioning coach. These guys showed us that, even though you may not have the speed of a Pearce Hanley, the size and balance of an Aidan O'Shea or the power of a Lee Keegan, there is always a way to improve and compete. It is the job of the coach to ask players the right questions. That necessitates taking the time and care to come to know and understand your players, as they are all different. It is then the responsibility of the player not to look in a straight line, but to find the corner and go around it.

*****

As I said already, the outsider narrative never cut it with Johno. Poor performances were never blamed on others, not referees and not a non-existent cross-border bias which proved over time to be as mythical as any Mayo curse. Nor did he posture and trade off his own achievements. Here we were, a bunch of cocky, impressionable teenagers, being coached by a guy who would leave school to drive to Galway to manage a squad of generational talents like Padraic Joyce and Michael Donnellan. In teaching us, he never made it about himself. Often, he would captivate us with stories of Kevin Walsh or Sean Óg de Paor, but it was never about him. He never put himself at the centre of the story. Crucially, the prevailing lesson was always the same: talent was from the neck up. Padraic Joyce may have been one of the most brilliant young footballers in Ireland but by Johno's telling we learned it was because of his application rather than his ability.

My teenage years coincided with a renaissance in Mayo football. After Johno brought the county to the '89 final, there followed some difficult years before John Maughan took Mayo to successive finals in 1996 and 1997. After decades of being written off as the poor relations out west, that Mayo team of the mid-90s were the measure of anyone in the country. Watching them as a kid was formative in the sense that I saw Mayo – my Mayo – as winners. For a teenager, this was a game-changer. Ballaghaderreen had two players on those teams. One was Dermot Flanagan, son of possibly Mayo's most famous footballer Sean Flanagan, who captained Mayo to their last All-Ireland in 1951. The other was Kevin Cahill, a prince of a full-back who was among the best in the business on his day.

Ironically, Johno – the man who started that renaissance in the late 1980s – was at this time managing Mayo's fiercest rivals. The phenomenon of outside managers coaching counties not native to themselves was still a relatively novel one. The fact that Johno, who was pure Mayo, was managing Galway may have been controversial at the time but not to us. As a kid especially, you only know what you see: and what we saw up close, almost by accident, was history.

After losing back-to-back All-Ireland finals, Mayo were the team to beat in 1998. Out of nowhere it seemed, Galway, under Johno, came and wiped our eyes. What we understood as pupils in Nathy's was that there was nothing lucky about Galway's success. Johno was clearly doing with Galway what he was trying to do with us: demanding standards and holding players accountable. Teenagers need standards. If you messed with Johno, you were dropped. He never wavered on this. Punctuality in school and training was a minimum standard. If you didn't have the correct gear on match day, you didn't play, no matter who you were. There was no preferential treatment for the supposed better players. You gave 100 per cent. If you did your job at training, the result would look after itself, whichever way. Many of us struggled to meet Johno's high standards but, crucially, we learned and by learning we earned his respect. That was better than any victory.

When I think back on Johno as a key influence on my life at a vulnerable age, I never remember him mentioning goals. What stands out was his near obsession with standards. It has taught me that we cannot be afraid to demand high standards from our young players. In fact, we are doing them a disservice if we don't. I feel I am living proof of his philosophy. Of course, if the coach who demands those same standards does not live up to them himself, there will always be a chance of rebellion within the group. For all the naivety of youth, a smartass teenager will land you on your backside if he sees hypocrisy at play. I already see this in my own kids. I was no different. This was never an issue with Johno. Even before his All-Irelands with Galway, his reputation as a man of integrity was unimpeachable. His brand of leadership may not be so easily defined in today's language but to be there, to feel the weight of his disappointment if he felt you had let yourself down (it was never about the result), and to feel his pride in you when you fulfilled your potential – that was what Johno gave me.

★★★★★

After Mayo lost to Cork under Johno in 1989, there was an iconic photo of him on the field surrounded by Mayo fans, one of them holding a banner that read 'JOHN SAYS KEEP THE FAITH'. Not long after, as if in an act of defiance, John's wife Gerardine put up a sign outside their home that simply read 'Keep the Faith'. It was like something you'd see in deepest Texas in a town obsessed with high school football. The message required no explanation. Mayo was always a football-mad county, and that 1989 championship run gave belief to a team and a region that had endured decades of heartache and no little hardship. I'm sure when Gerardine put out that sign, she intended to take it down when Sam finally crossed the Shannon under Johno. Well, it did, twice. It was a measure of Johno's ambition and drive that unable to do it with Mayo, he went and succeeded with our oldest rivals, Galway. As a community, we felt great pride and joy in one of our own doing something so unexpected and remarkable.

The excitement of having the Sam Maguire Cup in Nathy's was something I will never forget. In a bizarre twist, it seemed somewhat fitting that one of Mayo football's most famous sons would bring back Sam to his home town just over the border in Roscommon, having won an All-Ireland with Galway. That summed up the paradox of Ballaghaderreen in one fable. I remember having an affinity with that Galway team, something I often smile at now given my own subsequent battles with them down through the years but, in the context of Johno's role in my life, made perfect sense. How could you not want to hear tell of the genius of Ja Fallon or the composure of Kevin Walsh? In school and on the pitch, we hung on Johno's every word. He was teaching us through the gaze of a man achieving history. We were learning first-hand what it took to be successful in football and in life. It was around this time too that I saw another side to Johno. The softer side. Once, he took home a pair of Adidas Predator football boots from Galway training and gave them to me. Any sports-mad kid in the late 1990s would testify to what a big deal that was. At St Nathy's, we may not have been his team of primary concern, but we never felt it. He went out of his way to ensure that we felt included and that we were on top of our schoolwork. He looked out for us.

I was a member of the Mayo minor squad that lost the 2000 All-Ireland final. Traditionally, the senior and minor finalists sit down together the following day. Galway had drawn with Kerry the day before and with a replay looming large I'm sure it was the last place Johno wanted to be. Regardless, he sought me out and took the time to introduce me to the Galway players, understanding what that would mean to 17-year-old me. Put simply, for all his achievements and obvious importance, this guy cared. It taught me a lot and set me up to realise that no matter how much I thought I had achieved, there were always lessons to be learned and, most importantly, shared.

★★★★★

If Johno represented objective, often brutal, honesty, my mother Philomena was the perfect counterpoint. As two major influences in my life, they share many admirable traits – loyalty and selflessness chief among them – even if they differ in their delivery. We grew up in Dalton Terrace, a council estate in Ballaghaderreen. Money was tight but we never wanted for anything. This was due to Philomena's incredible work ethic. So often, she would take overtime and extra weekend shifts in the local milk factory to make sure my two sisters, my brother and I had everything we needed. We had what can only be described as a wonderful, fun-filled childhood. When we got to the age of competing in sport, her motivation drove us. As a mother, she always took great pride in our achievements no matter the activity. She believed if you were going to do something, you did it right. If you wanted something, you worked hard to get it.

We are always looking for people to inspire and lead us. In my case, I had an incredible leader in my life from the beginning. When I finally understood this, I realised there are great leaders, coaches and people in all our daily lives. Yes, take clues from successful sports stars and business-people but if we take the time to look closer to home, those people are often there, hidden in plain sight. Often, their leadership is more effective and authentic. It is not contrived or driven by expectant or sycophantic audiences.

When reading this book, I ask you to think of the teachers/coaches you remember from your youth? Were they the coaches who chased trophies and titles or mentors who cared about you?

In a world where we are trying to make every kid a winner for just turning up, I believe we are missing a very important aspect of sport. Participation is undoubtedly crucial but once the kids are physically present, there is such an opportunity to teach the importance of effort, resilience, taking responsibility and, crucially, working within a team. This was Johno's greatest strength: by making you accountable, he put you in the best position to win, whatever the competition.

TWO

Repetition, Repetition, Repetition

'Repetition is the mother of learning, the father of action, which makes it the architect of accomplishment.'

– Zig Ziglar

BEAUTIFUL tales often have ugly beginnings. The Mayo story of the 2010s captured countless imaginations and lit up many championship summers throughout the decade. That we ultimately did not succeed in winning an All-Ireland during my time – our definitive goal – is a criticism that could be easily thrown at us. In the context of the 'win or die' prism of elite sport, this criticism is entirely justified. We did not succeed. Loath though I am to use the f-word, we failed. In my 17 seasons as an inter-county footballer, *I* failed. That is top-level sport in its purest, most straightforward form. When you're the one in the arena, that narrative drives you on season after season. It's healthy if only in the sense that, when in pursuit of victory (excellence), you continually strive to get better. You play to win. The closer you get to the summit, the more realistic your chances, the more you want it.

But, when it's over and you reflect on the journey, the narrative changes. I don't believe this is true for everybody, nor do I believe this change in thinking is conveniently omitting the fact that we – *I* – did not win. Put simply, now that I have stopped playing, I can't affect the result anymore. In accepting that fact, I have reflected and asked myself if I regret not winning an All-Ireland with Mayo? I realise the question is nonsense – the word 'regret' implies a choice. The only choice was to empty everything into trying. I feel we did that. We never chose not to win. But if the question is nonsense, the answer is not: I regret nothing. The words 'journey' and 'process' carry their own baggage. But choose whatever word you like. My time as a Mayo footballer was the greatest experience of my life to date. Had I won an All-Ireland in 2004 or 2006, in my early 20s, would I have been better off? I strongly believe that no, I would not. That is not to say I didn't want it. Would the long-suffering people of Mayo have been happier? Probably. For a winter at least. I'd be a fool to think otherwise. There are elderly Mayo folk all over the world who have spent their entire lives waiting to see us win just once.

Perhaps I didn't appreciate that great longing enough when I was a younger player, but it was something of which I became increasingly aware as I travelled with Mayo teams, especially to London and New York. Whenever I played, winning was always the goal. Now that I'm done, I realise that everything good I took from it came from the struggle. I would never swap that now, not for any medal.

Back to ugly beginnings. It's May 2011, and we are in Ruislip to play London in the first round of the Connacht Championship. Mayo have never lost to London in championship football. Some ten months earlier, we had crashed out to Longford on a miserable Saturday evening, a loss that down brought the curtain on John O'Mahony's second term in charge of Mayo. It was a sad and sorry end to Johno's involvement in Mayo football and a ten-year stretch that had seen us reach two All-Ireland finals as well as winning a National League and an All-Ireland U21 title. James Horan, himself a two-time All-Star, took over a team at a critical crossroads. He was young by intercounty managerial standards but seriously ambitious. Despite his excellent work as a manager with his native Ballintubber, his appointment was still deemed to be a risk by many commentators. After experimenting heavily during the league, we retained our Division One status. Confidence was steadily growing within the camp and, in theory, our trip to Ruislip should've been a formality. Instead, we found ourselves staring down the barrel of successive humiliating championship defeats. With two minutes to go, we are two points down and this London team can smell blood. In the context of the Longford loss, defeat in Ruislip would've ended quite a few Mayo careers. Points from Kevin McLoughlin and Trevor Mortimer brought us to extra-time. Over the next 20 minutes, our superior fitness told, and we ground out a win on a day that was forgettable but for two connected facts: we used four freetakers that day with very limited success and 19-year-old Cillian O'Connor made his senior championship debut for Mayo. Whether by accident or design, we had found a young man who would lead our attack. Still a teenager, Cillian took the responsibility off all our shoulders and placed it on his own for the next decade.

Cillian joined the squad as an 18-year-old as James took over in the winter of 2010. Not content to ease his way in, he immediately set his sights on a starting spot. He heeded the advice of his Ballintubber clubmate Vinny Keane who told him that, as he saw it, Mayo did not have a natural freetaker. Understanding that the physical side of his game would take longer to develop, Cillian should make place-kicking his first objective, said Keane. This would be his shortcut into the team. The message was compounded when Cillian later read a piece in *The Mayo News* by ex-captain Noel Connelly, who had shortlisted those who might be Mayo's freetaker under Horan. Cillian was not among the names mentioned. Not happy at the omission, he set to work.

He already had a head start. In 2010, Ballintubber won their first county senior championship. James was at the helm. He had introduced Kieran Shannon to the team as sports psychologist. Kieran worked closely with Cillian, developing scripts around technique and what changed in each scenario: dry-day scripts, wet-day scripts, variations-on-wind scripts. They worked on visualising how each scenario might look on game day, as well as setting long-term goals for Cillian's career. Cillian was doing this as a teenager long before he'd kicked a point for Mayo senior footballers. What happened next was almost inevitable.

When great goalscorers come along in soccer, or three-point shooters in basketball, or placekickers in GAA, we too quickly dismiss what goes into making them great. We somehow become bored or immune to the normalised brilliance they routinely display. All we see is the end-product: each swing of the foot is either a score or a miss. What we do not see are the hours of individual study and practice that go on when the lights are off. In that regard, Cillian O'Connor was peerless. With him, there was no mystery to his mastery. The evidence of his excellence was obvious to those like me who bore witness to it: hours and hours of top-quality work, all executed so that when he came to the biggest moment in the biggest game, he had a technique he could trust. In 2011, his debut season as a senior footballer, he produced performances that forced people to take notice. He made opposing teams fearful of conceding scorable frees, knowing they would be punished. This had an invisible and unquantifiable impact on the rest of us Mayo forwards as it suddenly gave us more space and freedom to do what we should be doing: creating and kicking scores. Cillian's arrival had the added benefit of signalling the end to the lazy trope that Mayo were 'missing a marquee forward'. Mayo had won enough big games to debunk this theory as little more than high-stool punditry. Cillian was different, though. To watch him score was to see someone who appeared born to do it, yet even that misses the point: his natural ability was one thing but his work ethic was out of this world.

Even as a young man, Cillian understood something many of us only came to learn through years of trial and error: practice is one thing, practicing the *right* thing is something else entirely and often much more difficult. Every great basketball player shooting threes blindfolded in a gym, every great golfer hitting wedges to a saucer green: they understand that the muscle memory born from *correct* repetition is the key to unlocking their potential. Repetition, repetition, repetition. Practicing the right thing requires intelligence and humility – a willingness to self-evaluate, to change, even if that change brings with it short-term pain. This is especially true of the best kickers. Theirs is a sacred art honed over thousands of hours of simple, painstaking repetition. To change your style, as Cillian later had to due to injury and other factors, is the hardest thing.

Cillian identified this and adapted. As knee and hamstring injuries bothered him through his mid-20s, he completely re-evaluated his freetaking philosophy and, in particular, his practice. Understanding that excessive kicking was contributing to his injuries, he focused on cutting the quantity of kicking he did on the training field and concentrated far more on quality. That may have seen him kick 15 frees instead of 50. At face value, that sounds like a simple thing to do but part of Cillian's rationale was that if he were to take fewer kicks in practice, more thought would be required to ensure each kick mattered more. In practice, no kick was to be wasted. This often saw him out on the pitches even longer than before because he was now incorporating visualisation and stretching into his routine. Recognising and making this adjustment is evidence of what a special player Cillian is.

As a top player you can always lift more weights. You can always work harder on your speed. You can always study more game tape. It's tough and requires sacrifice and commitment, but it does not require too much soul searching. There is no suspension of trust like there is with when a kicker is faced with the choice of changing something that is already working but could be better. I saw, through Cillian, that to risk changing your kicking technique was to risk your entire reputation.

Why do it? To be the best, of course. In that pursuit, he left no stone unturned. It almost sounds funny, but Cillian often practiced with headphones before All-Ireland finals. In his ears, *Come on You Boys in Blue* would be blaring. The field he was kicking on may have been an empty one in Clogher but in his mind he was facing a hostile Hill 16.

I completely re-evaluated my attitude to kicking because of Cillian. It's ironic, of course, that although the game is called football, we spend so much time obsessing about so many other aspects. I learned through watching him that I couldn't just take it for granted that, once in the correct scoring position, I could suddenly trust my kicking technique because I'd been doing it since I was a kid. No. Through him I learned it was both an art and science. It required a deeper understanding of the mechanics of every detail of the process; from the planted foot, through the position of the head and on to the follow-through. It was genuinely humbling for me, as an experienced player in my late 20s who knew he'd worked hard to evolve and reinvent himself as a player, only to witness Cillian, seven years younger than me but an old soul, leading the way.

★★★★★

I often think about Cillian's journey compared to mine – how I was able to learn in the shadows, to watch others I admired, pick out the good habits and bin the bad. Like most Gaelic footballers, I was allowed to fail in relative darkness. That's not to say it was easy for me: the hard part was learning from those failures and returning committed to improvement. The easier part was being able to do it in relative peace. Cillian and Aidan O'Shea never had that luxury. By virtue of their prodigious talent, they have always been judged by a different standard. It makes their achievements all the more remarkable.

Young, talented sports people can be easily corrupted. It's a story as old as time. Early success can lead to apathy, an expectation that success is a formality. Cillian O'Connor was a much talked about footballer in Mayo from a young age. In a county synonymous with producing prodigies, chances were his obvious promise might go unfulfilled. A decade on from his debut, we are left in no doubt: Cillian O'Connor surpassed all the hype and continues to be one of the finest footballers of his generation. Having had a ringside seat to view his journey, I know first-hand what it took to get him there and he alone is responsible for everything he has achieved. Whether it's a club game in front of two dozen people or an All-Ireland with millions watching, he brings the same unrelenting commitment to his performance.

On a personal note, I believe I gained more than any other player from Cillian's arrival on the Mayo scene. We became great friends and developed an understanding of each other's style, making both of us – and by extension, the team – better. As he established himself, his mere presence gave every other forward on the field an extra second on the ball. He undoubtedly drove up the standards of everybody around him. The hours he put in either side of training would almost make you feel guilty. I definitely kicked far more in the second half of my Mayo career than I did in the first. That was down to him. His standards forced all of us to examine our own.

To me, trust is the key factor in any team environment whatever the discipline, be it family, government or sport. It didn't take long for Cillian to earn the trust of his Mayo teammates, despite only being a teenager when he joined us. It was obvious quite quickly that he shared the team's core values. He actively sought responsibility. He always put the needs of the squad before his own. His application and willingness to learn were examples to all of us and, boy, is he tough. He is an animal in the tackle. It is rare to see this in a player so classy. These qualities saw him gain our trust and he never, ever, betrayed it. If any young sportsperson were to choose a role model, I would ask them to look at Cillian O'Connor. The only tool he needed was a ball. The rest was down to him. Go wherever he spent time alone, kicking his way to greatness, and I guarantee you you'll find his blood in the dirt.

*****

Note: In 2019, aged just 27, Cillian became the highest scorer in championship history. His record in semi-finals and finals at that stage was remarkable and it became even more remarkable in 2020. In seven final appearances he has scored 0-54. His semi-final stats are just as impressive: in 13 appearances, he has scored 14-73, an average of almost nine points a game. Far from free-taking padding a forward's numbers, I believe the added responsibility it puts on a player is grossly underrated. To me, he is as close to a complete forward as this county has ever produced. It was an immense privilege playing alongside him, learning from him. What an incredible teammate and friend.

The Best of Cillian O'Connor

When you're part of that story, it's sometimes hard to see it for what it is. It's as if you're an actor in a movie shot on a giant green screen and only when you're seated in the theatre at the premiere can you see the whole picture. It's all too easy to become consumed by your role in it and, as a result, miss out on some of the magic around you. One moment for which I was very much present, however, came as I sat on the Mayo bench, my race well and truly run, as the clock ticked down on the 2016 All-Ireland final against Dublin. We are a point down and on the verge of another heartache. I'm surrounded by other players who had run their hearts out and by unused subs, county board officials and 83,000 manic supporters. We need a single score to force a replay. One point seems so small in and of itself but in those suffocating final moments on the biggest stage, one solitary score becomes Everest. Despite the thousands of hours preparing for this very moment, every single player, whether in sky-blue or green and red, feels the weight of history. The game is 76-minutes-old and this is our final attack. We work the ball up Croke Park from our own kick-out, David Clarke to Colm Boyle. Boyler finds Stephen Coen, who plays a hand pass to Tom Parsons. Tom, in turn, finds Cillian O'Connor, who exchanges passes with Aidan O'Shea. Cillian takes the ball 60 yards out, facing the Dublin goal. This is his moment. He is 25 years of age, our captain. Watch it back – never once did passing the responsibility of shooting to someone else enter his head. Running at Darren Daly, he steps off his left foot, takes one bounce without breaking stride and strikes the ball from fully 45 yards off his right foot – a shot I have seen him make *over and over and over* again. The ball flies over the black spot. Sitting watching, I feel the stadium shake. Our captain has delivered. We have another chance.

THREE

The Danger of Pride

'Pride only hurts, it never helps.'

– Marsellus Wallace, Pulp Fiction

P RIDE is something Mayo people wear like a birth-mark. You may live in Ballyboden on the southside of Dublin or Bay Ridge in southwest Brooklyn but if your people are from Mayo, it can have a defining impact on your life. It is as much a part of us as the colour of our eyes. We don't choose it. There is no 'finding your tribe', we are already in it. The pride we feel long predates any momentum created by Mayo teams in which I have been involved. Regardless of the exploits of our footballers, Mayo folk the world over are naturally proud people. The same could likely be said for Irish people everywhere but there's something about being from the west that amplifies that sense of place, a fondness for home, a connection and, most crucially, an identity. Perhaps it comes with being an emigrant people. For centuries, Mayo folk have left Ireland, often forced away in search of a better life. That's why there are entire communities in places like Cleveland, Ohio, that span generations of Mayo families who still maintain a deep pride in where their people came from. It's just as true now as so many friends and acquaintances of mine have left to start new lives in far-flung places. Regardless of where we end up, our Mayo-ness unites us.

It's often said that you never feel more from a place than when you live abroad. The longer I played for Mayo, the more aware I became of what our sporting journey meant to people, especially those who had left home to build a life somewhere else. Whether travelling to New York, London or Philadelphia, I began to appreciate more and more the pride Mayo people feel for where they are from. On the one hand, I regularly think how lucky I was that it wasn't me saying goodbye to home – Gaelic football always gave me a reason to stay – but on the other, I always looked at those Mayo communities abroad and envied the sense of pride they felt in Mayo and us, their footballers. People who were brave enough to leave home and begin a new life somewhere else. Start businesses, raise families, thousands of miles away from the support networks so many of us rely on, yet they looked up to us for playing a sport? The pride they exhibited made me feel privileged and of course it made me feel proud.

Pride, however, has two faces. As positive an emotion as it can be, as useful a tool as it is to inspire us to achieve, it can also blind us to hard truths. This is true in all walks of life, and it is especially true in sports, both for supporters and players. The pride we feel in achievement, though gratifying, can often make us complacent and stymie our development. It can also diminish our humility, especially when we are held in such high esteem by those people around us in our clubs and communities. It's one thing to fall victim to pride in an individual pursuit, when others don't rely on you, but it's quite another to do so in a team setting.

As a young footballer, I often fell victim to pride, long before I'd earned the right to. Our Mayo minor coach JP Kean often did not pick me. JP was a very well-regarded footballing man who had done a lot to establish Mayo as a force in underage football. Seventeen-year-old me never got the fuss. Why? Put simply, JP often overlooked me and instead of figuring out the reasons, I sulked and deflected.

Instead of seeking out constructive criticism on how I could improve my game and bring more to the team, I allowed myself to form the unsubstantiated opinion that he 'just didn't get me' and that not picking me was his loss. I certainly wasn't the introspective person then that I hope I am today. In hindsight, it was a wasted opportunity to be more self-critical, to learn from players and a coach who had a lot to offer me at a hugely formative time in my young life. Such stubbornness and pride are common in teenagers. I hope reading this might show them having the humility to find out the 'why' is a much more constructive avenue to travel down than that of blaming others, as I often did. I always had an answer ready when people asked me why I wasn't playing. I always protected my own ego and pointed the finger elsewhere. It was a foolish endeavour. JP Kean did more than perhaps any other underage coach in my lifetime to develop footballers in Mayo. I wouldn't have been the first kid ever to have too high an opinion of himself but to fall victim to that weakness when the opportunities to learn were so blatantly presented to me may have been extremely costly. Pride always allowed me to point to the fact that I wasn't the problem: JP, and all the other JPs, were.

★★★★★

If the drawn All-Ireland senior final of 2016 allowed me a ringside seat to Cillian O'Connor's greatness, the build-up to the replay opened my eyes to greatness of another kind, hiding in plain sight in the guise of our goalkeeper David Clarke.

Team announcements are intensely personal, selfish affairs, fraught with anxiety. Although you spend an entire season preparing to fight and die as a team, for those few minutes when the starting XV is being called out you just want to hear your name, whether you're a seasoned veteran or a first-year rookie. As soon as you hear it, your mind immediately switches back to the team again. You know you are playing, you can breathe, refocus and concentrate on the overall objective, but for those few moments before your name is called, you are vulnerable, almost childlike. David Clarke had been superb for Mayo that 2016 season, but for the replay our management decided on a different tactical approach, one that better suited the skill set of David's understudy, Robbie Hennelly. Robbie, too, was an extremely experienced 'keeper. His selection was a dramatic shift in strategy designed to unbalance Dublin. It centred around his kickout. It was a huge call. 'Keepers rarely get dropped mid-season and almost never get dropped for finals. I hear Robbie's name called out in the team meeting and I feel for Clarkie, but, deep down, I only worry about myself. I need to be ready. I need to be at my best. Being emotional about it is not an option.

Remarkably, at that moment, David Clarke understood this better than anyone. As I reflect upon it now, I'm sure this decision must have devastated him. I never asked him. He's 32, he's been around a long time, and he's just been dropped for potentially the biggest game of his life. The finishing line for him – and for me – is moving ever closer. All I remember now of that team meeting is how he handled it: there was no pride on show. He addressed the team, outlined his hopes for the game, wished Robbie well and allowed the group to immediately move on.

Imagine how he could have reacted? He could've destabilised the whole squad by letting his pride get the better of him, by lashing out. I often wonder how I would've reacted. I know how 17-year-old me would have reacted.

What happened for that final – David being overlooked – made a lot of headlines in the days, weeks and months afterwards. David's humility in accepting the management's decision enabled the team to focus solely on the game while allowing himself to prepare mentally if he were needed on the day. As fate would have it that day, he was. Robbie was black-carded just after half-time. If an outfield player is dropped unexpectedly, they can often harness their sense of injustice into a silent rage so that when they get their chance, they play with a point to prove. Goalkeepers can't play with that anger. They need to exude calm and control. David came on and played remarkably well. In the context of what he had experienced in the build-up, his performance was truly inspirational to witness. Knowing him as I do, it was also not one bit surprising.

David is a proud Ballina Stephenites man. For all his years playing for Mayo, his reputation as a committed club player preceded him. The example he set to young players coming through was of a guy who never saw himself too big for any team or any game, even an end-of-year, inconsequential league match. In 2005, Ballina won the All-Ireland club title. David had already established himself as a Mayo player but, after being injured earlier in the season, he lost his place on the Ballina team to John Healy. There are no foregone conclusions in sport but at that stage of his career few would have bet against David being Mayo's 'keeper for the next decade. Healy showed excellent form throughout Ballina's run to the final however, and David never regained his place. On St Patrick's Day, David is sitting in the stands watching as a sub as Ballina beat Portlaoise on what remains his club's greatest day.

Though he must believe himself to be the best goalkeeper in Mayo, there is no bitching from David, no moaning, no infecting the team with the negativity that can spread through a dressing room like a virus. Instead, he digs deep and sets about establishing himself as Mayo's number one 'keeper. A year after sitting in the stands watching his club win without him, David is in goals for Mayo in an All-Ireland final against Kerry. Fourteen seasons later, he's in goals in an All-Ireland final against Dublin. The years in between saw some quality competition for his place – particularly from Robbie (Hennelly) and Kenneth O'Malley, both of whom had superior kickouts, a skill that has become a more potent weapon as the game has evolved. David kept coming back season after season, a better version of himself than before each time. His willingness to break down every element of his game – be it his incredible shot-stopping, his kickout or his physical fitness – and improve, allowed him the longevity to have the career he had as an intercounty footballer. He won two All-Star awards in his mid-30s in an era of Gaelic football that was redefined by the consistent brilliance of another goalkeeper, Dublin's Stephen Cluxton.

That David was seen as Cluxton's equal, or superior on occasion, emphasises his ability and resilience as a teammate and leader. He rightly takes his place in the pantheon of Mayo's most celebrated and beloved footballers.

When you're on the inside of something, you're often ignorant to the perceptions people on the outside have about the group. Since retiring, I've always been amused to learn that many Mayo fans saw Clarkie as a very serious guy. Sure, he had an aura of authority about him but you'd rarely if ever leave any conversation with him without having a laugh. He was an observer of people and situations. This made him an interesting person to be around. On the training ground, he hit as hard as any man. It often surprised newcomers to the squad that our goalie was not just willing to mix it with everyone but that he was also built like a brick wall. He took pride in that.

How many times did David Clarke get dropped in his 20 years with Mayo? How many times could he have held grudges against the coaches who didn't believe in him or the players who replaced him? How many opportunities did he have to let pride get the better of him? He never flinched. What a lesson to young players! What an example to teammates! Were there moments when he felt sorry for himself when he was hurt or embarrassed? There must have been. The key thing with David – and for all of us – was how he reacted. He never allowed pride to get in the way of him becoming the best 'keeper he could possibly be. He picked himself up time and time again and sought out ways to improve: all of this in an era of Gaelic football when the role of a goalkeeper was evolving at a pace unmatched in the game's history.

David Clarke always got the bigger picture.

Every young person will at some stage not receive what they feel they are entitled to get. The nature of team sport is such that if you show talent, the expectation is that you'll always be picked. The same can be said in education with academics, or in our professional and personal lives with jobs and relationships. We become conditioned to expect to get what we think we deserve. Often, through no fault of our own, people choose to go another way and that hurts us. That hurt in turn can lead to anger and resentment and, ultimately, a failure to reflect on and figure out what we could have done better. I believe it's our job as teachers/coaches/parents to make young people aware that disappointment is part of life for all of us. As Mayo people, we know this better than any but there is only ever one way to get better: get up, get thinking and get working. There is always room to improve. Nobody better exemplified this than David Clarke. He always looked at himself first. We can all learn from him.

The Best of David Clarke

We are playing the All-Ireland champions, Dublin, in the 2012 All-Ireland semi-final in Croke Park, a game we are not supposed to win. Leading by three points with 66 minutes on the clock, Alan Dillon has the ball under the Hogan Stand. The game in the balance, Dillon is the man you want on the ball in such a scenario. He aims a pass to Cillian O'Connor but overcooks it. A small moment such as this can turn a big game. Dublin sense it and race into a counterattack. Our full-forward Alan Freeman does brilliantly to chase down and foul Kevin McManamon 70 yards out from our goal. The foul should give us a breather, a chance to get organised, but Dublin are in a hurry. Ciarán Kilkenny grabs the ball and hits an outrageous pass into Bernard Brogan, who has been left one-on-one with Ger Cafferkey on the 21-yard line under a heaving Hill 16. After not putting a foot wrong all afternoon, Ger is beaten by Kilkenny's pass. Brogan, one of the game's most lethal finishers, is already headed for goal as he collects. It all happens in an instant but in real time the moment takes forever. Our only hope is David Clarke. Before the ball lands in Brogan's lap, he is already on the move. As Brogan reaches the 14-yard line, Clarkie is almost on top of him and does what he has done since he was a kid in Ballina: mimicking Peter Schmeichel, he spreads, making himself as big as possible. Brogan opens his body to bury the ball and change the momentum of the game. Clarkie has other ideas. Staring down Brogan, he brilliantly saves with a strong right hand. In the context of the game, the opposition and the baying sky-blue mob behind him, it's one of the greatest saves I've ever seen. Brogan denied, Hill 16 can't believe their eyes. We hang on to win, a victory that sets us on our way to becoming the team we would become. Without the brilliance of David Clarke, it might have been a very different decade for Mayo football.

FOUR

To Be
or Not To Be

'Sweat more during peace, bleed less during war.'

– Anonymous

T HE hotel on the morning of an All-Ireland final
can be a window into a team's soul. Though the
collective goal is the same, individual approaches
differ dramatically from player to player and among the
backroom team. Some lads are bubbly and energetic, mad
to talk and defuse the tension. Some are the colour of the
milk they nervously pour into their tea. Others achieve a
trance-like state of meditative calm, built around a routine
years in the making. Playlists, video clips, mantras repeated
on a loop through headphones: no approach is absolute
and no approach is absolutely correct. Those guys who
have their regime meticulously planned can have it completely obliterated by a single missing sock. The guy puking
in the cubicle an hour before throw-in can be transformed
the moment he steps on the pitch. I should know. I've been
a version of every single one of those guys. From the fella
who couldn't shut up to the fella you wouldn't dare disturb.
For long periods of my career, I was unapproachable –
likely insufferable – for days before games. By the time I'd
finished, I had reached a more reasoned stage of acceptance.

Time mellowed me. It also made me more receptive to the moods of others and, crucially, to the fact that when it comes to team sports it takes all types: some players need the fury, others need the calm. There is no exact science.

One thing I learned for certain was the more I relaxed while playing, the freer I was to express myself. The theory of it makes perfect sense; the practice is harder to implement. The tighter a golfer grips the club, the more prone to mistakes they are. The more a placekicker tries to force a kick, the more likely they are to snap and miss it. Pressure does this. Overthinking. Forcing you to doubt your ability. That's why I placed so much emphasis on my own preparation. It was a controllable. One of the few.

Whatever the outcome of big games, people need to identify reasons to rationalise the outcome. Supporters, press and even players seek and often apply logical reasons to explain away our pain. Mayo lost because of this or that: a lack of 'marquee forwards', bad refereeing calls or because we painted a barn green and red in Manulla. I've lost All-Irelands by a single point (twice), by a goal and by 13 points. The reasons we lost or won were sometimes obvious but more often were a collection of tiny moments that culminated in victory or defeat. As people, however, we always need a reason. One thing that I believe can smother the dynamic of a group whatever the objective is tension. It can infect a team and disable it. One man who was completely immune to tension was Keith Higgins.

In the build-up to games, Keith was a sleeper. He would stroll into a pre-match team meeting as if just out of bed. There was nothing contrived or pre-rehearsed in his preparation. He was the same three hours out from a game as he was three weeks before it: calm, chilled out and, crucially, himself. The second he hit the field he came alive. A different animal entirely. Sleepy Keith was gone. 'Zippy', an appropriate nickname for one so quick, had arrived.

Keith began his senior football career with Mayo in 2005, while we were at IT Sligo together, and quickly established himself as a starter and designated man-marker. I often think back to the week of the National League semi-final that year against Armagh. Keith wasn't long on the team and would be marking Steven McDonnell, one of the best forwards in the game at the time. I remember the week of that game in college, how caught up in it all I was. Just like Keith, I was a student trying to balance studies and playing. Unlike Keith, I was deep in every and any process I thought would better prepare myself for Sunday. Keith took his football no less seriously but his approach to games couldn't have been more different. That Sunday against Armagh we were beaten but all the talk was about Keith. He had woken up in time and he had absolutely arrived.

Following our run to the 2006 All-Ireland final, Keith won Young Footballer of the Year. The next few years were tough for the team, but he was a constant, while playing hurling for Mayo at the same time. Then, in 2011, something happened, both for the team and for Keith. James Horan came in in the autumn of 2010 and slowly, slowly, the worm started to turn. In James' first year, we beat defending champions Cork after a stunning comeback before losing gamely in an All-Ireland semi-final to a 'Gooch' Cooper-inspired Kerry. After five tough seasons, a penny dropped for the team: the talent was there. New blood had arrived, and though nothing was guaranteed, if we could challenge ourselves, refocus and re-evaluate our training and preparation, there was an opportunity for us to contend. Change was needed. We all knew it, yet even though Keith may have been the most established and revered member of the panel – his place never in doubt – he was the one who most embraced change.

The perception may have been that somebody as naturally talented as Keith Higgins just is the way he is, especially because of the laid-back personality I just described. No change required; he just rolls with it. The reality was different: the reality is Keith made a conscious choice to change. He was so, so good already, but the changes he made saw him become great. They saw him win four All-Stars between 2012 and 2017. I recall being part of a conversation between Keith and our skills coach Ed Coughlan at some point in 2011. Keith was listening to Ed describe areas where he felt Keith could optimise his game when he suddenly interrupted him to say, "so, you're telling me I need to change?" In and of itself, this statement sounds insignificant. Sportspeople are always challenged to evolve and improve but taken in the context of who Keith was, his reputation as a footballer, the self-awareness he had to listen and understand there was more in him, seven seasons into an already great intercounty career, speaks volumes to me about who Keith Higgins is.

Not for a second am I suggesting that Keith was a bad trainer. As a dual player with Mayo, he trained every day of the week. He arguably trained *too* much. It was just his easy-going approach to things that could have prevented him from finding the next level. Nothing was really broken, so why the need to fix it?

Yet, fix it he did. In a converted handball court in Bally-haunis GAA Club lay a gym and that winter it became a second home for Keith. He had never really concentrated on this aspect of his performance before, probably because as soon as the hurling season ended, he would give his body a rest for the winter before it was time to go again. That winter he changed his training. It's far too simplistic to say 'he hit the gym'. What he did was seek the best help in identifying ways to optimise his obvious talents. Adding power to his game was chief among them. By winning his four All-Stars in six seasons, Keith established himself as one of the greatest defenders ever to play for Mayo.

Let's be straight: before Keith's moment of clarity in the winter of 2011, he had won an All-Ireland U21 title as captain in 2006. He had won Young Footballer of the Year the same year. In 2005, Keith won a Sigerson Cup with IT Sligo, giving a man-of-the-match performance in the final against Queen's University, Belfast. He had long been re-garded as an outstanding player and teammate. Blessed with unnatural pace, his ability to read a game and make match-winning plays made him feared as a dual threat in defence and attack. He could've easily continued as he was and had a great career, the kind of career Mayo lads could only dream about. Yet, he critiques himself. He listens to the constructive criticism of others. He studies. He goes to work.

The fruits of his work were evident as early as spring 2012. We were on a training camp in Portugal and a different Keith showed up. His laid-back, easy-going personality never changed, but his application certainly did. I could barely believe my eyes when I saw him out 45 minutes before training, stretching. Keith Higgins, stretching! Same when it came to those occasions we got to let our hair down together. He minded himself way, way more than he ever had before. Something had clicked in him, and he wasn't for turning. His new regime also allowed him to recover quicker. He wasn't as bothered by niggly injuries as heretofore. The power he developed elevated him as a player. As a result, he elevated us as a team.

Players like Keith are rare. I recall Donie Vaughan saying something about him which really stuck with me. Playing alongside Keith in defence, Donie said, was a game of trust. Realising that you could absolutely trust a teammate to handle his own man meant that you could fully commit to your own job and not instinctively doubt (the default setting of most defenders, I'm guessing). That split-second doubt was to concede a crucial half-yard to your own man because you were second-guessing your fellow defender. Keith's body language, even isolated one-on-one by himself in a full-back line, screamed 'TRUST ME'.

His game intelligence was exceptional. Though he was a leader more by deeds than words, when he did speak in a huddle he usually made the most salient point. As his own game improved, his influence on the team became greater. He never put himself forward as a leader. He just *was* a leader. He was also one of the toughest bastards I ever marked.

The beauty with Keith was that he was always his own man. Though an unbelievable teammate and friend, he was always happiest with his old Ballyhaunis school crew. He didn't rely on the approval of the group. He was so comfortable in his own skin. Even continuing to hurl for Mayo when I'm sure many – with his best interests at heart – would've preferred that he did not. He did it because it mattered to him so much. What an example of a man!

Teams, whatever the discipline, need contrasting personalities to succeed. As coaches and teachers, if we are egotistical and narrow-minded enough to try and mould a squad in our likeness, it can never end well. For all I feel I brought to Mayo squads, I shudder to think how little a team of 15 players like me would've achieved. Keith was so different to me in so many respects, but I loved his energy. Often that energy was low-key and completely at odds with my more high-tempo approach to pretty much everything. Yet, his presence calmed me. Like Donie said, the trust was there, established over countless hours together in the trenches. For all his calmness, there was no complacency. His ability to hear and take criticism was an example to anybody. Crucially, Keith didn't require a bad injury or being dropped to change. He didn't need a rock bottom to force that reckoning. By anyone else's standards, Keith was cruising. He changed anyway.

We tend to defend ourselves against criticism. We can say otherwise but our instinct is to bristle and repel. As coaches and mentors, we need to teach kids that critical analysis of where you are in your job, sport or life can make so much difference in terms of fulfilling your potential. We see far too many outstanding young people fall off their path because they resent constructive criticism. Instead, they rely on raw talent. Often, the more of that they have the less they want to be told. If there is one lesson we can learn from Keith, it's that even the slightest change to the most outstanding of talents can yield incredible dividends. Would Keith have won his four All-Stars without embracing the critique made of his game in the winter of 2011? Maybe, but the humility he showed in listening and accepting that he could improve even though, to an outsider, he looked bulletproof, was a lesson to me that none of us are so big we can't learn. To embrace criticism and evolve. We should never be afraid to commit to a change that will make us better. Keith is living proof of that.

The Best of Keith Higgins

As the changes in Keith's game became more apparent, so did his influence on matches. The traditional role of the corner-back was to man-mark, to neutralise the threat of whatever opponent came his way. To put out fires. To keep it simple. There was no need for any fancy stuff. If you had one who could kick, that was a luxury. There were notable exceptions. Kenneth Mortimer, Ryan McMenamin, Marc Ó Sé and Karl Lacey laid the track for players like Keith to follow but, put simply, a good corner-back was there to stop bad things from happening. Keith did all of that. What he also did was become a launchpad for so many of our attacks. His ability to read and intercept plays became a very potent weapon for Mayo. Not only did we have one of the best corner-backs in the business but we also had one of the best attacking players, period. The older he got, the better he became.

There was perhaps no better example of this than the drawn All-Ireland semi-final with Kerry in 2017. We are in injury time and Kerry are one point up. As often happens in the late stages of these games, things are getting loose. Paul Murphy has had Lee Keegan for company all afternoon but now, for the first time, Murphy is free, attacking towards our goal. Kerry inside forward Paul Geaney has been in incredible form and is exactly where you want him to be if you're from the Kingdom, isolated one-on-one with his marker on the Mayo 21-yard line. Only problem for Geaney is, it's Keith who's on him.

Murphy plays a lovely 20-yard handpass to Geaney who collects and angles to shoot. He is in a perfect position to execute. A supreme scorer off either foot, it's odds-on he makes the play to push Kerry two points clear, almost certainly sending them to the final. All he needs is a sniff. Keith has some decisions to make. Does he dive in and try to outmuscle Geaney, thereby risking the concession of a free and losing the game? Or does he stay on his feet, risking being made look silly by Geaney's footwork?

Nobody makes Keith look silly. Not even the best finishers in the business. Geaney initially moves to his right.

Keith, stuck to him, suffocates any chance of a shot there. Geaney goes again, jinking inside onto his left foot this time. Just as he's about to shoot, Keith reaches in and puts him off, forcing him to solo. For a microsecond, Keith is on his knees. Geaney goes a third time only to find Keith back on his feet, fully primed. This time, no doubt put off by Keith's dogged persistence, Geaney pauses and suddenly Higgins engages, smashes him and the ball falls loose. In equal parts desperation and frustration, Kerry concede a free.

Not quite done, Keith is on the attack. Throughout the final moments of the game, he is constantly demanding the ball, driving us forward, looking for ways to create the score we so desperately need. Finally, he finds acres of space on the Cusack Stand side. He carries the ball forward and feeds Paddy Durcan attacking off his right shoulder. Paddy exchanges passes with Donie Vaughan before kicking a famous equalising point. A week later, we beat Kerry in the replay.

Understandably, scores at the end of games get headlines. Ingenious corner-back play rarely does. That never bothered Keith Higgins. We trusted him. He delivered.

FIVE

Character

*'Be more concerned with your character than your reputation
because your character is what you really are, while your
reputation is merely what others think you are.'*

– John Wooden

SACRIFICE is a word synonymous with the GAA.
We love to use it, especially when comparing ourselves to other sports, many of which have their core
values complicated by the nature of their professionalism.
The fact that the GAA remains amateur is a source of great
pride for most people involved in the association, from
grassroots to great champions. We justifiably point to our
'love of the game' as the reason for devoting so much time
and energy to the sport. The sacrifice of the modern-day
intercounty footballer is a narrative that often amuses me.
I don't mean to belittle it but I always found that the last
people to talk about it are the actual players themselves.
Sure, there was plenty of sacrifice – of time, of opportunity,
of relationships – but there was also so much reward. We
got to live out boyhood dreams by playing for the team we
loved since before we could remember. Croke Park, once a
place of pilgrimage as a kid, became our playground.

The irony of the sacrifice narrative is that all intercounty
footballers are selfish even if we don't start out that way.
By the time I retired in 2019, I still hated not being picked
regardless of whether that non-selection was for my or the

team's good. Even as the tactic of the impact sub – or 'starting from the bench' – became much more palatable as the game and my career evolved, I still wanted to hear my name called out in team selection meetings. I just wanted to play. Like a 35-year-old kid. I wanted it so badly that even right until the end I never viewed the time devoted to my football career as a sacrifice. I saw it only as a privilege.

Ask most intercounty hurlers or footballers and they'll tell you the same. We are a selfish bunch. We do it for our egos, we do it for our families. Sometimes that sense of obligation to others can be suffocating, but we do it anyway. We keep doing it because we are petrified that the very moment we stop, the team will win it all without us. We try to be bigger than that, but it nags. For all the strength we condition ourselves to possess and retain, we are a fickle bunch. Yes, you are part of a team, but you are only one expendable part. Sure, there'll be days we resent it. Days when we send our partners off to weddings on the far side of the country without us. Days we miss kids' birthdays to sit on a bench in the rain in Ballybofey. But the flip side is immense. Crucially, we choose to do it.

The margins between first and last man on a Gaelic football panel are minute. You might be one of the best 'keepers in the country, but if David Clarke or Stephen Cluxton are ahead of you, there's little you can do. I saw plenty of lads pass through Mayo squads arguably more talented than me but due to bad luck or bad timing or a bad attitude, they didn't get their chance to claim a jersey. There were others though who, although not getting picked, served a much higher purpose than even they understood. Theirs is an entirely different kind of sacrifice. They do it with little of the adulation that goes with being a 'star' on a team like Mayo.

One such player was Caolan Crowe.

Caolan epitomised the true meaning of a team player. A quality footballer in his own right, he was involved in the Mayo team from 2016 to 2019. In that time, he only appeared eleven times in league and championship. That stat is not a fair reflection of what he brought to the team. As a versatile defender, good on the ball and bull strong, Caolan made most of his appearances in the full-back line, where he was vying with Keith Higgins, Brendan Harrison, Ger Cafferkey and Chrissy Barrett for a jersey. From a purely footballing standpoint, Caolan was more than comfortable in that company but his true greatness lay in his attitude. In the simplest terms, he always put the team first. Over the course of his Mayo career, he had more disappointments than anyone else involved in that group. He was an excellent trainer and had a hugely positive presence in the dressing room and on the field, but regularly he found himself just outside the match-day 26, often losing out to David Drake who offered more pace and versatility in the wide, open spaces of Croke Park. Whatever frustration he must have felt was surely amplified by the fact that many players, including me, felt he should have been in those squads. To my mind, both players could've been accommodated. Whenever we would attempt to commiserate with him, telling him how hard done by we thought he was, his response was always the same:

"I will be fine, concentrate on the game, see you after the match."

They say a quiet priest never got a parish. I would not have been so accepting of my fate if it were me being left out. Was that a weakness on Caolan's behalf? I don't think so. I see it as the opposite. I see it as an incredible act of strength that he took those mini-defeats and responded the way he did.

How did he respond? One way was by making me better.

Caolan's 'team first' attitude was best emphasised during a team-building exercise we did prior to the 2017 All-Ireland final. Our psychologist Niamh Fitzpatrick asked each player a simple question: "What is your promise to the team to help us prepare and win?"

At this late stage of a gruelling season during which he had given everything, Caolan knew he wasn't going to make the squad for the final. His answer, however, epitomised his character and why he had such a high standing within the group: "I promise to get whoever I'm marking at training this week ready for Sunday."

No table-thumping. No posturing in front of a management whose mind he could not change. No whining about being left out. He did exactly what he said he'd do. He trained harder than ever that week. I should know. I still have the scars.

If Caolan's answer during that team-building exercise was him saying out loud what he was going to do for the team, the work he had put in for two whole seasons up to that point was the physical manifestation of those words.

That same season, 2017, I won Footballer of the Year. While it never made up for not winning an All-Ireland, it was a huge personal achievement for me especially since it came so late in my playing career. Caolan's role in that award cannot be overstated. If I can credit myself with one thing, it was being smart enough at that stage to identify who could make me better. That's why I chose to mark Caolan in training so often. I quickly learned this guy had my number. He knew my runs, he was physically stronger than me and he could attack. One of the things that makes A v B games so challenging as a forward is that the officiating can be a little loose. Crucially, there are no umpires to monitor any off-the-ball stuff! The upshot was that you were ready for whatever was coming the following Sunday when a full set of officials and the prying eyes of TV were there to protect you. While Caolan wasn't dirty, he was the type of player I hated marking. Quicker defenders often had larger egos and wanted to attack more, which suited me as I knew I'd get more freedom to do damage closer to goals. Caolan knew me too well. I was the sole focus of his attention. No matter if he was in the match-day squad or not, he always brought an incredible attitude. No sulking, no bitching, just in to get the job done and get home. When it came to marking Caolan, I always had to bring something new to compete: changing the direction of my runs, shooting off my weak side, timing my movement better. He constantly challenged me to find ways to beat him. I had some rough hours during those in-house games marking Caolan.

Far from demoralising me though, those encounters gave me the confidence that no matter who I came up against in Croke Park, the challenge would often not be as difficult as what I had gone through with Caolan. That may sound like an exaggeration but trust me, it isn't. For those sessions, there existed a silent contract between Caolan and me, the terms of which were undiscussed but very simple: he would do everything in his ability to have me ready. Maybe it was his own frustrations at not being picked being taken out on me (he battered me) but whatever it was, it made me and the team infinitely better.

When I look back on those individual successes I had in 2017, I sometimes feel a guilt that they weren't shared. I know the work Caolan put into preparing himself mentally and physically and the knock-on effect his application and craftmanship as a defender had on getting me ready for the Roscommon, Kerry and Dublin games. Sometimes you would love to share individual awards with teammates who don't ever see that limelight. I hope Caolan looks back with great satisfaction on his contribution to those Mayo teams with which he was involved and knows that any success I had in 2017 was as much down to him as it was to me.

★★★★★

I often hear talk about why these boys continue to do it. Do they stick around just to be associated with something successful? For the holidays? The gear? Nonsense. First, no manager I've ever played under would entertain one player they didn't feel added value to the group. Quite the opposite. The nature of intercounty football is so ruthless that the second you are deemed surplus, you're cut. Secondly, their task is so thankless I don't know how they keep going. I don't mean that in a condescending way but they do so much heavy lifting for the group with very little relative reward. That's a real sacrifice in a team setting. The notion that it's anything else is just plain lazy.

I never spoke to Caolan about this, but I doubt he saw himself as inferior to any defender already on the team. His competition for a starting place was a group of seasoned All-Stars. He obviously had to rationalise his situation to keep playing such a pivotal role. However he did this, he never relented in his application or his commitment. He showed real character.

★★★★★

The Team. The Bench. The Others. Three distinct groups within one squad. Three extremely different emotional experiences yet we reaffirm the message that we are all in this together. There's a moment in Pat Comer's documentary *A Year 'Til Sunday* that poignantly captures Galway manager John O'Mahony telling player Robin Doyle that he will not be on the match-day squad for their upcoming All-Ireland final against Kildare. The conversation is silent to us, the viewer, but we don't really need to hear the words, as Doyle's face tells its own brutal story. As Johno walks away from him, Doyle is suddenly left alone with his thoughts, juggling an O'Neills' football as he grapples with the disappointment. In those moments, the loneliness is never just about the individual and their ego. It's about the drive home from training. It's about telling your partner whose own life has been on hold for nine months while you've been training and playing. It's about the phone call home to your parents who, in turn, mask their own disappointment even though they've been waiting for this day since they first drove you to training as a child.

There are always ten or so players who must hear this news before big games. Ten or so guys asked to put a brave face on it for the sake of the team. That's why culture is so important. Reading it on a page or in a tweet is one thing but identifying the need for it and developing an effective process to teach it to players is the challenge of a great coach. How do we engage those young players who find themselves on the periphery of a playing group? Asking them for their opinion. Giving them homework for games – analysis of opposition, critique of our own team. All these seemingly innocuous gestures count. If those guys are willing to devote their time for relatively little reward, they deserve the same respect as the first name on the team sheet. Exclusion breeds resentment.

Much is made of teams sweeping dressing rooms after games. I get it. However, the worth of the act is then devalued by it being exploited for reputational gain. But, at the core of that philosophy are humility and respect. The idea that when the lights are off, we are all equal within the team. What we do when no one's watching matters more than what we do in front of 82,000 people in Croke Park. One enables the other. The omnipresence of social media has seen reputation become more important than character. Reputation can be manipulated and presented. A person's character cannot. Guys like Caolan Crowe epitomised this. They put in just as much as everyone else and, come Sunday, they had to take a back seat. When the great teams win, they rightfully acknowledge those players, realising their success would not have been possible without them. It sounds clichéd but they're easily the truest words they'll speak.

When you look at the most successful teams of the modern era – Dublin footballers, Kilkenny and Limerick hurlers – you just know immediately they have got the culture right. You know they have a half-dozen Caolan Crowes willing to put the team first, but also ready if called upon.

The Best of Caolan Crowe

In March 2018, we travelled to Ballybofey knowing a defeat to Donegal would mean relegation from Division One football for the first time in 20 years. Understandably, our poor form in the league had us in the spotlight, leading many to believe we were on the wane. Donegal, too, were fighting for survival. With it being the last round of the league, the entire game had a championship feel to it. In the dying moments, a point down, Kevin McLoughlin kicked an incredible score off his right foot to tie it and, crucially, to save the team from relegation. It felt like a victory.

We had taken so much pride in our league record, we didn't want to be the team to lose that status especially on live television on a Sunday afternoon. If Kevin's score was the defining act, there was an intervention moments before that was just as important. Donegal's Patrick McBrearty is a real threat throughout. Caolan picked him up for the whole game and limited him to just two points from play. Now, with Donegal a point up and looking to close, McBrearty is on the ball on our end-line and trying to manufacture a shot or, even better for them, a scorable free. Caolan is on him and knows any mistake or lazy hand results in a tap-over score and our relegation.

Instead, Caolan stays disciplined, tackles with his near hand and forces McBrearty back out on his left foot. Under immense pressure from Caolan, McBrearty shoots, Caolan stretches and gets his fingertips to the ball, taking the pace off it and it drops into the waiting arms of our 'keeper David Clarke. Inspired and disciplined defending by Caolan, something I witnessed at very close quarters throughout our time sparring with each other. Mayo attack, Kevin McLoughlin takes over and the rest is history.

Division One status secured, so too Caolan Crowe's status among the team as a guy you could count on.

SIX

Quality

'However ordinary each of us may seem, we are all in some way special, and can do things that are extraordinary, perhaps until then ... even thought impossible.'

– Sir Roger Bannister

A S COACHES and supporters, we can obsess over talent. I've spoken already about the impact Cillian O'Connor and Aidan O'Shea have had on Mayo football, transitioning seamlessly from exceptional underage players to incredible senior footballers. With guys like them, it's almost as if their paths were mapped out by some higher power. Watching them play minor football, you could tell they had long careers ahead of them. Of course, it's easy to say that now. Their paths were mapped out by nobody but themselves. Being a brilliant minor is no guarantee of anything apart from added pressure. The history of football in Mayo is littered with hundreds of examples of young guys burning it up at underage level, only to fall away for a multitude of reasons.

How many teams of players could you pick of lads from the county who were brilliant underage players but subsequently never 'made it'? As a county, we have a proud underage record. One by-product of being consistently competitive on a national stage is that our underage squads tend to be the focus of selection for our senior teams. I benefitted from this. Though well regarded, I was a peripheral player on the minor teams with which I was involved but just by being there, I put myself on the radar. For me, it opened the door to progression to the U21s. It grabbed the interest of college and university teams who were recruiting for Sigerson. It gave me status within my club. Crucially, it validated a lot of the work I had already done on myself and gave me the confidence to push on.

By the time I played U21 for Mayo, I felt comfortable with the surroundings and personalities that could otherwise prove intimidating. That allowed me to relax and concentrate on the reason I was there – to play football. In many respects, my path, though unscripted, was the perfect one for me. Although I certainly thought I should've been the star of every team I played on, by not being that guy, I progressed at a gradual and sustainable rate. I set my own targets. Better players came and went but I trusted I would outlast them because I had confidence in my own potential. There were no external eyes upon me nor was there anybody surprised when I broke through. I may have been 'one to watch', but I was one of 50 lads around the county 'to watch'. There was a lot of work to do, but the foundation was there. The rest was up to me.

I often wonder what would have happened if I had been missed by the system and never been selected for a minor squad? Would I have stuck at it or fallen away? Maybe I would have resigned myself to accepting that I was not part of any grander plan and pursued other interests. If my form for Ballagh' were good, would the fact that I had never played underage for Mayo count against me? It's all obsolete now but I constantly think about it in the context of younger players and their development. The underage structures are such that young talent should be spotted and developed wherever possible. It's human nature, however, that some develop later than others. Everybody's circumstances are different. Some young lads freeze when they walk into a county dressing room, the only player from a club with no-one going to bat for them. They sit down quietly and look around at players who know each other from school or previous teams: guys at ease in each other's company, shooting the breeze and cracking jokes. It can be an intimidating place. Through no fault of the player they can underperform, and their chance is lost. It shouldn't be the end, however. There is plenty of evidence to the contrary.

★★★★★

Lee Keegan is the best footballer I have ever played with. I say this having spent many days and nights in the trenches with Ciarán McDonald, Keith Higgins, Alan Dillon and Cillian O'Connor, each one of them special players who would have graced any team in the country.

Lee is just different. He went from being a guy who never played minor for Mayo to being the Jesus nut of the senior team. He became our beating heart. His performances from 2015 to 2017 were nothing short of incredible. When Lee first arrived on the Mayo scene in the winter of 2011, he immediately stood out. He was burning lads on runs from day one. His physicality was immense.

He had played a lot of rugby in his teens, and it told in the attritional way he played football. He may have been a little late to the set-up but when he came in, he wasn't intimidated by anybody. He drove us. His arrival made a lot of more experienced lads take notice. Lee was just a different breed. The one word I always think of with Lee is quality. He had it in spades. The talk around the camp after he came in was all the same: "Where has this guy been?!". On top of everything, he seemed like a sound fella. The bastard had everything! Well, not quite everything. Taking his first couple of seasons in isolation, you'd say Lee was an elite player almost immediately but the improvements he made between 2012 and 2015 saw him become the best wing-back in the game since Tomas Ó Sé.

One inconsistent element of his game was his shooting. He could score and never lacked the confidence to shoot, but he was erratic. Although never an easy lad to mark, he lacked the guile in the opposing half which would allow you (the forward) to take a risk and let him wander, gambling he'd screw up the shot while leaving you free. So, he dug deep and focused on his kicking, often by himself before and after training. The fruits of that endeavour were plain to see. Over the course of those three epic seasons from 2015 to 2017, Lee scored 4-10 from the quarter-final stages on. These games were played against the likes of Donegal, Kerry and Dublin. The scores came off both feet and were often of his own creation. They mostly came in clutch scenarios – a period in games when we were drifting and needed something.

A case in point is his score off his left foot in the 2016 quarter-final versus Tyrone. I had watched Lee take on that shot so often at training. I swear he missed every time. Yet, when we needed him and he needed to execute, he nailed it. Critical to Lee's development were a few shrewd additions James Horan made to his backroom team. In 2011 and 2012, Cian O'Neill, Ed Coughlan and Kieran Shannon came in. All three had a hugely positive influence on the group but the arrival of Donie Buckley in 2013 was a game-changer for Lee in particular. Donie is a strong character, not one to be pushed around. The work he did with Lee in channelling his aggression and improving his skills elevated Lee's performances immensely. Lee always trained as if his life depended on it. Along with Donie Vaughan, he was the fittest player on the panel. All these coaches, in their own way, taught Lee how to better manage his energy. They harnessed what he already had and allowed him to focus on his softer skills – his shooting, kick passing and footwork.

The most remarkable thing about Lee's scoring performances in big games was that almost without exception he racked up those totals marking the opposition's best man. He did so without ever abandoning his defensive duties. He went out to outplay and outscore his opponent. Man-marking usually means sacrificing your own offensive performance to nullify the other team's main threat. It's a cancel job. Not so with Lee. He was always marking the danger. He sought out the confrontation. He thrived on it. Who can forget his battles with Sean Cavanagh, Diarmuid Connolly and Ciarán Kilkenny, three of the best players this century? Ask those boys, they'll tell you all about marking Lee Keegan.

What made Lee horrible to play against was he simply did not want you – his opponent – to touch the ball. He wanted to ruin your day. He kept Ciarán Kilkenny – effectively Dublin's point guard – to eight possessions in the 2017 final. Think about that. When marking Diarmuid Connolly he played in his face, front on, and man to man. His aim was to frustrate opponents by making every ball a scrap, a battle. Many defenders are happy to defend a player once he is in possession. Lee just thought differently. He never once allowed you a soft possession. That was one half of his mantra. The other was that once he beat you to it, he would make you pay by transitioning immediately into attack, creating or kicking a score himself. I never came across a player who combined such raw animal aggression in defence with an instinct and ability to attack so devastatingly.

The confidence Lee brought to the team in the biggest games was palpable. We knew going out that we didn't need to worry about their best player. We also knew that if we were in trouble, Lee would pop up. This happened time and time again.

The other area where Lee markedly improved was his combativeness. Early on, he'd tear the head off an experienced lad like Kevin McLoughlin at training, but the same aggression would be absent in the bigger games for Mayo as if he were unaware of his own strength. Only he knows what changed but, by 2015, Lee had turned into an animal. He was the most ruthless player I've seen. Physically, he was afraid of nothing. Mentally, he developed an incredible big-game temperament. He was built for Croke Park. The bigger the game, the better the opposition, the more Lee thrived. I remember him commenting after the All-Ireland final loss to Donegal in 2012 that he loved every minute of it. I don't think that ever changed. He had a psychic energy that's hard to explain.

You always got the sense from Lee that as much as he loves football it wouldn't weigh on his mind unduly. He wouldn't overthink it. He genuinely loves the craic, the few pints. And, boy, is he loyal. Lee Keegan would bury the body with you. I've no doubt about that.

★★★★★

Undoubtedly Lee had attributes that would have seen him excel in many sports such as rugby, soccer or athletics. What is often overlooked is the work he put in to get himself to a level that has seen him become the highest-scoring defender in championship history. That's where his greatness lies. That, and the fact that he showed up every single night with a smile on his face. The smile would still be on his face an hour later as he'd skin you alive in a drill. It was odd to watch him become a figure of resentment outside of Mayo as his reputation as an uncompromising defender evolved. If you knew him, you'd know he couldn't care less. What he did care about was his teammates. He was never too big to help another player who needed it. And he was never too big to put in the work on himself. Natural ability may get you a long way towards the top but it's not enough to keep you there. Lee is an example of that.

Mayo have a tradition of producing attacking wing-backs going back to Noel Connelly, Fergal Costello and later, Peadar Gardiner. Each one of them left clues a hungry Lee Keegan devoured. To me, it's no coincidence that just a few years after Lee burst onto the scene Mayo produced another All-Star wing-back in Paddy Durcan. Paddy brought huge energy to the set-up in his 2015 debut season, displaying an aggression and precision in defence and attack that was straight out of the Lee Keegan playbook. Another man who could dig you out of a hole with a score when the team needed it: his equaliser against Kerry in the 2017 semi-final will live long in the memory of Mayo supporters. There was nothing lucky about that score. It was a perfect example of Paddy's fearlessness and quality as a footballer.

Only Paddy can say how much he learned from Lee, but as a county we are blessed to have had both. Paddy's performances throughout a fractured 2019 season were among the best I've witnessed from any Mayo player in a single year: from nullifying Shane Walsh in our demolition of Galway in a crunch Super 8s game to his outstanding display on the irrepressible Ryan McHugh in a must-win clash against Donegal a week later. He did so kicking two outstanding scores, always offering the team an out in clutch moments. His most memorable performance was perhaps his last of that year as we fell to Dublin in the semi-final. Paddy was given the job of marking Jack McCaffrey, the best footballer in the country at that time. Not only did he completely dominate him but he kicked a couple of points in the process. His performance that day was nothing short of defiant. Just as with Lee, none of this happened by accident. Paddy had the talent, but more importantly, he had the desire to work and learn. In Leeroy, he had the perfect teacher.

The Best of Lee Keegan

When contemplating Lee Keegan's greatest hits, a man is spoiled for choice. His performances against Dublin, Tyrone and Kerry in Croke Park easily rank among the best delivered by any Mayo player in championship football. For me, however, there is a less obvious one that stands out more than any other.

In 2017, after two epic finals against Dublin the year before, we limped through the championship. First, we are dumped out of Connacht by Galway, a shadow of the team that had ended the previous season. We follow that loss with too-close-for-comfort victories over Derry and Cork. I say victories but they barely felt like them. We are a team in a funk and are unsure of a way out. Somehow, we find ourselves back in Croke Park, where a hungry Roscommon are waiting to put us out of our misery. If one game is to epitomise where we are that season, it is that one.

We are all over the place, stuck to the ground. Roscommon have the run on us. Their backs are on top, preventing us from getting any easy possession and building scores. Their forwards too have the upper hand. We can't get to grips with their kickout. We need something, someone to step up and drag us out of the hole we've dug for ourselves. On that dirty Sunday afternoon in a saturated Croke Park, Lee Keegan, playing midfield and marking Roscommon's best player Enda Smith, drags us through. We are on the verge of being beaten by a second Connacht team in a single championship season, and one managed by Kevin

McStay, himself a proud Mayo man. Losing this game may have marked the end of the team. Instead, Lee just takes off, scoring 1-3, while completely taking Smith out of the game. Carried on Lee's back, we scrambled a draw. The following week, we annihilated Roscommon, before beating Kerry after two epic semi-finals.

A season that was perpetually on life support turned out to be one of our most memorable. Not for the first time, it was all thanks to Lee Keegan.

SEVEN

Leave the Jersey in a Better Place

'Plant trees you'll never see.'

– Greek proverb

A FOOTBALL career resembles life in many ways. You start off innocent and relatively carefree. One minute you're a kid out messing with your mates. The next, you're part of a county set-up, mixing it with players you saw as heroes only months before. You fly by them at training, full of exuberance and enthusiasm, half-wondering what's taking them so long. You bounce into games while they stroll. They never look as old and tired as when you're training in the dead of winter, while you never feel more alive. Come summer, you marvel at their ability to perform as you start to learn the hard way what it is to time your run.

Innocence gradually gives way to insecurity as you enter the adolescence of your career. You are wiser to some things, increasingly paranoid about others. What does the manager really think of me? Who's this new young fella? You train harder not smarter. You inevitably take yourself too seriously. To perform to your potential, you need everything to be just right, in place and on schedule. Your world, which will never be as small, revolves around you. Your ego, which will never be as big, is perilously fragile. There is no greater representation of this than your belief that the team cannot survive without you.

If you are lucky enough to survive this delayed adolescence, maturity eventually arrives. It can come naturally or be inspired by an event such as an injury or a change in family circumstances like getting married or having kids. Slowly, then quite suddenly, you can see the game and your place in it for what it truly is: a release. The team – Mayo football – will endure beyond you. You prepare the best you can for games, but interruptions and miscalculations become an accepted part of life. Coaches and managers come and go. The young will saunter in hot and burn you in runs at training. Their numbers and stat lines would make you feel ten years older than you already are – if you cared enough to take notice – but you have a quiet confidence in your own ability. You trust your process no matter how flawed or fractured it may be. You stretch more, physically and mentally. You see the end even if you're not quite sure of the when or the how. It may sound clichéd but it's a cliché because it's true.

Most players exist in the minds of supporters only in the context of the 70 minutes they see them play on a Sunday. It makes sense that when those players drift away the only thing that's missed by fans is their performance between the white lines. As players get older, their playing minutes often decrease, making the transition from firm fan favourite to life without them a little easier, just like any breakup. What the supporters can never see is the influence of those players on the group they leave behind. If you are lucky enough to survive infancy, adolescence and maturity as a player in a county set-up, it's almost incumbent upon you to do the one thing that those on the outside will never see: leave the jersey in a better place.

One such player was Trevor Mortimer. The middle brother of three who represented Mayo with distinction over two decades, Trevor bled green and red. He had seen four management teams come and go by the time he came back for what would be his final season in 2011. He had played through many changes, not just in personnel, but in training regimes, nutrition and technologies. As the playing of the game evolved, so did the language surrounding it. By the time James Horan took over, video analysis, individualised training plans and GPS tracking were the norm. So much had changed in the decade previous it was sometimes easy to forget the core values of playing. Trevor represented these. In the simplest terms, he practiced what he preached: honesty. The ball is there to be won, you go and f**kin' win it. When the game is on the line you need action, not talk. Just do your job. Trevor took his role in the team very seriously. He was an incredible influence on a young group of footballers breaking through, many of whom would form the spine of a team that proved itself to be one of the best of the next decade.

Trevor was decidedly no-nonsense. As team captain in 2010, he led the team admirably in incredibly difficult circumstances. It ended an era during which we had contested two All-Irelands but were well short in terms of talent and application. The support for the team off the field and in the stands was disjointed if well meaning. There was a stress fracture running through Mayo football that was never severe enough to be diagnosed. Our defeat that fateful night to Longford in 2010 put us out of the championship. It ended Johno's second coming as manager and many intercounty careers. Not Trevor's. I've no doubt he felt the pain of that defeat even more severely than many of us and maybe the easier thing for him would've been to walk away, his duty done. Instead, he returned in 2011, determined to contribute. Adamant that he would leave the jersey – and the team – in a better place.

In positional terms, Trevor's playing years followed a curious trajectory. He first emerged as a bull-strong inside forward. Fearless and skilful. His animal fitness and work rate saw him develop into a tireless wing-forward during his middle years. By the end, he was playing wing-back, a position where he thrived especially as it allowed him to play ball facing the opponent's goal. As an opposing forward, you did not want to see Trevor jogging over to mark you. He had the aggression of a filthy corner-back and the ball skills of an inside forward. Sound like anyone who came after him?

An almost forgotten footnote of the story of Mayo football over the last decade is that Trevor kicked a crucial point in Ruislip in James Horan's first championship game. It was the point that drew us within one point of London as we fought to stave off an historic defeat. Had he not, we would have followed up the previous year's catastrophe in Longford with another humiliating loss. Nobody can know for sure, but the next few years may have had a very different complexion had Trevor and Kevin McLoughlin, who got the equaliser, not saved us that day. The following year, after a season-long apprenticeship, Lee Keegan stepped into Trevor's boots. Before too long he became the player we all now know him to be. A wing-back with the aggression of the filthiest corner-back and the ball skills of an inside forward. I often thought we never saw the best of Trevor Mort at wing-back as he only played one season there but, in hindsight, maybe we did – in Lee Keegan.

Trevor was never the most outwardly expressive. Never the most vocal, but the way he trained helped to develop the team of the next decade. Never was there a lost cause, never was a 50:50 ball not worth fighting for. Trevor was cut from a different cloth. If you wanted things easy, he was not the guy to be around. We hear constantly of certain 'one per centers' who make teams great. Trevor was ahead of his time, but in the most old school of ways. Everything he did, every day at training and every game he played for Mayo silently screamed, 'if you want it done, follow me'.

★★★★★

I was privileged to count Kevin Cahill as a clubmate. Kevin was a prince of a full-back who along with Meath's Darren Fay dominated the position in the late '90s. The traditional model of a physical, brutish 'stopper', epitomised by Mick Lyons, gave way to a more rounded defender – one who could read the game, mark his man and link play. Fay and Cahill shared octopus-like qualities which made them nightmares for an inside forward. Key elements of their greatness were their footwork and tackling. Like Lyons before them, they had physical presence, but they brought a subtlety and nuance to the position. If Cahill did a lot to evolve it, another Mayo man, Ger Cafferkey, came damn close to perfecting it on and off the pitch. Over a decade in the Mayo jersey, Ger experienced many highs including an All-Star in 2012, and some lows too, including a brutal hamstring injury that sidelined him for over a year. Caff gave his all to Mayo and in doing so understood a fundamental truth few others could: as a player, your first job is to make yourself the best possible player you can be. Your second job is understanding how you can make the team better. What can you bring to the dressing room? The first part requires selfishness. The second requires the opposite: a selflessness that enables you to sacrifice your own position for the betterment of the team and, crucially, the team's future. It also requires personality and emotional intelligence, both of which Caff had in abundance. He was always learning and always giving back to the team. He never rested on a good or bad game. There was always homework, always questions asked of himself first then others. He was a student of football. Some lads just showed up to train and play but that was only a fraction of what being a Mayo player meant to Ger.

When you are in a group, no matter your status, watching a player of Ger's class and ability dedicate so much time to better those around him is humbling. Whether he was first choice or battling to regain his place, his desire to positively influence his teammates, including rivals for his jersey at times, was something truly exceptional to witness. He drove a culture within a squad that left no room for self-interest. Given his personality, he did so in his own calm, almost academic, way. There was no table-thumping or bravado. His method of teaching was subtle but effective. It's no coincidence Mayo developed players like Brendan Harrison, Paddy Durcan, Padraig O'Hora (a clubmate of Ger's) and Stephen Coen while Caff was playing. They were his teammates but also his protégés though he'd be far too modest to claim them.

On the pitch, Ger was a class act. Never dirty, his ability to read his man and cut out trouble earned the trust of his teammates. Full-back can be a lonely and isolated spot on the field. In many respects, you're at the mercy of what's developing out the field. So many times, Ger found himself one on one with the game's best attackers and so many times he emerged on top. You'd never catch him hitting a 40-yard slider off the outside of his right peg – the man knew his limitations, but he also recognised his ceiling to improve. He never sought adulation, nor did he wallow in self-pity when he struggled for fitness or form. If the Mayo players of today are looking beyond themselves and seeking to improve the guys coming after them, it's because of Ger Cafferkey and his ilk. An admirable legacy to have left behind.

The Best of Ger Cafferkey

There is probably no better example of Ger Caff's brilliance as a player than against All-Ireland champions Dublin in the 2012 semi-final. His first-half performance on Bernard Brogan saw him at his best. Our forwards, led by Cillian, Jason Doc and Alan Dillon, are having a half to remember but the foundation for a great team display is being laid much further back. Brogan, easily one of the top three forwards in the game that year, gets the start any scorer wants by knocking over a couple of easy frees – they're always good for confidence. He follows that up by winning a superb delivery from Paul Flynn out in front of Ger. We know that if Brogan gets motoring the rest of the Dublin forwards will follow. A massive confidence player, it's clear his eye is in.

Ger has different ideas, however. The next ball into Brogan results in him dropping a shot short into David Clarke's hands under huge pressure from Caff. The next, Ger is out in front, winning the ball comfortably and laying it off in his trademark, no-fuss style. Not long after, Ciarán Kilkenny puts a beautiful ball out in front of Bernard. Usually bread and butter for him, he fails to gather clean ball as Ger gets the claw in and knocks it away. Each one of these moments builds confidence in us. Each interception initiates a Mayo attack. Twenty-two minutes in, Dublin register their first point from play from Diarmuid Connolly. Again, Dublin come looking for Brogan. The next ball sees a subtle nudge from Caff and another Mayo possession. The sixth ball into Bernard, it looks like his moment has finally come. He wins it out of front of Ger and, after playing a one-two with James McCarthy, he leaves Ger for what looks like dead. In games like these, such moments matter. As Brogan pulls the trigger, Ger comes from nowhere to execute an incredible block, denying a certain goal that would have changed the game. The confidence courses through the team. We go in at the break six points up. An hour later, we have beaten the All-Ireland champions thanks in no small part to an exhibition of full-back play from Ger Cafferkey.

EIGHT

Note to Oneself – Don't Be Afraid of the Maverick

'If everyone is thinking alike, then no-one is thinking.'

– Benjamin Franklin

I N MAYO, we love ourselves a maverick. Our recent history as a force in Gaelic football has seen us produce quite a few. Willie Joe Padden in the 1980s, Liam McHale in the '90s: these guys were household names in a pre-internet age. They were recognisable all over the country and not just because they were top-class footballers. They also had an X-factor. There was something different about them. Willie Joe was 5'11" but out-fetched midfielders half a foot taller than him. He also looked like a musketeer. McHale was 6'5" and moved with the deft feet of a dancer. His reputation as one of the country's best basketball players added to the mystique. That, and the fact he looked like he was from the beaches of California.

These guys were larger-than-life characters from my youth. They captured imaginations and divided opinions. All-Ireland winning teams from other counties came and went but few seemed to have those mavericks in their ranks.

But, as much as we love mavericks, we can also be suspicious of them. They are almost always the first, easy target for our anger when things go wrong. People's perception of players who are in any way 'different' is often an unforgiving one. The days we win, it's because of them. The days we lose, it's because they wore white boots. There is nothing new in this dynamic. When things are not going well, the maverick can be perceived as the disruptor. This groupthink can be a curse. I believe our lack of faith in players who are different has held us back.

Children, especially, are drawn to these players. Crucially, kids share none of our adult suspicion or scepticism. They are unaffected by rumour and conjecture. They believe only what their eyes tell them. Children see things in a different way and, consequently, maverick players can have a much more profound impact on us as kids than victories or defeats do. The pain and joy of those events pass very quickly. The memory of seeing a player doing something special stays with you for life. Children remember *how* their favourite players did things rather than *what* the outcome was. The act is everything. The fascination with results comes later.

I was lucky as a kid to grow up in a time when the number ten was king. European football became more popular on television. Watching Baggio, Totti and Del Piero play in Serie A in Italy had us all out on the green trying things we may not have attempted previously. These guys lit up our imaginations and taught us that to try new things was to improve. Failing was part of the process. It took a little time for the English clubs we all supported to become as trusting of these unique players as their European counterparts. I was a mad Liverpool fan growing up, so I took no joy out of watching Frenchman Eric Cantona morph from difficult misfit into a mercurial genius. It's a little ironic that it took a dour Scotsman in Alex Ferguson to see in him what so many other managers and coaches had missed or tried, and failed, to harness. Cantona's personality was that of the classic enigma, but he lit up a league that for so long had been resistant to temperamental outsiders.

As I transition from player to coach, I admire more and more the courage of coaches who find ways to integrate the maverick into their teams. The more diverse the skill set of our playing groups, the more potential they possess. Exposure to these players forces good players to look inward and examine how they can become better, just as we did when we were wide-eyed kids trying to mimic the classic number tens. Gaelic games have often treated these players as a luxury or an indulgence. Other sports have built teams around them.

In my time involved with Mayo teams, I've seen two players who fit the maverick profile. Two guys who once you saw them play, you got immediately excited at the prospect of playing with them, of testing yourself against them and of learning from them.

The first was Ciarán McDonald. Few players have captivated Gaelic football fans the way Ciarán did. The look, the skills, the attitude: he stood out a mile on every pitch he graced. I had the pleasure of sharing the field with him for the first few years of my senior intercounty career. Seeing him in action up close was as thrilling as you might expect. I don't think I've ever seen a player more at one with a football as Ciarán. He saw the game differently, the way great players in every sport do. I'm sure, given his 'temperamental' side, he was often difficult to manage. I wonder how much of that had to do with our unwillingness to trust him enough to build a team around his talents? His club Crossmolina did this to stunning effect, winning six county championships in a glorious ten-year spell. McDonald was the fulcrum for everything on that club team, sometimes to a fault but, if a club team is as dominant for a decade as Cross' were in a county championship as competitive as Mayo's, you have all the proof you need that trusting Ciarán was the right thing to do. He took that trust and he honoured it. It made him and, crucially, his club team, better.

Watching him play, you felt like that kid watching Del Piero. In 2003, I was playing a bit of soccer with Longford Town U21s. Our goalkeeper at the time was Gary Cassin, a Dublin lad living in Longford. He was mad to convince me to keep playing soccer. For me, it wasn't an option. John Maughan had just called me into the Mayo senior squad for the first time, so I knew soccer was going to get left behind. Cassin was always telling me what a crap sport he thought Gaelic football was. I told him one evening if he really wanted to see what the sport had to offer he should watch the number eleven for Crossmolina in that St Patrick's Day All-Ireland club final in Croke Park. Watch the player with the blonde hair and white boots, I told him. "You won't be disappointed."

Gary arrives out at the next training with his white socks pulled up to the knees (à la McDonald), shouting at me from the goals about how brilliant Ciarán Mc was. He spent the whole week driving us mad at training trying to kick the ball off the outside of his boot, just like McDonald. That was the power of Ciarán. He could convert the non-believers. Many people were drawn to him because of his image – the hair, the boots, the tan. But once there, they stayed for his talent. When he was on it, he was nothing short of brilliant.

In 2004, we were an ordinary Mayo team. Ciarán only joined us after the league, but he lit up that championship, carrying us to the final against Kerry. For a guy who was apparently a difficult individual, he made that team infinitely better. Looking back, I wished we better understood how to harness his maverick nature. I understand it's easier for a club to use a focal point like Ciarán to dominate given the talent differential at that level but I still believe we missed a huge trick by not embracing him more and en-abling him to do his thing while supporting the broader goals of the team.

Why is that? How would Alex Ferguson have handled Ciarán? No two players are the same. As coaches, we need to adapt to all personality types. If that talent eventually exhausts the patience of the team there's little more you can do, but I believe your job as a coach is to do your abso-lute maximum to make the team better. That requires the emotional intelligence to adapt your approach from player to player.

It must be acknowledged that Ciarán's peak coincided with a difficult time for Mayo football. It's hard to say ex-actly why that was even for someone on the inside like me. Although we reached two All-Ireland finals in the mid-

2000s there were issues that were hard to define and therefore impossible to sort. We all wanted the same thing – players, management, county board, clubs – but sometimes it was difficult to get on the same page. Integrating a maverick talent like Ciarán McDonald proved harder than it perhaps should've been. He was ahead of his time. I'd like to think we learned as a county and were a little better able to cope by the time the next star came along.

I had few if any regrets when I retired in 2019. Ciarán joined James Horan's backroom team the year after I left. How I would have loved to have picked his brain, me as a senior player, him as a coach! What a resource for that group to have.

★★★★★

A couple of years after Ciarán played his last game for Mayo, we were drifting as a team. Confused by our own identity and missing a star to follow. We had won an All-Ireland U21 in 2006 and with John O'Mahony back for his second stint in charge, the potential was there for us to do damage, but we just weren't clicking.

In the summer of 2008, our minor team lifted the county's spirits. We had lost to Galway and Tyrone in the senior championship so our minor team's run to the final was a welcome boost to morale. A talented bunch, they had a standout star in young Aidan O'Shea, 18 years old but already playing a man's game. In the final they met Tyrone who had a wunderkind of their own in Kyle Coney. If Coney was a silk-smooth inside forward, Aidan was a wrecking ball. His ability to dominate games with his size and ball skills made the whole country take notice. Mayo lost after two great games to Tyrone but we all left Longford after the replay believing we'd seen the next Mayo superstar.

Aidan was different in every aspect. His sheer physicality and size made him stand out from an early age. The way he played, carrying the ball, breaking up attacks, fielding high and kicking scores gained him immediate attention from those first big performances as a minor. His experience playing basketball gave him a more subtle quality in his play, the same thing Liam McHale had before him. He had good feet and quick hands which enabled him to distribute the ball as effectively as a player half his size. Many players shy away from the attention that can follow prodigious talent, but Aidan embraced and enjoyed it. Being so aware of it as a young fella, and then being able to handle it, pointed to an emotional intelligence rare in players so inexperienced. It was as if Aidan believed he was born to do this. Since making his senior debut in 2009, just one year out of minor, he has gone on to become one of the biggest stars the game has ever seen. He's done so while never sacrificing his team or his own application. Over the years, I have seen the pursuit of stardom obstruct the path of some potentially great players. They get obsessed with their profile and forget that their abilities as a footballer have gained them this attention in the first place. Their profile grows but their footballing performance declines. They can often become a distraction for the group. A manager senses this and will grow frustrated. Eventually that player ends up on the bench.

It leads to the question: when is the maverick truly accepted?

As I've mentioned already, my introduction to senior football was like that experienced by most other young players. There was no hype. The only pressure I felt was the pressure I put on myself. For the few guys like Aidan, it was a completely different scenario. He came in with a target painted on his back. Being a beast of a young fella only made him a bigger target. Literally.

Who does this pup think he is?

Yet he thrived on it. The positions he played too meant there was nowhere for him to hide. Always in the middle of everything, either at midfield, centre-forward or the edge of the square. He thrived on that responsibility from the moment he came into the senior set-up. Aidan always felt like he belonged at the top table. He apologised for nothing. His arrogance was very un-Mayolike and was refreshing. He lacked any of the torture that can hold back so many prodigious talents. He was sure of himself: that's one of his greatest strengths.

In many respects he was Mayo's first modern player. He was extremely aware of his own profile and far from that being a negative thing, it made him an asset to Mayo football on and off the field. He has helped to build the Mayo brand throughout the country and further afield. His ability and willingness to interact with children and the positive effect he has on the next generation of Mayo footballers are two of the greatest legacies he will leave when his playing days come to an end.

It's often been rather lazily thrown at Aidan that his personality has been a distraction for this team. It's a trope that usually gets aired after we lose a big game. Again, people crave simplicity and need easy narratives to explain why this or that happened. From my perspective the answer to that question is simple. When a player is consistently adding to the team through his performances, his uniqueness, his social profile and his different personality are all accepted by the group. Since his debut in 2009, Aidan has possibly added more to the Mayo team than any other player. All-Star awards at midfield, centre-forward and full-forward, he has excelled in every role he has been handed. He even coped brilliantly when asked to go to full-back to mark Kieran Donaghy in our famous semi-final victory against Kerry in 2017, putting his ego and reputation on the line. That's what teammates see. That's what management sees.

We have struggled with the independent thinkers in Mayo. I think it's one of the reasons we have not produced as many brilliant inside forwards this last 20 years as we should have. Could it be that we are spotting those differences in players when they're young and coaching the personality out of them? What a tragedy that would be. Imagine a Mayo with no McHale, no Ciarán Mc or no Aidan O'Shea to inspire the next generation after them?

I know that one of the challenges I will face as a coach will be how I handle the 'different' player. Should those nuances be encouraged or suppressed? I hope I have the courage of my convictions to recognise that if those individuals can potentially add value to a team, it will be my job to facilitate an environment in which they can flourish.

The Best of Aidan O'Shea

In the summer of 2015, Aidan O'Shea simply tore the Connacht Championship apart. He torched Galway in Salthill and then scored a hat-trick of goals against Sligo in the Connacht final in Hyde Park. As always with Aidan, his critics would argue his best performances have come with an asterisk; that the opposition he was up against were not of the quality to justify his reputation. So, when Mayo met Donegal in the All-Ireland quarter-final in Croke Park, those critics would get their answer.

Was Aidan really a big-game player?

Waiting for him was the best full-back in the country, Donegal's Neil McGee. McGee and his brother Eamon were huge factors in again making Donegal such a force in the game. Two brilliant defenders, as tough as any players I've ever played against. With all the hype about Aidan coming into the game, we knew they would've done their homework on him. It would've been the easy option to use Aidan as a decoy. Instead, we did the opposite. We embraced the attention. We went for the belly of the beast. Aidan was to be the focal point of everything we would do. He would be the tip of our spear. He wanted it. So, we gave it to him.

The game starts at a frantic pace. The first battle between McGee and O'Shea is won by the Donegal defender. Imagine, after all the build-up, the mindset of a weaker player than Aidan after losing that first ball?

The next ball into him, Aidan claims a huge win, earning a tap-over free for Cillian. In trying to protect McGee, Donegal deployed Mark McHugh as a sweeper in front of Aidan. The ripple effect of that move for us was oceans of space out the middle of the field. This allowed Seamus O'Shea time to pick his deliveries into Aidan and for us to feed off him. Crucially, Aidan was a willing target man. As the half wore on, he became more influential, putting Jason Doherty through on goal to leave Mayo up by two approaching the end of the first half. Donegal respond down the other end and entering injury time Mayo only lead by one. Again, Seamus finds himself in the middle of the park advancing into space. He picks a glorious pass into his brother who is being double teamed by McGee and McHugh. Regardless, Aidan collects, and, in that moment, the world and its mother know what is coming next. Aidan leaves McGee in his wake, fires McHugh to the ground and buries the ball past the giant frame of Donegal goalkeeper Paul Durcan. His fourth goal of the championship but the one that matters most. We go in at the break leading by four. The only story is the utter domination of Aidan O'Shea.

Donegal use the break to re-strategise, moving the other McGee brother, Eamon, onto him. It makes no difference. Diarmuid O'Connor finds Aidan out in front. He wins the ball again and now the runners are streaming off him. The ball is switched across the field and Lee ends up getting Mayo's second goal. Next time, Cillian directs an angled ball to Aidan. He wins it again. This time he drives at Eamon McGee and Paddy McGrath, beats the two of them and sets Lee through the gap to win another handy free. It's 2-8 to 0-6, and we are now pulling away. The teams exchange the next two scores, and in the 46th minute Tom Parsons pings another one to Aidan. They have no answer to him at this stage, he manufactures the space and Keith Higgins drives over a score to put Mayo nine points up. The game is as good as over, a famous victory.

The gravity of what Aidan achieved that day should never be underestimated. Between the 35th and the 47th minutes, Mayo scored two goals and three points. Aidan, who was brilliant throughout, demolished Donegal in those 12 minutes. Against one of the most physical teams you could meet, he dominated and destroyed them even though they were ready for him. Marking two of the best in the game – the famous McGee brothers – he ripped them apart. His critics well and truly silenced, there was no ear-cupping from Aidan. No pointing at the stands. No 'up yours' to his detractors. He just did what he has always done for Mayo – showed up for his team.

NINE

The King of Adversity

'My comeback will be stronger than my setback.'

– Tom Parsons

A S PARENTS, we preach the virtue of dealing with adversity in our children's lives but how often do we pause to practice it? Deep down, we know that losing and getting hurt are part of growing up. We know that by experiencing the pain of setbacks we grow as people and learn lessons that will stand to us later in our lives. We know it but, still, when it comes to our own kids, we often struggle. We don't want to see them hurt. We don't want to see them not picked. We don't want to see them lose. So, sometimes we let them quit too soon rather than face the pain of rejection and the learnings that come from it. Why is that? Is it the guilt of peer pressure we feel as parents that if our kids are failing – especially in public – we are somehow failing them? Is it an overcorrection from our parents' generation, many of whom believed 'suck it up!' was the appropriate response to any expressions of self-doubt from us, their children?

Whatever the reason, it has drastically changed how we see the role of sport in young people's lives today. Personally, I agree with prioritising participation over achievement among younger age groups... to a point. Every kid should get the opportunity to express themselves without the 'fear of failing'. Every kid deserves equal minutes. Every kid needs to learn how to play before they learn how to compete. But as I learned during my adult life on and off the field, the lessons sport taught me as a kid about dealing with adversity stood to me time and time again, even if I hated learning them. By depriving young people of the life lessons that come from winning and losing, particularly in a team environment, I believe we are doing them an injustice. Kids need to learn that sometimes another team or player might just be better than them. Helping them understand this one simple life lesson can greatly enhance their ability to handle failure later in life. We all fail exams. We all get dumped. We all interview for jobs we don't get. Competitive sport teaches us how to fail and, crucially, how to bounce back.

In Mayo, we know a lot about adversity. Historically, our county has arguably been ravaged to a greater extent than any other county by recession and emigration. In that context, losing All-Irelands is hardly a burden. Being from Mayo, however, gives you an edge and it's an edge I needed more than once. In September 2011, a few weeks after losing to Kerry in an All-Ireland semi-final, I broke the fibula in my left leg at International Rules training in Parnell Park. At the time, it was the worst injury of my career. I was lucky. The season was over, and the nature of the injury allowed me to recover and rehab quickly. Aside from the International Rules trip to Australia, I didn't miss a game.

Worse was to come for me, however. Eleven months after my leg break, I tore my cruciate ligament against Down in the All-Ireland quarter-final. Weeks later we beat defending champions Dublin to set up a final date with Donegal. Although I felt ready to physically tackle my comeback, mentally it was the toughest thing I've ever gone through. The torture started straight away. As euphoric as I felt for our guys beating Dublin in the semi-final, I also was hit with this confusing sense of despair. It wasn't the obvious 'I can't believe they will win it without me'. I never felt that way. I was desperate for us to win regardless of my absence. I felt incredibly proud of being part of that team and, thanks to James Horan and his management, I felt part of the team as much as anybody else even when I was injured. This despair came from a different place. I felt a profound sadness, the source of which was my sense that the team needed me to win it. I know that might sound narcissistic, but it was much more complex than that. The feeling was genuine and hard to compute. That was only the beginning of the struggle.

Immediately after we lost to Donegal, I was at my lowest point. With my knee just operated on, I had a long winter of rehabilitation work ahead of me and suddenly the season was over, ending on the cruellest possible note. Standing in the hotel lobby on crutches after the game, putting on a brave face for my teammates and well-wishers, I was dying inside. The next few weeks were rough, I won't lie, and I can only imagine what they were like for those closest to me. As my physical recovery progressed, my mental rehabilitation lagged a couple of steps behind. I was 28 and in great shape so, in a sense, my body was ready for the challenge.

The loneliness was a terror, though. I spent a lot of hours with our skills coach Ed Coughlan on the top pitch in Castlebar as the team trained, often within view. Even though they were only on the next field, they felt a world away. Still, I got there. There were setbacks, like when I started running again and my knee swelled badly and as the knee swelled so did the doubt. But, with the help of the Mayo support team and especially my wife Jennifer I got there. By the time we faced Galway in Salthill in the Connacht quarter-final in May, I was on the bench and ready. I came on, scoring a goal in an emphatic 17-point win. There are photos of me celebrating the goal that in any other context might be funny such was my over-exuberance, but the relief I felt was profound. The journey was not over, however. Coming back from that injury, I hit many plateaus in my recovery, my subsequent playing form and my headspace. That was a long, hard season, one littered with self-doubt and paranoia and one I'll explore in greater detail later in the book. Rest assured, it was probably the most formative year of my footballing life.

★★★★★

One of the key lessons I learned from that year was just how fortunate I was. Fortunate that I had learned hard lessons about myself in my youth that I wouldn't just quit when things got tough and uncomfortable. Fortunate that I had such incredible people in my life who loved and supported me when they saw me struggling. Fortunate that my injuries were such that there was a clear way back. Many before me had done what I was trying to do. I later saw an example of a man who was not so fortunate and who, when dealt the cruellest blow imaginable for a sportsperson, had every reason to quit. Instead, he chose the other path and in so doing became a beacon of positivity and a living, breathing lesson on how to overcome adversity.

It's May 2008, and we're playing Sligo in a Connacht semi-final. John O'Mahony includes three debutants on our starting team – Colm Boyle, Kieran Conroy and a young midfielder with a curly mop of hair from Charlestown, Tom Parsons. Just 20-years-old, Tom goes out and cleans Sligo's talisman Eamonn O'Hara as if he had no idea who he was. Kickout after kickout, Tom rises above him and plucks the ball from the sky, displaying a natural ability to jump, hang and fetch. His raw athleticism makes him stand out. In his first championship game for Mayo, marking an All-Star midfielder, he wins man of the match. It is some arrival. The rest of the year is a washout for Mayo. We lose to Galway and Tyrone and the season has few positives, but Tom's story is one of them.

Later that year, he is selected to represent Ireland in the International Rules series, the youngest player on the squad. He looks set to lead Mayo's midfield for the next decade but it doesn't happen for him. After playing U21, senior, Sigerson and International Rules, Tom struggled to adapt to the new demands ushered in by James Horan and got dropped from the panel in 2011. Suddenly, he goes from being part of five teams, to being left with only one: his club Charlestown, who, as luck would have it, have just been relegated from senior football. Mayo pushed on without Tom.

The cruelty of sport and how you can be king one minute and forgotten the next. Many would've sulked. Maybe Tom did, but it never showed. Suddenly, without all the football that had defined his early 20s, his life faced further changes as he moved to Cardiff for work shortly after being let go by James, commuting regularly over and back to play for Charlestown. Tom has spoken about the pain of being dropped but also how that time away matured him greatly, allowing him to put football in perspective. Suddenly, football was no longer the centre of his world. Living away, the circles he moved in knew nothing about who Mayo were playing in the next round of the league. His world got bigger and, as it grew, so did he. If he harboured bitterness about being dropped, nobody heard about it, and you always hear about it. It takes maturity to realise that all players achieve when they bitch and moan about not being picked is prove the manager who dropped them was right. I say this as somebody who did bitch and moan, especially when I was younger. Tom took the higher road.

Instead of feeling sorry for himself, he dug deep, worked on his game and sought a way back. The way back for him was playing for his club. By the time Tom returned to the panel in 2014, it was clear to all of us how he had handled the adversity that came with the crippling rejection of 2011. He returned in the shape of his life. His physicality and athleticism were at another level. Furthermore, his attitude and personality had a hugely positive impact on the dressing room. King TP was back, and this time he was ready.

★★★★★

Over the next four years, Tom became the midfielder all of us had hoped he would become when he first arrived in 2008. He formed a formidable partnership with Seamie O'Shea, both lads perfectly complementing each other. As the team's personality and identity became stronger, Tom was happy to let others have the limelight. His priorities were clear: how could he help the team? Each year after we lost finals or semi-finals by the tightest of margins, it was always Tom asking before anybody else: why did we lose? Always looking for the answer. Always challenging players to improve. Always challenging himself. He used his difficult experience to not just help himself but the younger lads as well. He was the perfect teammate.

As fate would have it, Tom's tussles with adversity were not yet over. The biggest test was yet to come. In May 2018, against Galway, he ruptured three of the four ligaments in his left knee, tore the fourth and dislocated the knee while also sustaining tears to his calf and hamstring. The footage of the horrific injury is distressing to look at and was much worse in reality. In the early days after the injury, medical experts doubted whether Tom would ever walk again. Weeks later, he was plotting his comeback. The road he travelled was long and tortuous. Three heavy surgeries at Santry Sports Clinic followed over a period of three-and-a-half months. He had grafts taken from his hamstring and quad to reconstruct the knee ligaments, plus a cadaver's ligament – an Achilles from a deceased donor.

Sleeping proved difficult. Tom's wife Carol is a physio, which helped his rehabilitation process. Unable to work, he would spend up to five hours per day rehabbing the injury. The process involved using ice and electrotherapy machines, getting a soft-tissue massage and then spending around 90 minutes on rehab exercises. He'd often do that twice a day. He wore a brace and was in crutches for four or five months. The impact on Tom's mental health must have been immense. So, too, on Carol's. She gave up her job for a year to support him. At every point in this process, nobody expected Tom to play football again. Sure, we hoped for it, but we didn't expect it. All the while, Tom and Carol worked away. He was always coming back. Fifteen months after almost losing his leg, he came on against Dublin in an All-Ireland semi-final. The game that had twice tried to break him had twice lost. In times of adversity, community is everything. The sports community is large but the trauma of an injury is universal to all of us.

Tom received support from South African rugby legend Jean de Villiers and Connacht rugby player Eoghan Masterson, both of whom had suffered similar injuries. De Villiers wrote to Tom and his physio went so far as to correspond with Carol, sharing programmes and exercises. Masterson took it upon himself to visit Tom. These gestures were not done for plaudits or PR, but out of respect for a fellow competitor who had put his body on the line and suffered horribly for it. I know how much Tom appreciated those gestures. I know too that without Carol the road back would've been infinitely more tortuous. Tom Parsons is a special man. There is an incredible amount young people can learn from his ability to handle adversity. To get hurt. To bounce back. To carry on.

Tom's example is not just a sporting one. While out injured, he was brave enough to change career, moving from one very specific field, engineering, to another, occupational wellness. Since retiring from football, he has been brave enough to change careers once again. In the summer of 2021, he was appointed as the CEO of the GPA. Each career move has been a progression in a new direction. I vehemently believe that whatever he does next, Mayo football will benefit from having a man of Tom's charisma and personality around the game. We are sometimes far too willing to cast the net afar when the people we need are right in front of us. To me, he is one such person.

The Best of Tom Parsons

Tom's performance against Dublin in the 2017 All-Ireland final was arguably his best in a Mayo jersey. Marking Brian Fenton, one of the best midfielders the game has ever seen, the battle between them was an epic clash between two men at the peak of their powers. Tom's style of play was not too dissimilar to Fenton's: both incredibly mobile and athletic, both able to affect decisive plays at either end of the pitch. Instead of seeking to nullify the threat of Fenton, Tom went toe to toe with him. If we were to die that day, he knew we could not die wondering.

What best epitomised this spirit was his brilliant chase down of James McCarthy. The game was 13-minutes-old, and after an early goal Dublin were leading by a single point. As Tom is tracking Fenton, James McCarthy, the other Dublin midfielder, spots a gap in the Mayo cover and hits the gas. TP would've been quickly forgiven if he decided to stay tracking Fenton, especially given Fenton's prowess at engineering scores. Instead, Tom decides to hunt McCarthy. Leaving his man, he pursues him like a cheetah would his prey, knocking the ball from McCarthy's hands and, in the ensuing scramble, somehow breaks the ball away to Keith Higgins. Moments later, Kevin McLoughlin kicks a gorgeous point to level the game.

Since retiring, Tom has talked about the emotions he felt after that game. He spoke of that feeling that although he was devastated by the loss he felt at peace because he understood we could not have given more. That is something we often preach – leave it all on the pitch – but it's usually elusive. Witnessing up close how Tom played that day, I understood how he came to feel it. He left it all out there. The only way he truly knew.

TEN

Stay Calm, Be Patient and Start Being Productive

'The measure of who we are is how we react to something that doesn't go our way.'

– Gregg Popovich

W E LIVE in a time of perpetual impatience. All of us have become accustomed to getting everything we want, now, or at least expecting to. When we send messages, we look for blue ticks and immediate responses. We go to concerts and games and feel compelled to share the experience with people we don't even know as it unfolds in front of us. We scroll our phones and feel connections with people we've never, ever met. Our expectations for getting what we want are completely skewed. As a kid born in the '80s, I was part of the last generation to grow up without mobile phones and access to the internet. Being bored was absolutely forbidden and would likely earn you a clip round the ear.

Now, I find myself part of the problem. I use social media to promote my businesses and to keep track of current affairs and politics. I participate in a media world constantly finding more innovative ways to put itself in people's pockets. Everything is now and I am an impatient person. I was an impatient player too. It was undoubtedly a flaw. Reflecting for this book on many of the games I played, the memories of the growing anxiety I felt during matches came creeping back. I always wanted early touches to relax myself, to grow into games. If those touches didn't come, I got antsy. I rushed plays and, fatally, I forced shots. It was the biggest defect in my game, a failing born from impatience and anxiety. If it looked like I played frantically, it was because I did. I was always in a hurry and sometimes it served me well; more often it didn't.

I often look at younger players and wonder how difficult it is to be patient in the context of making a team. If the breakthrough isn't immediate, is it easier for them to walk away because they have more options in their lives? Similarly, on the field, having the composure and forbearance to bide your time, especially as a forward, are qualities that need to be better pushed by coaches. Too often as a younger player, I didn't trust myself.

One teammate who never suffered from impatience was Alan Dillon, Mayo's ghost assassin. His numbers are phenomenal, but they only tell part of his story.

He played senior football for Mayo 134 times, 66 of those appearances coming in the championship. He scored 3-225 in the green and red. At different times he was our freetaker and our captain. He was always a leader. He won eight Connacht Championships and two All-Stars. More than all of that, he had the respect of his opponents and teammates. Over 14 seasons he cemented his place as one of Mayo's greatest ever forwards. His longevity was only matched by his utter class as a footballer. He had vision, balance and two great feet. As his pace declined, as it always does for an aging player, he refined his game to optimise his most potent weapon – his brain.

Alan was a prodigy. By his mid-teens it was clear to those who knew him that he would not only play for Mayo but with the right application and guidance he had the potential to do so for a long time. It's no exaggeration to say that for 12 seasons for Mayo, his was the first forward's name on the team sheet. Despite his relative lack of size, he was never out of his depth. He was playing a different game to everybody else. While the rest of us were running around like lunatics, Dillo was playing chess.

"Composure, composure and composure," Martin Carney said in co-commentary as Alan rounded Kerry 'keeper Diarmuid Murphy to score a goal four minutes into the 2004 All-Ireland final. He was 21 and with practically his first touch he found himself one on one with Murphy. With a single hop and a ridiculous step, he dances around the Kerry shot-stopper and slots into an empty net. No thoughts of a fisted point to settle his nerves. No blasted shot to get the moment over with. Even then, it was as if his mind were working in slow motion, two moves ahead. Back then, he looked like a kid, but he played like a veteran.

Two years later, he was at it again on the biggest stage. While Ciarán Mc and Kevin O'Neill dominated the headlines that famous day, it was Dillon who gave a masterclass in forward play from start to finish in an incredible semi-final win over Dublin. He was literally everywhere. Linking defence and attack. Pinging passes. Kicking scores. He oozed class on a day that will be remembered for a lifetime by Mayo supporters.

Normalised brilliance often sees exceptional players like Alan taken for granted. The next four seasons for Mayo saw little joy but Alan, along with his sidekick Conor Mort, kept producing when the team was struggling to find its way. His standards never, ever dropped. He never ceased to be productive.

A year older than me, Alan, too, would've felt the pangs of anxiety that come with approaching 30 and guessing what a new manager's motives might be. As a clubmate of James Horan, Alan no doubt realised the new manager certainly wasn't the sentimental sort. Dillo's reputation may have been well established, but the pressure was on all of us to respond to the new challenges being put in front of us by James and his team. Alan, given his standing in the group, could've been forgiven for being precious. Instead, he rolled up his sleeves and set to work. In 2012, he played some of the best football of his career, earning his second

All-Star. His trademark move of ghosting around a team-mate to take an offload and kick a point off his right instep had long been established. That season he perfected it. If you didn't know your football, it may have looked like he was kicking soft scores but the artistry it took to read the play two steps ahead, to track the pass and loop around off the ball-carrier, to lose your man and then execute the kick, was poetry in motion.

Like all players good and great, time played its part in slowing Alan down. He found himself on the bench more and more during the 2014 and 2015 seasons. The trend continued during 2016 when Alan – and the rest of us – thought manager Stephen Rochford had decided he was surplus to requirements. Mayo's greatest forward of the previous decade, who came into the squad and was immediately a starter in 2003 and stayed as a starter for the next eleven seasons – suddenly, he was now a sub. His style of play was such that he was never really deployed as an impact player, either. His influence on the game was more subtle but no less powerful. It was a harder sell from the bench. What's a killer in those situations is watching the team develop and win without you. Watching the older guys you came up with, clinging on for dear life, everyone trying to convince the management they matter more than the next guy. More than any other, Alan would've been forgiven a sulk. Instead, he waited, patiently.

In 2016, as we picked our way through a series of qualifiers after losing to Galway, the team was gathering momentum. Wins against Fermanagh, Kildare and Westmeath saw us build confidence. In each game, Alan got some playing time but for a player who for so long was the first forward on the sheet, being reduced to the role of a sub must have been a difficult transition.

Bigger tests were coming. Waiting for us were Tyrone.

Preparing for that quarter-final, Stephen and his management team took a gamble. We knew Tyrone deployed two defensive players sitting just in front of their full-back line. One would be Colm Cavanagh dropping back from midfield, the other Justin McMahon falling back from his centre-back berth. The idea for Mickey Harte was to protect

KEY INFLUENCE: St Nathy's College, All-Ireland Senior B Colleges champions 2000. A good coach can steer your life in many ways. Johno helped me in more ways than one. Front row (from left): Stephen Drake, Ollie Towey, Sean Mangan, John O'Mahony, Keith Mahon (captain), John Carty, Andy Moran, Eamon Towey. Middle row (from left): John Mitchell, Michael Solan, Liam Regan, Thomas Naughton, Kenneth Duffy, Derek Moran, David Jordan, Keith Johnston, John Ginty. Back row (from left): David McNulty, Dermot Corrigan, Kieran Lynn, Barry Regan, Colm Towey, Derek Barrett, Joe McCann, Paul Freeman, Michael Cooney.

TAKING IT ALL IN: Our greatest ever performance, in my opinion – the All-Ireland Senior Championship final 2017.

Photo: Seb Daly/Sportsfile

LAST WORDS: Croke Park, 17 September 2017.

Photo: Piaras Ó Mídheach/Sportsfile

REPETITION, REPETITION, REPETITION: Practice gets you ready for the big moments. Cillian perfected his technique through obsessive practice. Here we see him kicking the equaliser against Dublin in the dying moments of the 2016 All-Ireland Senior Championship final. *Photo: Dáire Brennan/Sportsfile*

READY FOR BATTLE: The Mayo team before the 2017 All-Ireland final.

Photo: *Eóin Noonan/Sportsfile*

THE BEST: Three of the best to go to battle with. It was great to share special victories like this with Clarkie (left), Tom Parsons (centre) and Jason Doc (right).

Photo: Ray McManus/Sportsfile

ON THE BALL: In the right place at the right time, as he so often was for Mayo, Keith Higgins escapes with the ball to see out the victory against Dublin in the 2012 All-Ireland Senior Championship semi-final.

Photo: Dáire Brennan/Sportsfile

CHARACTER: What do your teammates think of you? Your character is what you truly are. Caolan Crowe (left) always put the team first. Aidan O'Shea acknowledges that in the tunnel beneath MacHale Park. *Photo: David Maher/Sportsfile*

NEVER GIVE IN: A photo that symbolises Tom Parsons' career.
Photo: Sam Barnes/Sportsfile

**LEAVE THE JERSEY IN A BETTER PLACE: Ger Cafferkey is a
student of the game. The knowledge he passed on to others is still
felt in the dressing room to this day.** *Photo: Dáire Brennan/Sportsfile*

QUALITY: Lee doing what Lee does. Performing on the biggest stage.

Photo: Sam Barnes/Sportsfile

APRIL 2012: Two of the best wing-forwards of the decade, Alan Dillon collides with Paul Galvin in the league semi-final.

Photo: Brendan Moran/Sportsfile

SETTING US ON OUR WAY: Kevin McLoughlin's moment of brilliance against Cork in 2011 was the turning point for the decade that followed. *Photo: Dáire Brennan/Sportsfile*

WRITE YOUR OWN SCRIPT: After Lee was sent off against Kerry in the All-Ireland Senior Championship semi-final in 2014, Colm Boyle was not willing to accept the fate that many felt was waiting for us. Like so many times before, he wrote his own script. *Photo: Pat Murphy/Sportsfile*

CAPTAIN COEN: The man who sacrifices his own game for the team to achieve is indispensable. Stephen Coen is not just a leader but the minder on the field of play.

Photo: Piaras Ó Mídheach/Sportsfile

ROCK SOLID: As always, protecting… Other players got the plaudits but Seamie was the foundation that the team was built on.

Photo: Brendan Moran/Sportsfile

BIG BIRD & THE SHOE:
Barry 'Big Bird' and Donie
'The Shoe' having a laugh
in Croke Park.

Photo: Brendan Moran/Sportsfile

4 August 2013: After the heartache of the 2012 All-Ireland defeat to Donegal, Mayo needed a big performance against the same team in 2013. Donal Vaughan led the way.

Photo: Stephen McCarthy/Sportsfile

ALWAYS FINDING A QUOTE!

Donie and me posing on a night away in Donegal.

THE MAVERICK:
Aidan celebrating his goal to cap a breathtaking performance against Donegal in the 2015 All-Ireland Senior Championship quarter-final.

Photo: Stephen McCarthy/ Sportsfile

against Aidan and Cillian doing serious damage in the inside line. The extra defensive line could also push up as required on our attacking half-backs as they sought to exploit space and do what they did best.

What the Tyrone set-up did was free up space between halfway and the edge of the D. Who did we have who could play there? Which Mayo player could demand the ball, see a pass nobody else could see, retain possession and come up with a critical score when we needed it?

Stephen knew the tactic was an audacious one and it required a special player to execute it. Many players may feel they have the confidence to pull it off but among us only Alan really had the ability and, crucially, the intelligence. The fact that his body was betraying him at this stage may well have helped him because as the old saying goes, '*an té nach bhfuil láidir, ní foláir dó a bheith glic*' (the one who isn't strong had better be clever). A cute tactic is only as cute as the player who executes it and Dillon was the perfect man. He led Tyrone, and Justin McMahon in particular, a merry dance. For 35 minutes it seemed like he owned Croke Park. Like a quarterback playmaking in the pocket, he plotted attack after attack, dismantling Tyrone's game plan. It was brilliant foresight from Stephen Rochford and his team. All season it looked like he was putting Alan quietly out to stud, only to turn to him when the team really needed something different. Alan was patiently waiting, ready to do what was necessary. Mickey Harte had made his play: Stephen had double bluffed him.

I suspect Tyrone knew this very early on and this may have panicked them into taking off Justin McMahon just before half-time. The final irony came when, shortly after McMahon was substituted, Tyrone's game plan in tatters, Tom Parsons replaced Alan. That was all Alan's body could give and it was more than enough. His job was done. He had befuddled Tyrone and given Mayo a platform to win the game. Like a placekicker in American football, Dillon was wheeled in to do a specific job and wheeled out again when that job had been done to perfection. As sweet as the moment must've been for him, it may have been frustrating too because just as the season up to that point had unfolded largely without his influence, so did the remainder of the season thereafter, culminating in a one-point loss to Dublin after a replay. In that last significant contribution against Tyrone, Alan Dillon proved his greatness, and his loyalty to the cause one final time.

At times we need to sit and be patient, be that on the bench or in the shadow of others. The responsibility we have to our team in our professional and sporting lives is to be ready when the opportunity arrives, not to sulk when it doesn't come sooner. Alan, who had absolutely nothing left to prove to anyone, chose to be patient. He took a step back, refused to feel sorry for himself and stayed productive. In 2015, Alan saw no game time in our quarter-final against Donegal and our two semi-finals against Dublin. Another player may have taken this as a sign that his time was up. Instead, after 14 seasons, during which he was often our best forward, he learned a new way and when the opportunity arose he acted like he played. He watched. He read the situation. He timed his run, looping around to take the pass he somehow knew would come. When it did, he pulled the trigger.

The Best of Alan Dillon

Mayo versus Dublin in the 2006 All-Ireland semi-final was memorable for a multitude of reasons. There was a remarkable energy about the day from the atmosphere on the streets *en route* to Croke Park to the unforgettable Battle of the Hill before throw-in. Even before a ball was kicked, it felt like the match itself could only be memorable. The highlights reel will always climax with Ciarán McDonald's epic winner but the winning of that game was in the margins and Mayo's master of the margins was Alan Dillon.

Kicking four points from play, he pinged passes and linked play all day, winning breaks and finding space like only he could. He had a habit of making the difficult look very simple so while Ciarán and Conor Mort were renowned as the flashy finishers, Dillo, moving around the field like a ghost, put himself in the right position time and time again.

His first point after eleven minutes was a mixture of skill and dogged determination. Using his low centre of gravity to collect a ball running away from him, he gets separation from his man Paul Casey before hitting his trademark instepper from a full 40 metres. His next touch is another ingenious one. His back to goal, he flicks a handpass from Ciarán over his head and over the bar. The Dubs are rattled and Dillo is purring.

Moments before half-time Alan turns provider. Winning the ball on halfway, he patiently waits for the runner before hitting a daisy cutter into Kevin O'Neill who gathers and hits a screamer. On 55 minutes, with Mayo desperate for a score, Aidan Kilcoyne is suffocated by a hungry Dublin defence. Who pops up in support only Alan, looping around to take the pass before calmly popping over. Minutes later, Aidan is on hand to assist Alan again. Deceptively strong, Alan takes the pass on the run before stepping inside Bryan Cullen and kicking an equaliser.

Alan Dillon did everything that day. In the most claustrophobic of atmospheres, he kept his head while pretty much everybody else was losing theirs. The headlines went elsewhere, lost to the noise of the Hill and the drama of the McDonald winner, but for that one glorious Sunday afternoon, he owned the stage. Our ghost assassin.

ELEVEN

The Water Carriers

'Individual commitment to a group effort
– that is what makes a team work.'

– Vince Lombardi

A S KIDS watching sports, what we see is formative. I remember watching the 1994 World Cup and the legendary RTÉ commentator Jimmy Magee remarking during a random Brazil game that "Dunga carries the ladder while Romario paints the beautiful pictures". To be clear, I wanted to be a Romario, the painter of the pictures, not Dunga. Scoring goals was what mattered to me, but I understood the sentiment. Romario was arguably the star of that World Cup triumph, just as Zidane would be four years later for France. Both artists had unbelievable foremen to carry their ladders – Dunga for Brazil and Didier Deschamps for *Les Bleus*. Neither man sold too many jerseys I'm guessing but neither team would've triumphed without them. It was not that they just did the dirty work – the tackling, the second balls, the mopping-up – it was the example they set for their teammates. 'I do this... so you can do what you do.' While goal-getters and match-winners can often be sprung from the bench, a good ladder carrier is the first man on the team sheet.

Deschamps is a prime example. Swapping water for a step ladder, the phrase "the water carrier", was used about him not as a compliment but as a term of abuse by his compatriot Eric Cantona after he (Cantona) had been omitted from the 1998 World Cup squad. No doubt he was appalled that he, King Eric, was not deemed good enough to be included while Deschamps, a 5'7" mongrel of a footballer, was not only picked, but as midfield general and team captain was central to everything France did. Over a decade, Deschamps became one of the world's most decorated footballers, winning three Champions Leagues, as well as skippering France to a World Cup and a European Championship.

It takes balls to assume the role Deschamps did. Like Roy Keane after him, his lack of flair and size no doubt forced him to re-evaluate early in his playing career what role he saw for himself in the team. He had the foresight and drive to go and do it. The immediate adulation often goes elsewhere to the goalscorers and the creators but history is usually kind to those who do the heavy lifting behind the scenes.

In Gaelic football, we tend to categorise our emerging players when they are very young. Is he a back, a forward or a midfielder? Much of the early decision-making in that regard is done according to size and skill. If you are a naturally bigger young fella you may excel at underage, but by the time you hit senior football that size might even count against you. You may fail to develop other areas of your game. Your peak may have been at 16 when you could physically dominate your peers. That same size may initially give you some protection among the big boys but to excel you need to ask the right questions of yourself: How can I make a difference? How can I become essential to this team? The novelty of size wears off quickly in the big leagues.

You think you're big?
So what?
What else can you do?

Seamus O'Shea is one of the biggest specimens of a man I've ever seen. As an underage footballer, he had the ability to dominate his opponents using his size alone. Did that make him lazy when his opportunity with the seniors came? Not one bit. He assessed his abilities, surveyed his role in the group and decided on how he could make a positive difference to the team – and executed.

That execution required hours and hours of extra work. A guy like Seamus excels in the gym. Like all of us, the area where we shine is the one we tend to spend most time because it comes easiest. It also makes us look good to outside eyes. The hardest thing to do is concentrate on the facets of our game with which we most struggle. For me, it was recovering my aerobic fitness after injuries, which unfortunately became more frequent in my 30s. That was a red line I had to cross, however, to regain my place on the team. Seamus could have pumped iron all day and all night and likely still made the team, just as a lesser version of himself.

Instead, he chose the harder road, spending hours on shooting and kick passing. He also developed a defensive acumen that saw him fill an invaluable role in the team. He plugged holes defensively to allow Lee Keegan, Donie Vaughan and Keith Higgins to become potent offensive weapons. This was not Seamus' natural game. He was a more offensive-minded player blessed with a phenomenal engine, great hands and an eye for a score but the set-up of our team required somebody who had the discipline and ability to hold. Seamus saw the gap – literally and figuratively – and he filled it.

For a lot of his Mayo career, he did so while partnering his younger brother Aidan at midfield. Although a big personality himself, Seamus always seemed most comfortable out of the limelight. It suited him to allow others take the accolades. His role in the team was a quiet one but he was brilliantly effective. This may have been missed by those watching with the naked eye. 'Big plays' are what draw us in be they scores, turnovers or high catches. Seamus had many of those down through the years but his true worth was in the water-carrying he did, allowing those around him to shine.

In another era, Seamus O'Shea may have been a different player for Mayo. Given his size and reputation, he could have put himself at the centre of things much more, not for the good of the team but for the good of himself. His ability to see the bigger picture, to read the room in the sense of understanding where he could make himself most useful, was half of what made him great.

The other half was his commitment to the doing.

As with Deschamps and Dunga, the term 'water carrier' could initially be perceived as a pejorative one – a throwaway moniker for a guy who doesn't do the fancy stuff but look closer at these guys and you will inevitably find a team's oxygen. For Mayo, Seamus was our seventh attacker and our seventh defender. He gave the team maturity and balance, things we lacked without his presence.

The water carriers may not have the largest followings on social media. Their role requires patience, intelligence and discipline, not least because many watching will never praise them for what they do. Footballers are fickle beings. We need our egos massaged just as much as our calves. Having the mental strength to identify a role for yourself that yields little credit from the terraces is a brave thing to do. The supporters may not know your worth, but you can be guaranteed your team will. When it came to Seamus, we all knew.

Every team wants a Seamus O'Shea. There can be no greater example of what Seamus brought to us than his performance against Kerry in 2017. In Gaelic football, as in most team sports, it's unusual for the underdog to win a replay. The accepted wisdom is that you had your chance the first day and you blew it. Time and time again we see the inferior team fall away. Mayo have fulfilled this prophecy too often, most recently in consecutive semi-finals to Kerry and Dublin in 2014 and 2015, and in the final (to Dublin, again) in 2016. When we drew with Kerry in the 2017 semi-final, it was understandable that many assumed we would stay true to recent form and come up short in the replay. Our manager Stephen Rochford had a simple philosophy on how to attack Kerry – hammer the hammer or, to put it more specifically, go after their big players. All eyes were on the use of Aidan O'Shea at full-back, picked there specifically to combat the threat of Kieran Donaghy. Few took heed of the role played by the other O'Shea, Seamus, in nullifying Kerry's princely midfielder David Moran. Seamus and David were good friends from their college days at UL, so they understood each other's game well. Stephen had correctly identified the supply line of ball from Moran to Paul Geaney and Donaghy as the biggest threat to us. Our plan was simple: deny the ball at source and they can't score.

Seamus attacked Kerry 'keeper Brian Kelly's first kickout and won it cleanly, setting down a huge marker. Moran is usually majestic in the air so depriving him of clean ball off the Kerry restart was imperative for us to achieve dominance. Their second kickout was again broken away by Seamus. As often happens when Plan A is not working, a team can look rattled. After Cillian made the game four points apiece, Kelly once again kicked long to the middle where it was again gathered by Seamus. He worked the ball to the attacking Colm Boyle who found Kevin McLoughlin who, in turn, kicked us a point to the good. Moran's ball-winning ability in the middle third had been an attacking platform for Kerry all season long. Mayo, through Seamus, had flipped that on its head.

Later in the half, desperate to assert his authority, Moran carried the ball directly at Seamus on the 21-yard line, cutting in towards the Mayo goal. Using all his pace and power, Moran couldn't find a way past Seamus who forced his college buddy into a tired shot that fell wide on the near post. In close games, these moments carry greater significance than they otherwise might. By selflessly doing the job of two men, Seamus laid the foundation for a famous victory.

★★★★★

There are some players whose worth to teams is only ever fully appreciated by those who play alongside them. In Mayo, we like our footballers to be dynamic and full of personality. We pride ourselves on wearing our hearts on our sleeves. This desire for connection between fan and player can often see the worth of the water carrier ignored. Some of the best footballers I've ever had the pleasure of playing alongside barely ever kicked the ball – Kevin Cahill and Ger Caff being two who cared little for the aesthetic or how they were perceived externally. They just cared about their job and the team. Everything else was just noise. Another whose worth is fully appreciated in the dressing room is Stephen Coen, whose influence may be invisible to the naked eye but who has captained almost every team for which he's played.

Of all the strange sights to see in a Mayo senior football dressing room, a lad in a school uniform is right up there. Certainly, it was guaranteed to make a veteran like me feel old! Sure enough, fresh from winning an All-Ireland Minor Championship as captain the previous September, Stephen Coen joined the senior panel in early 2014. The team had been on a three-year run under James Horan and, as with all cycles, fresh blood was needed to energise the squad. One of James' greatest strengths is his desire and ability to blood new players. As older players, the introduction of youth keeps you fresh and on your toes. It rids a dressing room of complacency. It takes courage as a coach to trust players who can easily be written off as being too 'green'. There is a freedom that youth brings to a team – there is no baggage. No historical trauma. It still takes guts to trust them. Patience, too, as those players often need time to get it wrong before they get it right. In Stephen and his great buddy Diarmuid O'Connor, James had two guys who'd need very little time at all.

From the first day he walked through the dressing room door, Stephen Coen oozed class. His credentials as a footballer had been established but it was his attitude and demeanour that caught the eye more than anything else. Forget that he was just doing his Leaving Cert, Stephen looked at home.

Success at minor level guarantees you nothing. While Stephen looked perfectly comfortable in his new surroundings, that trust that only comes from spending time in the trenches with teammates had yet to be earned. Unfazed, he set about achieving that, doing whatever was asked of him in his now-typical, no-fuss and no-nonsense manner. That trust is won not in Croke Park on All-Ireland Sunday but in Castlebar on bleak January nights. Even then, it takes time. It can't be forced or rushed. Nor is a senior inter-county squad a charitable retreat. No matter what you may have done as an underage footballer, the grace period only extends so far. You must earn your right to stick around. I can't speak for James Horan but from his very first winter with us, Stephen Coen proved to his teammates that he was the real deal.

To the outsider, Stephen's qualities as a player may not always be so obvious. When you are flanked by visually spectacular players like Paddy Durcan and Lee Keegan as Stephen often is, the priority for the team is for him to pro-vide stability. This is a priceless asset to a team whose re-liance on scores from wing-backs is long established. One can't happen without the other. Stephen Coen, like Seamus O'Shea, is a trusted water carrier. His role is in no way di-minished by his willing acceptance of the fact that the head-lines are unlikely to be about him. By the age of 22, he had captained All-Ireland winning minor and U21 teams, and a Sigerson Cup team. No headlines required.

So often we see younger players content to just fit in. They attain a goal but forget that is just the starting point. Their performance level stagnates rather than evolves and suddenly they are left behind. Stephen Coen was the an-tithesis of that.

We only get one chance to make a first impression on a group. He may have been in his school uniform but, boy, did he make it count.

The Best of Stephen Coen

Few Mayo footballers get to win one All-Ireland. Still fewer have two. Stephen won both of his three years apart, as captain of underage teams. In 2016, as Mayo supporters bounced out of Cusack Park in Ennis after beating a much-fancied Cork team in the All-Ireland U21 final, it was easy to focus on the superb goals from Liam Irwin, Conor Loftus and Diarmuid O'Connor. The tenacious defending from Seamus Cunniffe and Eoin O'Donoghue, the energy and speed of Mattie Ruane, Shairoze Akram, Fergal Boland and Michael Plunkett. For all of that, there was one player who made it all stick together – Stephen Coen. When his team needed him most, when the ball needed to be won at the death, he was the one who went after it. The skipper read four breaking balls one after the other. No fuss, no ego, just did his job like he always does.

That victory typified Stephen's way. The game was memorable for its crazy scoreline (5-7 to 1-14), a chaotic end-to-end battle that defied logic, save for Stephen, 21-years-old but an old soul, a calming presence at the centre of it all.

TWELVE

Think More, Run Less

'You play football with your head, and your legs are there to help you. If you don't use your head, using your feet won't be sufficient.'

– Johan Cruyff

GAELIC football is forever evolving. The discourse surrounding this era being better than any that went before is as futile as chasing shadows. Nostalgia, too, can be a dangerous emotion. When I first broke onto the Mayo senior panel in 2003, a quiet footballing revolution was occurring. While the blue-blooded royalists of Kerry were experiencing their own cyclical revival, up north Armagh and Tyrone were changing the game by embracing a more abrasive style of play, combining enhanced physicality through tackling with ball-playing ability. As Kerry and Tyrone went on to dominate the decade, Cork emerged in the late 2000s in a manner that once again challenged how teams like Mayo approached training and playing.

They may have only won one All-Ireland (2010), but their ability to combine size with outrageous athleticism brought about changes in football that are still relevant today, more than a decade later. It's no coincidence that the style of football with which they won had its greatest exponents in players like Graham Canty, Pearse O'Neill, Paudie Kissane and Nicholas Murphy. These players were blessed with size and pace. I saw at first-hand how they trained, collectively and individually. The decade would later be dominated by Dublin but that Cork team lay down a marker. Part of their legacy was a change in what coaches felt they needed in players. One thing was for certain, it made it much harder for the slower guy, the smaller guy, the thinker.

Look at the Mayo team from 2011. Seamus and Aidan O'Shea. Donie. Jason Doc. Leeroy and Tom Parsons. Even David Clarke, the 'keeper. All possessed immense size and athleticism. All were physically dominant players. In keeping with the game's evolution, they became the spine of the team. Still, we needed others. Those 'others' needed to do more to survive the revolution. To work harder. To channel different attributes that weren't so obvious. One such 'other' was Chrissy Barrett. Small in stature and of average pace and physical presence, Chris was a natural centre-back who had to adapt as the game changed. A sceptic by nature, he always sought to understand rather than just go with the flow. He always asked why, especially when it came to tactics or a game plan. His scepticism was never disruptive. Rather it forced us all to think more about what we were about. Chris needed the answers. He may not have been the quickest or the biggest but he made himself one of the smartest.

Needs must, and as our half-back line became an increasingly potent attacking weapon with Lee, Colm, and Donie, Chris provided invaluable cover along our full-back line. Our game plan caused him to constantly question what contingencies we had to offset our attacking strategy, and the defensive gaps it left:

When the half-backs go, who's covering?
Which midfielder is dropping back to mark the space?

Questioning tactics was just one part of it. In 2019, my last year on the team, I was coasting a little, happy to accept my role as an impact sub. Mid-summer, Chris pulled me into the medical room in MacHale Park for a quick word.

"What the f**k are you doing?" he asked me.

"What do you mean?"

"You were Footballer of the Year two years ago? You're just giving up your place. You're still good enough to play. What the f**k are you at?"

I was shocked but Chris being Chris, I realised this wasn't some spur-of-the-moment conversation, but something he had thought about and wanted to say. He was right. It was just the kick up the arse I needed.

Dogged by injuries early in his Mayo career, another player would've packed it in, especially as his path was not an obvious one. But not Chris. He was a warrior. He sought out ways to improve and he set to work.

I marked Chris a lot in 2011. He gave me a torrid time in A versus B games all summer. I dreaded seeing him coming. I remember thinking, how is this player not on the team? I knew what a good footballer Chris was. I knew how well he knew me as a player and how much he relished the opportunity to give me another lesson. I always learned from those sessions and went out the following weekend certain that nobody would mark me like Chris did.

Chris was the best tackler I ever encountered. His timing was impeccable. He had an ability to read a play and engage at just the right moment without fouling. Where others used their size, Chris always used his brain. His ability to get his hands in and out without fouling was phenomenal. He worked on it tirelessly.

He was brave too. Not just physically – that was always a given with him – but in his decision-making as a defender. Good decision-making was imperative playing in the full-back line for Mayo. We set up in such a way that our last line had to be confident playing one-on-one, especially in the biggest games against the best attackers. Chris was not afraid to take risks. In the wide, open spaces of Croke Park, he was often left alone on an island marking Dean Rock or Paddy Andrews. His confidence at being able to read what was in front of him, allied to having the courage to play on the shoulder or out in front of top-class forwards, were possibly his greatest strengths. He backed himself. Always.

He feared no-one. In 2017, Jim Gavin pulled a potential masterstroke by starting Eoghan O'Gara in the final. We weren't expecting it and suddenly we found ourselves with one of our smallest backs on O'Gara, a 6'2" beast of a man with a track record in finals against Mayo. Undaunted, Chrissy went toe to toe with him. O'Gara was replaced at half-time. Two seasons later, he repeated the trick in the 2019 league final against Kerry. In a planned matchup, Chris picked up the behemoth Tommy Walsh who stands 6'6". Chris dominated him with precise positioning and trademark tigerish aggression. Walsh was substituted after a scoreless 54 minutes.

As an attacking player Chris' timing was also impeccable. He was brilliant at coming off the shoulder of a teammate and rarely if ever carried into blind alleyways. Less was always more for him, nothing was done for show or for the sake of it.

It might have gone a different way for Chris. Blighted by injuries in his early years with Mayo, he was at a crossroads by the time James Horan arrived in late 2010. Perennially injured players can become a drain on a squad. It seems cold to say it but if you have players bursting to get their chance, it's counterintuitive to keep waiting for a guy to pull through when there are other alternatives available. To James' credit, he viewed an investment in Chris as an investment in the team. He was patient and his faith was rewarded by the brilliant Belmullet man as he became one of our most important defenders for the next eight seasons.

He had other, less obvious, qualities too. There was a crankiness about him, an aloofness that could be attributed to the part of Mayo he was from on the shores of Carramore Lake, not far from the parish of Kilcommon. It's a raw and beautiful place. He played the same way for his club Belmullet as he did for Mayo. He took no shit. He was man of the match in the 2006 Comórtas Peile na Gaeltachta final for his club at the age of 17. He was fearless then and it never left him.

He was a man of few words in the dressing room. He never sought attention or affection. He was only interested in the battle.

Perhaps because of the early injuries, Chris was the player who thought more and ran less. That is not intended as a negative, quite the opposite. He was almost an intellectual footballer. He thought his way through games. He played with his head. He never doubted his own ability, which is most unusual for a Mayo man.

What I learned from Chris was something that served me well as we continued to play together. I didn't need to get bigger to compete. I just needed to use my head more. During that 2011 season, he out-thought and out-fought me more times than I'd like to admit. It forced me to reassess what I was prioritising in my game. He was struggling to regain a place in the team at the time. His dogged persistence forced James and others to take notice. Once he got himself fit, he wasn't going away again.

When you consider the dominant teams of the last decade you think Dublin, Kerry and Tyrone. Tyrone and Dublin have had four managers between them in the last dozen seasons. We've had five in the same timeframe. For all that change, newly appointed managers have consistently gone back to a core of the same players. Chris was one of those guys. As every new manager came along, they might have looked at him and assessed him as too slow, too small or too injury-prone. Instead, he made himself indispensable.

The Best of Chris Barrett

In 2013, fresh from the heart-breaking loss to Donegal in 2012, expectations are high in the county that we will continue to assert ourselves as a force. In the semi-final, we meet a Tyrone team that still commands serious respect thanks to the three titles they claimed between 2003 and 2008. To everyone else, we are still wet behind the ears. As players, we see a huge opportunity. Early in the game we face a sliding doors moment when our scorer-in-chief Cillian O'Connor goes off with a shoulder injury. Approaching half-time we are seven points to three down and struggling. Our forward line is lacking the leadership Cillian had started to provide. In moments like this, teams need something for which they haven't ordinarily planned. In Mayo's case, it seems we have these moments far more often than other teams, and, more often than not, an unlikely hero emerges.

Today is Chris' day. Punctuality may never have been his thing but his timing in battle certainly is. A couple of minutes before half-time he takes the ball off his great friend Seamus O'Shea on our 65 and drives forward. Approaching the Tyrone 45, he's engaged by Ciarán McGinley. Without breaking stride, he steps inside McGinley before hitting an outrageous score with the outside of his right foot. Feeling a momentum shift, we win the next ball and attack. Lee Keegan kicks another score, and our tails are up. Sensing the Tyrone boys want half-time to come quickly, Chris steps up again, this time taking up a position off the ball in our attack. Tom Cunniffe collects the ball off Alan Dillon and sees Chris making the kind of run across the line that Dillon himself would usually make. Tom ships it to Chris, and with his back to goal he steadies himself before kicking a beauty over his left shoulder. The gap is down to one and the momentum has swung in our favour. We needed something. Chris delivered.

In the second half, inspired by Chris, we come out a different team and go on to beat a fine Tyrone side by six points. Chris even kicks another to cap a brilliant performance. Cometh the hour, cometh the man.

THIRTEEN

Supply and Demand

*'Good teams become great ones when the members trust
each other enough to surrender the Me for the We.'*

– Phil Jackson

IN CHRIS Hadfield's book, *An Astronaut's Guide to Life
on Earth,* he tells how he would constantly move around
with his family during his training. Each time he moved,
he would need to learn how to work with a new team. He
may have been top dog at his last post but suddenly he
would be a nobody within his new group because they had
no idea of his skill set, his personality or his abilities. Despite
what he knew about himself, there existed no trust between
him and his new teammates. So, he developed a strategy: instead of barging in, over-imposing and trying to take charge,
he realised that there are three basic levels you can fall into
when joining a team: a minus one, a zero or a plus one.

"Over the years, I've realised that in any new situation,
whether it involves an elevator or a rocket ship, you will almost certainly be viewed in one of three ways. As a minus
one: actively harmful, someone who creates problems. Or as
a zero: your impact is neutral and doesn't tip the balance
one way or the other. Or you'll be seen as a plus one: someone who actively adds value."

He explains that, at first, on a new team or in a new situation, his main goal is to avoid being a net negative contributor. Rather, he seeks to be a 'zero'. At face value, this can seem counterintuitive, especially in the context of a sports team. When you are called into, or join, a new group you want to stand out. You want to make those on the sidelines with the clipboards remember you. You want the respect of those you're playing alongside and opposite. When you come into something new you want to make your mark. Immediately. While I don't entirely agree with Hadfield's assertion that you should aim to be a zero, I see huge merit in his thesis that you should not try to always or immediately be the hero.

If, on day one, you look to be a plus one it can cause negative ramifications almost straightaway. The veterans on a team may be jealous, wondering 'who does this guy think he is?' Hadfield's assertion is that you should aim to win your peers' confidence and trust by being a zero instead. This means pulling your weight, humbly showing up, not trying to be in the spotlight, doing your job professionally, asking questions and learning the ropes. In time you will earn a teammate's respect and can progress from being a zero to a plus one contributor and someone others will want to follow. This may be the longer play but it's far more effective in gaining confidence in the long run.

In sport, especially underage, this is a hard philosophy to adopt, particularly if it is not taught. It would take a young man or woman of immense self-awareness to trust that even if they are not the brightest, shiniest player out there on the field their value will not only be appreciated, but they will be the cornerstone of a team's success if they persist. As I see it, I don't read 'be a zero' as submitting to being a foot soldier or an unquestioning follower. I see it as an act of humility that, in time, allows you to become a leader organically. Not forcing it, not shoving it down people's throats.

I say this because, as with many of the lessons in this book, I learned it the hard way. As an underage footballer, through college and during my early intercounty career, I was always in a hurry. Always eager to impress, sometimes to a fault. I believe my heart was in the right place – I don't think I ever made noise for the sake of it – but I often lacked the self-confidence and vision to understand that if I kept doing the right things, if I kept aiming to make positive contributions, my worth to the team would not only be realised but amplified. I may have got there eventually but if I did, it was in large part due to learning from others around me.

★★★★★

It may come as a surprise to Mayo supporters to learn that the most important teammate I had throughout the second half of my career was Jason Doherty. I say it may come as a surprise because the body of work he has left, and continues to leave, is there for all to see but it may not always have been so evident to the outside eye. In some respects, he suffered for standing out too much when he first emerged onto the senior team. He gained a well-earned reputation as a goal-getter (something we were sadly lacking at the time), scoring seven in the 2011 National League campaign. His performances as an inside forward had many believing he was the answer to the 'Mayo lack killer instinct' narrative. Thereafter followed a dip in form, which would've seen him undoubtedly written off by the same high-stool experts who built him up in the first place.

Undeterred, Jason always took a longer view. There exists a baseline in quality that intercounty footballers will always meet. Jason far surpassed that with his natural abilities. But what propelled him beyond it was a maturity that ensured that regardless of whatever early setbacks he encountered, regardless of any outside noise doubting his value to the team, his worth would win out.

He also had a hunger to develop our on-field relationship. I recall the day before an FBD match in January 2017. The two of us met in the upstairs of the gym and sat discussing how we could better link up on the pitch, mapping out runs and match-day scenarios. My aim was to score more goals. His aim was to better understand how to win better primary possession along the attacking 45 and convert it into scores. My strength was winning the ball. His was finishing. We were learning from each other.

As a footballer, Jason evolved from an inside man to a classic modern forward, a player who could do a little of everything but do all of it very well. Without the ball, he was brilliant at protecting the full-forward line when opponents started to drive up the pitch. His incredible engine allowed him to track back multiple players, affect turnovers and initiate attacks. Further out, his fielding ability always made him an extra option in the middle third for kickouts. His willingness to win dirty ball was without equal. For a big man he could pick the ball off his toes, usually under immense pressure. When the team was flagging, he selflessly acted as an extra defender. He would do all of this, often in a single game, and still come good for a score off either foot when the team badly needed it. If I were to sketch out a team forward as a coach, Jason Doc would be it.

As often happens in life and sport, someone's worth is only truly felt when they are unexpectedly absent. During my last season with Mayo, Jason suffered a season-ending cruciate ligament injury early in the second half of our Super 8s clash with Donegal. His performance on that greasy dirty evening in Castlebar was one of his best for Mayo. It had been a long, tortuous season to that point for all of us. MacHale Park was heaving and as often happens, as the rain fell the tension grew. Donegal were hotly fancied to challenge Dublin later in the semis. Mayo, by contrast, were seen as a team on the wane, thanks mostly to a humbling at the hands of Kerry under a hot summer sun in Killarney.

That wet Saturday night in Castlebar, we emerged triumphant thanks in no small part to Jason Doc doing Jason Doc things. A brutally honest footballer, he was like a platoon sergeant consistently digging his lieutenants out of the shit. Few on-the-whistle match reports ever mentioned his name but while he was on the pitch that night, he best epitomised Mayo's dogs-of-war mentality. Cruelly, he suffered his injury doing the ugly work of which few others were capable, winning a kickout at a key moment. If ever a moment epitomised a man, it was that. Knowingly or not, Jason Doc was always willing to be a zero. Ergo, he has always been so much more. He became what every player should strive to be to his team: irreplaceable.

★★★★★

Another in the selfless mould of Jason was his great partner-in-crime, Kevin McLoughlin. A Swiss Army knife of a footballer, he could do pretty much everything. In his early days, he was arguably a victim of his own versatility. Of all Kevin's abilities, his most enduring one was that of availability (like Donie Vaughan, as I mentioned earlier): from his match-saving cameo in Ruislip in 2011 to the end of 2019, he played an unbelievable 52 championship matches in a row. An achievement like that is no accident. His discipline in looking after himself was an example to every young player. This allowed him to be durable and reliable – two traits all management teams value in a player. That discipline complemented a work ethic that saw him constantly identify areas to work on and improve his game.

To the untrained eye, he looked incredibly gifted. Blessed with a remarkable turn of pace, his trademark dummy solo, his side-step, his ability to kick off both feet and his outstanding capacity to play in literally every outfield position – but it would be lazy to suggest that all of these skills came so easily to Kevin. I was privileged to see the work he put in honing those skills and can only guess that much of what he possessed, he had worked on since he was a kid. How much of this was down to where he was from, I wonder? His club Knockmore is a special place. A proud footballing parish, like many in rural Ireland, the GAA pitch is the centre of a little universe. Knockmore itself is a crossroads: a shop, a pub, a church and a pitch, that's more or less it. They breed them tough in Knockmore. Many players have come from the club and represented Mayo with distinction – Padraig Brogan, Peter Butler, Raymond Dempsey, Kevin Staunton, and another Kevin, the one with the genius left peg, Kevin O'Neill. Every one of these guys had individual qualities that Kevin McLoughlin went on to possess. He is an incredibly tough footballer, an attribute for which Butler, Dempsey and Staunton were famous. He is incredibly gifted, just as O'Neill and Brogan were. He worked immensely hard on his game, just as I'm sure all those lads before him did. He was also one of the most intelligent footballers I've ever played with.

I've no doubt Kevin was a product of the footballing environment in which he grew up. I can't imagine being a young cocky footballer, a know-it-all, and surviving in a Knockmore dressing room. Kevin has a strong personality, sure, but his is a quiet intelligence, just as his presence on the field is often defined by a quiet excellence. He was responsible for some big scores in big games for Mayo – relegation-defying points in '17 and '18, saving the day against London in 2011 and many others – but, more profoundly, his consistent presence in the team for almost a decade provided an unbroken chain of excellence.

Alex Ferguson was often quoted as saying that "hard work will always overcome natural talent when natural talent does not work hard enough". Kevin had all the natural talent a player could wish for but on and off the field he gave you everything. He played that unbroken run of games under four different managers. Each manager saw the same thing all of us did. For us to be the best version of ourselves, Mayo needed Kevin McLoughlin.

★★★★★

If Caolan Crowe was the man I credit most for getting me right on the training field in 2017, it is Jason Doherty and Kevin McLoughlin I must thank for being my protectors on game days. When I broke back into the team in 2016, it was clear to management and me that I wasn't aerobically able to compete with most of the athletes then playing the game. Stephen Rochford justifiably kept me on the bench for a lot of that season, figuring my best impact would come from there as opposition legs tired and the game got looser. As frustrating as it was, I understood it. Our high-tempo approach required total immersion in every aspect of the game: defenders defended and attacked, forwards attacked and defended. The physical toll of this was immense. As the 2017 season evolved, a facet of the game we were struggling with was winning and retaining the ball in the full-forward line. This had become my trademark. Although my ability to cover every blade of grass had waned, I prided myself on making intelligent runs, winning ball and executing good decisions thereafter. Those skills themselves required huge energy, just a different kind. To Stephen's credit, he identified me as a solution while also acknowledging my inclusion on the team would require compromise elsewhere. Attacking corner-backs were becoming more of a force in the game so we knew if I were to play and be effective, having me cover their runs was not an option. Step up, Kevin and Jason. Without so much as a murmur of complaint, they did step up. Together they covered my defensive duties, sacrificing the sexier sides of their own games in the process. Without them, I wouldn't have regained my place on the team, never mind won Footballer of the Year. They were not doing it for me, just as they weren't doing it for themselves. They were doing it for the team.

As I begin my life as a coach, I reflect on how players like Jason and Kevin changed Mayo football for the better over the last decade. Just like young, impressionable players, coaches, too, need to win and impress early to feel more secure and confident in their roles. The tendency is for quick fixes. What I learned from my teammates was to always consider the long game not only when assessing my abilities as a coach but also when looking at players. What do they offer off the pitch? In the changing room? On long trips to faraway matches? Leaders wear many faces. It's our job as coaches and mentors to recognise them.

The Best of Kevin McLoughlin

In the summer of 2021, Kevin McLoughlin played his 100th competitive game for Mayo. This remarkable run has seen him play in practically every big game for Mayo for over a decade. It's also seen him score many points in clutch moments. As the decade wore on, and our rivalries with Dublin and Kerry grew, some of the more formative wins of the team's adolescence drifted from memory. One such game was our All-Ireland quarter-final victory over defending champions Cork in 2011. Just a couple of months earlier, we had been brought to extra time by London. The Cork game was one we were expected to lose. Always willing to fulfil a prophecy, we found ourselves four points down after 20 minutes. We were a young team, early in James Horan's first reign, so losing to Cork would be disappointing but expected. As players, you constantly guard against accepting such defeatist outcomes, but sometimes these thoughts are inevitable. You can literally feel games slipping from you as a team but are somehow powerless to stop the rot as an individual. This was threatening to be one of those games until Kevin Mc flicked the switch. Taking the ball in traffic on the Cork 45-metre line, he shows a turn of pace and a jink that would become his trademark over the coming years. Shrugging off the attentions of Cork defenders, travelling at top speed, he bursts the net from just inside the 13. In typical Kevin style, there is little or no celebration, just a fist pump. The head down, Kevin sprints back to his position. It's only a moment, but suddenly we are back in the game. We feed off his energy, and the lift he has given our supporters. An hour later, the All-Ireland final champions are out, and we are one step closer to coming of age.

FOURTEEN

The Entertainers

'Try to enjoy the great festival of life.'

– Epictetus

W hat truly makes the GAA different from other elite sports? This is a question I've asked myself many times, first as a player and now as a coach. There is no one answer but the more I reflect on it, the more I realise that the answer lies in the people who play, coach and support in the stands, at home, behind the scenes. When the dressing room door closes on a Tuesday night before a championship game, there may be 50 people there. Each of them after coming from their day jobs. From their kids. From their studies. Look to the left and you might have an engineer who was out on site all day. To your right, a scientist fresh from ten hours in a lab. There were boys laying bricks and lads teaching kids. Suit jackets hung up on pegs alongside garda uniforms. Boys who had driven from Belmullet and boys who had driven from Dublin. There were wives, partners and kids all waiting for us to get home. Yes, we were a band of brothers bound by a footballing code, united in our pursuit of excellence and glory but, much more than that, we were all different people from different backgrounds who for the hours between training sessions went about our daily lives, working our jobs and caring for our families.

Far from being a matter of complaint this made the dressing room a more interesting place to be. Because playing football was not our job, it served as a release. There was pressure – overwhelmingly so at times – but we were not playing for contracts, lucrative transfers or bonuses. Self-interest played a part, sure, but the primary motive was love of the game and love of our county. One of the greatest rewards was the craic we had along the way.

Nobody plays intercounty football for the craic. Nor do lads begin an intercounty career and think to themselves "I'm going to make myself undroppable as the joker in the pack". No, these things can only happen organically. When you have a garda warming up alongside a teacher, both after putting in long weeks in their respective arenas, stories will be shared, and laughs will result. Nowadays, there exists a multi-million-euro industry around team-building and leadership development. I can't deny the merits of some of what's taught but from experience I also believe you can't recreate or force the bond guys develop by sharing buses, hotels and changing rooms with each other. Professional sports teams do this too, but to me the difference is that we come to train and play, bringing our lives with us, sharing them even if it goes against our natural way. If the group of which you are a part is strong enough, players can be vulnerable within it. With that vulnerability comes trust. Once trust is there, anything is possible.

What is probable is that you will come across some of the rarest characters imaginable. Quiet lads who'd floor you with a one-liner, messers who'd mimic the entire squad, fearless about the consequences. You can't just walk through a dressing room door and stop being who you really are. A healthy team should want the opposite.

The concept of culture in team sport is not a new one but the branding of it certainly is. As society becomes increasingly obsessed with image and public relations, the manipulation of 'what goes on behind the curtain' for likes and shares is pervasive and, in my opinion, disingenuous. The ethos – or culture – of a team, should be personal to the group. By opening it up, exposing it to critique and outside opinion, the integrity of the idea is compromised. If you are doing the right thing to gain approval from others outside the group, your motives have been compromised. As for the fun element, this is something that cannot be manufactured. Encouraged and nurtured, sure, but not manufactured. It certainly helps when there are a few born comics in the group. There was no shortage of those throughout my years in Mayo. Some boys were born for the stage, others a little more subtle, but there was nobody on a level with Mickey Conroy.

It almost reads like a disclaimer, but no conversation about Mickey C as an entertainer can happen without first acknowledging what a brilliant footballer he was. From his debut season in 2004 all the way to his Indian summer in 2015, he proved himself a quality forward who could run, score and create but that was only the tip of the iceberg with him. A Mayo career that spanned a dozen years. Three All-Ireland final appearances. Not one start in the Connnacht Championship. He reckoned himself that this was the very reason he was called 'Mickey C'– Mickey Croker. He only played the big games in Croker – "any fool can play in Connacht!" The man defied definition off the field and was a complete force of nature on it.

Every extra-curricular thing that happened when Mickey C was part of a Mayo squad, he was stuck in the middle of it. Every wind-up, every illegal session. He never once shirked his responsibility for his role in any of it. The beauty of Mickey was that nobody could stay mad at him for too long. He had a way of defusing any situation with a quip that I've never seen matched. He was called up by six separate Mayo managers, all serious men. Each one knew his reputation as a footballer and a character. Each one saw through the bullshit, no doubt realising that he offered a double threat: not only could he do serious damage in front of goals, but he was also part of the glue that bound the team in the dressing room, too.

He had the wonderful ability to appear utterly blessed and wide-eyed in his surroundings while simultaneously adopting a leadership role. There was never anything nasty or mean-spirited in his antics. He'd never target a rookie and make them feel small. His humour needed no props or protagonists. He was a storyteller, pure and simple. He would have you in stitches in the back of the bus even though you knew there was a generous degree of poetic licence being applied, especially as you might have been a witness to the original story yourself! I'd hate to see Mickey on the stand at a war crimes tribunal. He'd take everyone down with him, most of them innocent.

He tells a great one about the fallout from an impromptu day-long session that followed an apocalyptic league loss to Donegal. However bad the loss was, manager James Horan's post-mortem poured salt into an already open wound. So, as often happens to teams when they're hurting, some of the boys go on the beer. Sensing an air of guilt the following Tuesday night, James asked the perpetrators to own up to the breach in discipline, take ownership and the matter would be closed. Mickey's was the first hand up, his false remorse so convincing I nearly believed myself that he was sorry. To all our horror – but especially Mickey's – some of the boys misread the room and not only owned up to one day's drinking but the second day as well! Mickey had already prostrated himself once and wasn't going to do it again. The lads sat alone on an island of guilt as Mickey shook his head in disgust at their – albeit honest – naivety.

"I thought I'd schooled them better than that!" he'd later say, "Never admit to the double day! Never admit to the double spill!"

Mickey was as much at home down the back of the bus as he was twisting defenders in knots. His prime time was not on team holidays and organised get-togethers but before, during and after some unmerciful floggings, be it at a training camp in the Catskills or a bootcamp in the Curragh. The guy had a knack of spotting the funny in the absurd. More than once, you'd find yourself on your hands and knees, killed out after some drill, and Mickey would be there, twice as worn out, winking at you. He'd rob you of the last air from your lungs with a quip. A second later, we'd be up and gone again.

These moments would become the inspiration for a hundred table-thumping tales later. It was the beauty of having a guy like Mickey Conroy in the trenches with you. He knew the pain. He was a serious player and a brilliant team-mate. He wasn't there for morale: he just brought it naturally. It's who he was. He felt comfortable enough to be himself in our group, and we were all the better for it.

★★★★★

Fear is a constant in any team sport. There's the fear of failure, as in not winning, and also the fear of not making it. Your fate is very much in other people's hands. The contracts that protect professional sportspeople do not exist for amateurs, even if the dedication required is similar. As an intercounty footballer, you are an expendable piece of a large puzzle. A dip in form can see you go from first man in to first man out. There is no transfer to a team that wants you. There are no payouts when you leave. You constantly run the risk of annoying loved ones, frustrating employers and disappointing yourself, all based on the whims of a manager who doesn't like the look of you anymore. This fear is real and at times it can be suffocating.

For this very reason, I always believed there had to be more to playing for Mayo than just winning. There simply had to be for the journey to last so long and mean so much. If it was only about winning, there would have been no Mickey Conroys. That's not to say Mickey wasn't a winner, far from it, but the obsession with results and the metrics around them can often reduce the game to a bunch of numbers, a mathematical equation. To me, that misses a huge point – play and train to win, sure, but do it while allowing people to breathe. To support each other. To be united in the pain of a loss and together in the joy of victory. Again, I feel this is an impossible ethos to force but there must be room for it to grow.

Barry Moran was another who just knew how to read a room and land a killer punch. The high stool was Mickey C's throne; the back of the bus was Barry's kingdom. A hugely decorated club footballer, Barry was a constant around Mayo squads for more than a decade. A beast of a man, he was in direct competition with the O'Shea brothers, Aidan and Seamus, and Tom Parsons for two midfield spots. Ironically, his most memorable performances for Mayo came as a sweeper against Donegal and Tipperary in consecutive seasons, executing the role brilliantly in both games. I have no doubt Barry was frustrated by a lack of minutes, but it never affected his relationship with any of the squad. His best buddies were his rivals for places. In any case, if he couldn't always dislodge them from the starting team, he was lethal at landing any man on his arse the second they stepped on the bus.

In 2006, one of our coaches, the late John Morrison, had the temerity to, er, politely explain to me that I was carrying a little more timber than I perhaps should be.

"You're too fat, Andy," he said, in his broad northern accent.

Every Saturday morning before a big game in Croker the team bus would pick me up in Ballagh' *en route* to Dublin. The second I stepped on the bus, there'd be a roar coming from the very back, in a familiar, thick northern accent "YOU'RE TOO FAT, ANDY!"

It sounds like nothing, but it meant multitudes: it meant the start of a huge weekend together as a group. It was an icebreaker for me, a reminder not to take myself too seriously whatever the challenge. It was also a reminder of how lucky we all were to be part of something so powerful. We were on a journey, figuratively and literally. 'Big Bird' Barry's attitude to those journeys was unique and refreshing: he saw them as a weekend away with your friends with a huge match against Dublin or Kerry in the middle of it. He was no less dialled-in because of this approach. He spent far too much time on the pine for his own liking, yet he always delivered when he was sprung. He was some servant to Mayo football, and some teammate to us all.

★★★★★

Barry was a great man for settling nerves before the game; Robbie Hennelly was without equal in boosting morale after it. Though we still won many more games in Dublin than we lost, those journeys home after losing the All-Ireland finals were as painful as you might suspect. Your hopes destroyed. Even though you knew it was coming, the season is suddenly over. That journey west is often a conflicted and confusing one. Regrets from the game fresh in the mind, doubts over the future already ruminating in your head, the group is wounded and vulnerable. That's when Robbie was immense, be it with a song, a story or a sketch. Robbie's interventions were a timely reminder of why there was more to our journey than the destination.

Robbie's pain in those defeats was no less acute than mine or anybody else's, yet he had the emotional intelligence to understand his worth in those moments. The teams were about to break up. Uncertainty, disillusionment and even bitterness can linger when those journeys end. Robbie's ability to put those disappointments behind him and feed positive energy back into the group through humour and song was a testament to his character and leadership within the group.

Back in 2012, during James Horan's second season in charge, we headed to Portugal on a training camp between our league semi-final victory over Kerry and the final against Cork. It was a curious week not least because the team was unsure of where exactly it was at. The management team were still finding their feet too, evaluating the group and trying to identify good and bad influences within it. Our first season under James had been a good one and a lot was expected of us. As a result, there was what I could only describe as a tension that lingered undefined and undiagnosed until one night during a team-building exercise, Robbie stood up and brilliantly mimicked James and coach Cian O'Neill, two very intense characters. It was an unexpected moment of levity during an incredibly tough week. The pressure valve was suddenly released. Everyone had a laugh at themselves, from the manager to the most junior rookie. It was a seminal moment for a group that until that point was still seeking its identity. That was Robbie's gift.

★★★★★

As kids, we primarily play sports for fun. That's what draws us in. We want to be with our friends or make friends or make our Mums and Dads proud. The more we play, the more the hunger to compete and win evolves. Regardless of what level you reach, however, if fun is not central to what you are doing, what is the point? Whether in the dressing room or boardroom, whatever the stakes, an ability for a team to enjoy themselves while driven to achieve can only enhance the experience. When the stakes are high and fear is a driver, there needs to be escapism. For me it came in the form of the craic provided by Barry, Mickey and Robbie.

The leadership books will tell us about the leaders who were intensely driven, ultra-competitive and often humourless. They will likely never mention the characters who made the journey enjoyable. As coaches, parents and mentors, we need to encourage kids not to feel that they must be something they're not just because they read it in some leadership book. Instead, they should be encouraged to be the very best version of themselves. If that version is full of energy, enthusiasm and humour, it is our job to enable them to use those qualities to make the team better.

The Best of Barry Moran

In our epic 2012 All-Ireland semi-final battle with Dublin, Barry, along with Aidan O'Shea in the middle of the park, gave a first-half display for the ages. Their performance gave us the platform to set a target for the defending champions to chase and chase it they did. In the second half, the Dubs redressed the balance at midfield with Michael Darragh MacAuley catching ball for fun. As the clock ticked down, we were hanging on for dear life.

Leading 18-16 heading into injury time, our goal is being bombarded by Dublin artillery. With a crucial kickout in front of the Hill, Clarkie has no short option available to him, just a wall of sky-blue jerseys pressing. His only option is to go long and hope that one of our twin towers can secure possession. It's a risk as Dublin have owned the skies and another concession would see another attack on our goals. As Clarkie kicked, Kevin McStay on co-commentary speaks the words everyone watching is thinking, "this is a crucial possession". After taking a battering for the second half, Barry knows the importance of the kickout and with eyes glued on the ball and impeccable timing he sails through the air and fetches cleanly, drawing a relieving foul from James McCarthy in the process. Moments later, the siege lifted by Barry's catch, Seamus O'Shea kicks a score to put us three up and sailing towards an All-Ireland final. Big Bird had bided his time and delivered a match-winning moment when the team needed it most.

FIFTEEN

Seek Out the Challenge

'Every journey begins with a single step.'

– Maya Angelou

AS VALUABLE as the entertainers are, every great team needs a straight shooter just as every town needs a sheriff. A guy who will resist the invitation to go on the beer when the team is hurting. A guy who wakes himself up in the middle of the night to hydrate. A guy who dedicates his adult life to being in peak physical condition when called upon. You can't have a team of entertainers – well, you can, but the seasons would be very short, if eventful. You can't have a team of robocops either but having a couple of clean-living specimens always helps to give a group balance. They silently lay down a marker for everyone else by their very presence. Lads in dressing rooms always pay attention to the physical conditioning of others. It's human nature. Some lads are sleeper agents: they might not look in the best of nick, they may even enjoy the few pints but run into them on a dirty night in MacHale Park and you'll learn never to do it again.

Others flatter to deceive. They may have the disco muscles but they're soft underneath – these boys always get exposed when it matters. Then you have the exceptional few.

The freaks. Lads who look carved from granite and live up to it on the field. Pure athletes who are aerobically elite and built like Olympians. Unless you have the formula to create them in a lab you will never have a team of Olympians. Theirs is a talent just as rare as Cillian's or Leeroy's. These boys are few and far between simply because the work it takes to get in that condition is alien to most of us. I always took pride in my preparation, in discovering new methods and testing out new theories. I said it earlier, I could never do it the Keith Higgins' way – never rock up to training literally just out of bed but, as meticulous as I thought I was, there were some men on another planet entirely. Diet, training, rest, recovery – and that's before you got to skills and ability.

Speaking of ability, one of the most underrated abilities in life and sport is availability. All the physical conditioning and talent in the world is useless if you are not ready and willing to perform. This is not just a matter of hanging around and waiting for your chance. It's much more about working hard on developing your game, on remaining patient when you're being ignored and, most crucially, being ready when the chance presents itself. Of the 16 All-Ireland semi-finals and finals Mayo played between 2011 and 2019, just three players started every game: Cillian O'Connor, Aidan O'Shea and Donal Vaughan. While you would likely expect to see Aidan and Cillian on that shortlist, Donie's may be more of a surprise to those outside the group. To players who saw him in action up close, his inclusion makes perfect sense. The guy was a machine. Arguably the best prepared Mayo footballer of his generation, his dedication to always being available in the best possible condition was unrivalled.

Like all sportspeople, footballers are curious beasts. We plead humility and sacrifice for the greater good, as I believe we should, but lurking behind the thin veil of selflessness is ego. That ego partly drives our hunger to succeed. It's that ego that keeps us out on the training field longer or in the gym lifting heavier. We want to earn a reputation for this or that but, once gained, it's imperative we strive to live up to it. Donie was one such beast. He quickly earned a reputation for being a phenomenal athlete. It was his desire to sur-pass people's expectations that made him the player he was for Mayo for a decade.

Donie, like Keith, Leeroy and Kevin McLoughlin, played in a variety of positions in huge games from full-back to centre-back to midfield. This was a testament to his foot-balling dexterity. Casual observers may have only seen an athlete covering vast amounts of grass, but Donie was much more than that. He possessed excellent game intelligence, posed a constant attacking threat thanks to his incredible engine and his ability to read a situation and proved a night-mare for opposing forwards. He never, ever stopped going.

In the 2009 Connacht final, Donie was a 21-year-old newcomer not renowned for his man-marking qualities. In the first half of that game, Galway's Nicky Joyce was tearing us asunder. At half-time, Johno, to pretty much everybody's surprise, called on Donie to step in at corner-back and do a job curbing Nicky. I recall thinking it was a huge risk, throwing Donie in to stymie such an in-form player. Rookie players had perished on similar rocks many times before. We recognised Donie as an attacking half-back not as a guy who'd sacrifice his game to disrupt and destroy. Donie re-assured the dressing room he had it covered. He went out and rewarded Johno's faith in him, proving wrong any doubters on his team or in the stands. By marking Nicky out of the game, he played a key role in Mayo becoming Connacht champions.

Donie, as evidenced above, craved responsibility. He al-ways wanted the opposition's main man. He always wanted a central role. This was recognised by successive managers from Johno all the way through to James Horan at the tail end of the last decade. They all saw in him what he gen-uinely saw in himself: a leader whose style was to lead by example.

In all my time playing, whether with Mayo or IT Sligo or getting exposure to International Rules teams, I never saw a guy more professional in his conduct. He lived and breathed it. He most likely recognised that he was not the most naturally talented footballer among us – I'm guessing that only drove him harder.

I remember coming back down from that fateful league loss in Ballyshannon early in 2012, the game that inspired the session which, in turn, inspired a famous "double day, double spill" comment from Mickey Conroy that I'll come back to later. We were all hurting, especially after getting justifiably berated by James Horan for our attitude. Chatting to Donie afterwards, I remarked that I needed to work harder on my shooting. Quick as a flash he was on to me: "When?"

I told him I'd be at the pitch in Ballaghaderreen with a bag of balls at 11am the following day. At 10.45am the next day, my doorbell rang. It was Donie, after driving for an hour, ready to go. We stayed 'til three o'clock, doing a full weights session as well as an amount of kicking practice. From that day, through to that year's league final, he scored in all but one of our games. For him, the Donegal loss was not something to be forgotten. You couldn't just simply 'move on'. There had to be a lesson. As some lads took to the high stool to blow off steam, he took to the field to go again. That summed him up.

There was no judgement by Donie of the lads who had other, more relaxed methods of release. He knew himself. That was enough for him.

★★★★★

In those early James Horan days, I remember saying to the group that I saw Donie as a guy who would captain Mayo in the coming years. It likely didn't happen due to the presence of Cillian and Keith but that was the esteemed company he was in when it came to leaders within the group. He gave us direction. He was an ethical compass. He existed as a model athlete and player within the squad, a yardstick against which we could all measure ourselves. If you thought you were doing enough, all you had to do was look at Donie. You'd quickly realise there was always more to do.

Season after season, Donie's passing and shooting got consistently better. He kicked huge scores in big games – three points on Declan O'Sullivan in the 2011 semi-final, goals against Galway and Donegal in 2015 as well as the point before Cillian's famous equaliser in 2016, a game in which he was undoubtedly our best player. Donie always sought out the team's burden. Donie truly believed that the better he got, the better the team got.

As with all men of immense character, there were dark days too. In the 2017 final, following a rush of blood to the head, he was uncharacteristically sent off after an altercation with Dublin's John Small. As I've said plenty of times before, every game needs a retrospective narrative to help explain away the pain of losing. For many that day, it was Donie's sending off. I don't think a single teammate would accept that reason. Sure, Donie's momentary lapse didn't help, but to us and I'm certain to himself, it did not define him.

Donie was the team's natural protector. Our mantra that day against Dublin was to never take a step back. Don't concede an inch in any battle. His eagerness to rush after Small's hit on Colm Boyle was just another example of this but one he would be the first to admit he timed wrong.

These days, such totemic moments are replayed on a loop on social media to the point of absurdity. A thousand little mistakes are a much less attractive proposition to dissect than one big one. Donie took a lot of unwarranted abuse after that game, all from anonymous strangers who wouldn't dare say it to his face. Knowing him as I do, I trust he didn't worry about himself in any of it. His only concern would've been for his family who, in turn, I have no doubt, were only worrying for him.

It's a side to Donie I was privileged to get to know. I don't often talk about such things, but I recall on the night of my wedding my father was unwell. As I danced the first dance with my new bride Jennifer, Donie had the presence of mind to seek out my Mum and take her out to the dance floor. A young man in his mid-20s at a wedding, surrounded by his buddies and teammates – yet that's what he thought to do at that moment. That is who he is. I always said that he was the guy you'd be delighted to see arrive home with your sister. He was also the guy you wanted beside you in battle. It's rare that those two qualities exist in the same man.

By the time Donie retired in 2019, he had played in five All-Ireland senior finals. Along with Lee and Colm Boyle, he was part of one of the most respected half-back lines in recent footballing history. He played in every position for Mayo from number two through to 12. Injuries deprived him of the Indian summer his career most definitely deserved but even his departure was a testimony to his professionalism and class. Thirty-two is young for an intercounty footballer of Donie's physical conditioning to retire. In typical Donie fashion, he did the math, looked at his life on and off the field and decided his race was run. I think, for him, there was literally no way to continue without pushing himself to the absolute maximum as he had done for every day of his footballing life.

He was truly a unique character. For all the advances in sports science and medicine, for all the minding of players that can happen to ensure their efficacy on the biggest stage, he remains an outlier for his freakish conditioning and his dedication to his craft. Too often when players retire, we say we may never see his likes again. With Donal Vaughan and Mayo, I am certain of it.

The Best of Donal Vaughan

Although I had been playing senior football for Mayo for almost eight years, 2011 was a time of great innocence. James Horan had just come in, bringing with him a sense of freshness and revolution that gave great cause for excitement for almost all of us within the squad. Throughout the league and Connacht Championship, the team gradually found its identity even if we hadn't fully caught up with our tactical approach. Having faith that one would follow the other, we resolved that we would become the most hardworking team in the country. The innocence quickly gave way to reality after a brush with catastrophe in London, that near miss providing us with the wake-up call we needed. As the summer matured so did we, winning a Connacht title before dumping defending champions Cork in the quarters. To a team in the first year of a progressive cycle, the season was already a success. Waiting for us in the semi-final were Kerry, no doubt smarting after watching Cork triumph the year before. Ultimately, we came up short against a superior opponent, but that loss was as important as any of our victories that year. It gave us a taste, a free shot at the big boys and served as a day of arrival for the likes of Cillian and Donie. Marking the mercurial Declan O'Sullivan, one of the most gifted centre-forwards the game has seen, Donie, aged 22 and completely fearless, went toe to toe: no sweepers, no support, just green spaces in O'Sullivan's playground. Not only did he prove a nightmare in his defensive work that day, but he also broke forward at every opportunity, kicking three points from play and bringing the game to Kerry. It was the start of something special.

SIXTEEN

Write Your Own Script

'You define your own life.
Don't let other people write your script.'

– Oprah Winfrey

THE Mayo footballing story is a polarising one. Being consistently second best for nearly a quarter of a century made us the butt of much satire and sarcasm from some, as well as being the recipients of great respect for going so close so often from others. Our inability to finish a season as champions while being consistently competitive inspired many theories from the spiritual to the psychological to the tactical. In keeping with every great story, the need for narrative endured. We didn't breed enough scoring forwards. We lacked the bottle on the big day. The team overtook a funeral driving home 70 years ago. People always need reasons for things and the more binary and black-and-white, the better. To me, as someone involved in six final losses over 17 seasons, the only thing I'm certain of is that there is no one reason why we didn't win it in my time. I have my own ideas on why which I will get into later. It's just as important to me, however, to reflect on and learn from all those I played with who exhibited qualities in their personalities that made them admirable footballers and great people.

We never wore our losses like victories. Each defeat stung more than the last. There was no joy taken in the fact that we had reached finals only to lose by the slimmest of margins. We were a proud group and losing hurt like hell. We were certainly aware of much of the noise that followed our losses, good and bad. Paper doesn't refuse ink and as much as all the criticism hurt, we didn't need to read it. We knew ourselves where we had not performed and what hadn't gone our way. The question for us as a group and individually was always what we could have done better. There was rarely any self-pity and if there was, it didn't last long. A defining characteristic of our teams has been that many of the players have had second comings, me included. We do not have the population of Dublin or the winning history of Kerry so it's imperative for young players to always remember that if the door is closed on you once, if you want it badly enough you must be prepared to kick it back down. Coming back again and again is a quality synonymous with Mayo teams and resilience a trait famously inherent in Mayo people. We should be proud of it.

★★★★★

Sometimes, a journey has a totem. If the theme of our journey was resilience, one of its greatest embodiments was Colm Boyle. At the age of 21, Colm was enjoying his first full season as a Mayo senior footballer when he went through one of those experiences that could have easily finished him. Picked corner-back in his first Connacht final against Galway, Colm endured a torrid afternoon chasing forwards like Michael Meehan, Nicky Joyce and Mattie Clancy. Moments after Galway scored their second goal, Colm was hauled ashore just before half-time, always a bitter pill for anyone to swallow but especially for a young player finding his feet. It was Colm's last game for Mayo for four seasons. Another player's career might have been over. In fact, it was less 'might', and more 'probably'. Deemed too small and too light for the demands of the modern game, Boyler was shunted aside for the younger, more physical players coming out of a minor team inspired by the emerging talent of Aidan O'Shea.

As a young player, Colm's passion and intensity were there for all to see. However, just as he was breaking through, the dynamic of the intercounty game was shifting. Change, driven by Cork, Tyrone and Kerry, saw bigger and more physical athletes dominate the field. Big men had roamed the earth before but not like this. Training and conditioning were evolving so that a new breed of player was emerging, one with size, speed and skill. To survive, you needed at least two of the three.

And so, after a bad year for Mayo, Boyler got cut. Mayo moved on without him. New players like Donie Vaughan and Ger Cafferkey emerged, giving the team an edge that saw us slowly turn a corner. Meanwhile, back in Ballindine in south Mayo, Colm Boyle had gone to work. Along with his teammate and friend Mickey Conroy, they set about changing their games to get back into the intercounty scene, setting a goal to bring their club to county intermediate glory in the process. They did more than that. In 2011, Davitts won the Mayo intermediate title and then Connacht, driven on by their centre-back and talisman Colm Boyle. By that summer, Boyler was back in the Mayo squad. The energy and intensity were the same; the player was different. Colm had used his time away to add serious physicality to his game. That would be the defining characteristic of the next decade of his career.

Immediately back on the team, Colm went on to win four All-Stars over the next six seasons. By the time he was 21, he had played at every grade for Mayo – minor, U21 and senior. Then he was rejected. Far from wallowing, he took time and space and came back a different player. He became a hero of Mayo supporters. He was tough as nails and sometimes that toughness overshadowed his footballing ability. Just as easy to overlook were his willingness to learn and his game intellect. He constantly refined his approach, looking for ways to become an even better defender. His first act may have been a short one. By 2021, his second act was still going.

*****

The idea of space, particularly in the context of allowing ourselves some, is something many of us struggle with in our lives. Even if we do believe in it, we can convince ourselves that it is for others to practice i.e., those with the actual space and time to do so. We finish school and can't wait to get to college. We finish college and rush to get a job. We lose our job and can't wait to get another one. The same goes for relationships: marry first, buy a house, have kids. We finish playing and we rush to fill the void with something else. Sometimes you don't have a choice, however. Sometimes it just gets foisted upon you when you least expect it, like when you get rejected from a team for which you love playing – you have no choice but to grieve, hurt and think. That time, that space, if used properly, can be transformative. It can be the difference between good and great. Colm was good. He took the time and space he likely never wanted, and he became great. He wrote his own script.

★★★★★

For a lot of Colm's journeys, Boyler had a great sidekick in Mickey Conroy. Both proud Davitts men, they were inseparable but also opposites. I never saw a more nervous man before a game than Colm Boyle. He would be the colour of milk. Mickey, by contrast, would be full of life. You couldn't shut him up. Mickey had a remarkable Mayo career that spanned from 2004 to 2015. He had electric speed, was a great ball winner and possessed an eye for goal. He was an exceptional player and an exceptional teammate. The character of the group who lit up every situation with his wit and humour, as I've said already.

The Best of Colm Boyle

The greatest example of Colm Boyle's fortitude came in the drawn All-Ireland semi-final between Mayo and Kerry in 2014. Nine points to five down at the break, with Lee Keegan sent off just before half-time, we were in serious bother. As a team, we relied so heavily on our attacking half-back line. Losing Lee and being a man down surely spelled the end of the road. We needed something, a spark, and who better to ignite it than Colm Boyle. In the words of the commentator Marty Morrissey, "look at him bouncing off the ground." That summed him up.

Just after the break, each team picked off a score, James O'Donoghue at one end and Alan Dillon at the other. Following Alan's score the resulting kickout broke to the ground and the ball was about to be gathered by the Kerry wing-forward, Michael Geaney. Colm had different ideas. Outsprinting Geaney, he got a boot to the ball, knocking it away from the Kerry dangerman. Next up Declan O'Sullivan who sprinted toward the ball around the centre-half-forward position. This was a big moment in a big game, and there was only going to be one winner. Boyler crashes into O'Sullivan, gets to the ball first and wins the free. The tone is set. The comeback is on. We narrow the gap to 11-8. The next play is vital. Aidan wins a free from the next restart and plays a one-two with Boyler. Big Aido attacks through the heart of the defence and brings three Kerry players with him. He shovels it out to Jason Doc who finds Boyler on the 45-metre line. In front of him stand the three biggest Kerry players – Donnchadh Walsh, David Moran and Anthony Maher. Boyler, standing at 5'8", sets himself and goes straight at them. Beating the first tackle, he slaloms through the two midfielders and pings one straight between the posts with the outside of his right foot. In typical Boyler fashion, he turns, punches the air and sprints back to mark his man. With that, Geaney is replaced by Bryan Sheehan, brought on specifically to curb the influence of our flying wing-back. It's too late though. Boyler has sparked us into life. We are ready to fight and Boyler is leading us into battle.

On so many occasions Colm Boyle was the man to spark the comeback. The player who put his heart and body on the line for the team. We had just seen arguably our best player sent off and up stepped Colm. He gave us the energy on the field, he inspired the supporters off it. The game finished in a draw and was memorable in its own right, but the second-half performance of Colm Boyle was something that will live long in the memory of all Mayo supporters.

SEVENTEEN

We Are in This Together

'When you cease to dream, you cease to live.'
– Malcom Forbes

MY FATHER was not a football man. Not in the traditional, Mayo sense. Ours was not a football house the way others around us were. My love of Gaelic football was self-made. I grew up in a time when John O'Mahony led Mayo to their first All-Ireland final in 38 years, in 1989. I was only five years old. The colour and pageantry that went with the build-up to that final against Cork are among my earliest memories. Our club, through Johno, Dermot Flanagan and Noel Durkin, were strongly represented in '89. The legacy of that final appearance against Cork was a renewed pride in Mayo football. As a child, you could feel momentum building. Going to games with my brother Vinny in Castlebar, or the Hyde in Roscommon, came with a loaded sense of excitement and anticipation. Tailbacks and traffic jams in rural country towns. Ordinary things that would usually drive your parents mad only added to the sense of occasion and of being involved in something bigger. Even as a child, you knew you were part of a movement.

Just as I started secondary school, Mayo, under John Maughan, began writing another chapter. If winning in 1989 was borderline unthinkable and reaching the final an achievement in itself, the Mayo team of the mid-'90s was among the best in the country. Losing consecutive All-Irelands to Meath and Kerry, the first in hugely controversial circumstances, brought sharper focus on a football-mad county that had not tasted ultimate success in four decades. Increased media focus highlighted the drought. The much-hyped curse was wheeled out as an easy story to explain away our perceived bad luck. Coming into the 1998 season all eyes were on Mayo to see whether they could reach an unprecedented third All-Ireland final on the trot. In a bizarre game of football in MacHale Park, Galway – managed by my old friend Johno – shocked Mayo and as if to compound the feeling of injustice, curse and bad luck, supporters were beginning to feel, they went on to win the All-Ireland the same year, ending their own 32-year drought.

I had my own reasons to be happy for Johno and Galway but, across the county, watching our closest rivals wipe our eye just as we had again established ourselves as a force was a particularly bitter pill to swallow. Mayo's victory over Galway in Tuam the following summer – our first there since 1951 – once again raised hope that we were getting closer to the summit. I was still a fan at this point and going to the games watching my clubmate Kevin Cahill and an idol like Ciarán McDonald do their thing made me more and more want to wear the jersey. Although we kept falling short at the death, the teams we were producing and the football we were playing never filled me with anything other than hope and excitement for each coming season.

Long before I was involved with the minor team, I never bought the hard-luck story of Mayo football even after watching us lose three All-Irelands in eight years. What I saw was a team competing at the highest level. That team set an example, a standard for me, and others, to follow. I watched Mayo beat Kerry in Croke Park. I saw us beat the All-Ireland champions, Galway. I watched when we won the National League. I only viewed heightened expectations as a good thing. Maybe it was Johno's influence in school but there was nothing to be feeling sorry for ourselves about. Quite the opposite. I saw us win far more matches than we lost. Yet, as the team came close again and again, a story was being written.

Mayo are bottlers.
Mayo are cursed.
Mayo are unlucky.
Poor Mayo!

I don't buy it. I never bought it. Not as a fan and not as a player. Only once as a player did I feel we gave it everything and lost. That was in the 2017 All-Ireland final loss to Dublin and even then we were beaten by a better team. Every other loss in a big game, no matter how well we played, we still came up short either on the field, or off it, or both. Sometimes in our preparation, sometimes in our execution, sometimes the hill was just a little too steep for us to climb. I understand the romance aspect of it, and I know that lends itself to amplifying the notion of bad luck or a curse or some sense of injustice, but those feelings were only ever fleeting for me. I felt those losses just as acutely as anybody but I always – eventually – found the positives.

We did so much right.
We got in a position to win.
We beat everybody to get here.
What can we do more?

The golfer Padraig Harrington finished second 29 times in his career. His story was like that of Mayo footballers before he won the first of his three majors in 2007. The moment he triumphed, the narrative evaporated. Like him, I see the fact we came so close so often as us doing a great deal right a huge amount of the time. When we finally do win, those losses will not have been in vain.

★★★★★

Twelve months is a long time in football. In June 2010, we lost to Longford in a qualifier in Pearse Park. There was, of course, a travelling Mayo support there but, after four tough seasons since our last All-Ireland final appearance, they most likely numbered in the hundreds rather than the thousands we came to expect in subsequent years. That night was humiliating. We let ourselves down. It sadly ended John O'Mahony's second stint as Mayo manager. For those few there to witness it, it must've been a tough night. As a team we were probably blessed that the Mayo crowd numbered a paltry figure.

A little over a year later, as we ran off the field after our first-half performance against the champions, Cork, in an All-Ireland quarter final in Croke Park, we were still in the game at just two points down. We had opened poorly but had fought our way back with some brilliant football epitomised by Kevin McLoughlin's superb goal. There were only 20,000 fans in Croke Park that day and those who travelled from Mayo did so more in hope than expectation. We had not won in HQ since the Dublin semi-final in 2006. Cork had beaten us plenty in the years in between and although there were good vibes coming from James Horan's first summer in charge, the bar was set in that a good performance would be a victory in itself.

What lives in the memory is not the final whistle that day, nor a defining moment in the game, but running in the tunnel at half-time. Although we were a couple of scores down our tails were up. We were playing well and had weathered a storm that would've seen us done for in the couple of seasons previous. As we ran for the dressing rooms, we received a standing ovation from the Mayo supporters. Compared to other years, there were not that many there but that made it even more special. The hairs stood on the back of my neck as I entered the dressing room. I recall chatting about it with my teammates afterwards. It felt like there were 80,000 Mayo people in Croke Park that day. We took their energy, fed off it and recorded a famous victory. That ovation remains one of my favourite memories as a footballer. For the players and, I believe, the fans, a corner had been turned.

★★★★★

If we as Mayo people are to accept the congratulations for being a support that follows its team like few others, then I feel it's only right and proper we acknowledge that it hasn't always been a bed of roses. We have the diehards like most counties do: the men and women who will travel to Omagh and Clones and Killarney without a moment's thought. Those guys were there before the team's popularity grew in the 2010s and will still be there no matter what happens in the future. They take wins and losses personally, as the team does, and because of that a little tension can exist when things aren't going so great (2007 to 2010 is a good example). That tension is a consequence of caring that I understand all too well. They invest a large part of their lives in following the team. It's understandable that they feel let down when the team fails to live up to their expectations. You can be sure the players' expectations are just as high if not higher.

That Cork game aside, we were always a great county for travelling to Croke Park. Some counties go the opposite way but for Mayo and its supporters there was an element of ritual and privilege about it. In the late 1980s and 1990s that was marked by stops in Harry's of Kinnegad and sandwiches in the Phoenix Park before the game. Six-hour journey home that evening. As kids, it was often our only outing to Dublin in a given year. The country seemed bigger then.

In the 2010s, something changed. The pride in and love for Mayo football was always there but, just as a new, young team emerged, so did a different breed of support. This was post-Celtic Tiger Ireland. The arrogance of the late 2000s had given way to a realisation that we needed each other way more than we ever thought. This feeling was as true in sport as it was in families and business. Tens of thousands of young Mayo people had migrated to Dublin for studies and work. In previous decades the movement may not have been to the capital but further to England, the US or Australia. As the Mayo population grew, so did our support. Saturday evening games in Croke Park took on a life of their own, becoming far more significant events than just a game of football. They were legitimate social gatherings. You saw people you'd only ever meet at Christmas, a wedding or a funeral. The more games we won as a team, the longer the summer lasted for our supporters. The connection was real and it grew with every game.

I knew from my travels with the team, and from my friends and family, how much the idea of Mayo identity mattered outside the county. Forget football, people from the west of Ireland see themselves as a forgotten people. That chip on the shoulder can be healthy if it doesn't make you cynical and I think, for the most part, we have worn it with plenty of perspective and humour. Often, on the way through the city to games in Croke Park, we would see more Mayo flags hanging from houses than Dublin ones. As the decade grew, so did our following, proving that if you have a good core – and we always did – everything else can flourish.

There is another side to the Mayo support network that must never get left behind or forgotten. I've seen first-hand in cities like New York, London and Philly how passionate Mayo people are about football. It was always a great source of pride and wonder for me to see people so far away from home care so much about the team. I've heard the lengths to which people go to watch matches. I've often imagined how that sense of isolation and loneliness that comes from being so far away from loved ones must be suddenly exaggerated on the day of an All-Ireland, knowing their families are gathering to watch it or to travel to the game. I know too that the traditional emigrant destinations of the east coast of the US and the UK are a thing of the past and, like all Irish people, young Mayo folk are now settling in parts of the world of which many of us have barely heard. As a former player, I believe it is imperative these communities are always included in Mayo football as much as possible.

When we went as a team to New York in 2019, we brought about 10,000 supporters with us. It was a remarkable occasion not least because so many supporters who came were reunited with loved ones living in New York and the east coast, many of whom could not travel back to Ireland themselves. It was remarkable too to see the goodwill of Mayo people abroad. I feel lucky that I got to witness it at the end of my career with my family, instead of as a young pup mad to see the Manhattan nightlife! Being older and a little wiser, I savoured it, and understood that these people living far away from home were as important to the future of Mayo football as anybody else.

★★★★★

As a young man growing up in the west of Ireland, I can attest to the need for ritual to fill the emotional gap that comes with the territory of being Irish and male. Being openly emotional, especially in matters of the heart and family, is not in our DNA. We tend to express ourselves a little differently. I saw so much of this in the faces of parents and their children, infant and adult, throughout my time playing for Mayo. This was a family thing that would not have had a medium to grow if we had been losing every game. I genuinely believe Mayo being successful brought families closer. It allows us to be together without having to overthink it. I had it with my own Dad. From the time I first started playing for Mayo, I could see how my involvement gave him so much enjoyment and pride. He went to every game, dressed up in a suit – don't ask me why! As I look back on it now, I realise it only added to the sense that we were all part of something together. I know I gave him great joy when I played for Mayo and that makes me proud.

Another source of pride is knowing how much the Mayo team I retired from meant to a county. A new generation of Mayo people belonged to something. We felt it out on the field in Croke Park in big moments. We honestly felt it in the depths of winter on mucky training fields too. The love was reciprocated. We, the players, understood it wasn't contrived or the product of media spin. Sure, there was often condescension from outside, but we knew where we were from, and we knew the people we represented. Results will show that the team fell short but the story is much more complex and beautiful than that. We were there, time and time again, and we came back as a team on the field and supporters in the stands.

There is nothing unfortunate or unlucky about this story. The unity and resilience we display as a county are blessings in my eyes, never a curse. Our day will come.

EIGHTEEN

The Support Team

'I am because we are.'

– African philosophy of *ubuntu*

WHATEVER the walk of life, whatever the endeavour, people need support to achieve. No successful person is an island no matter how much they protest otherwise. Whether it's heading out the door to do a night shift, or flying overseas for work, each one of us needs people to support us on our journey, especially if we hope to be successful. If and when we are successful, much is said of the sacrifices we made to 'get there'. In the case of the intercounty footballer, those sacrifices are easily defined, tangible things: we sacrifice our bodies, playing with and through injuries, often without even thinking about the consequences that may occur later in life. We miss a lot of things that are routine, everyday things to our friends and family. Weddings and birthdays and family gatherings and holidays. We spend large parts of our adult lives travelling in cars and buses. Getting home from training at 1am, back up at 7am and out the door to work. There are many casualties of this lifestyle, some personal relationships among them. This is a tale well told. It's as easy a crutch for players to lean on as it is a story for papers to write. The fact that we are amateur players only amplifies the message. We do it for our families. We do it for the love of the game. We do it for Mayo. We do it for glory.

All the above may be true but what is certain is that we could do none of it without our loved ones behind us – our parents, wives, partners and girlfriends. It's a well-worn cliché, flogged to death by every actor who ever won an Oscar, but, like most clichés, it's 100 per cent true. They are the invisible blanket that comforts us during our losses. They act as therapists when we are dropped or paranoid about the mood of a manager suddenly not talking to us. They are proxies in our absence at weddings and funerals. They will rarely get sympathy for their role either, because, in Mayo, footballers tend to be regarded as the beatified few. To some, our partners are the lucky ones to share in *our* journey. I see this thinking as a little backward. The opposite has always been the case – we are the lucky ones to have them support us.

In material terms, what do they get? At best, a fancy team holiday at the end of the year. The rest of the time is spent captive to our schedules. So often for Mayo, that meant starting in November, ending ten months later in September, before a few less intense weeks of club football. Often, footballers will meet their life partners – as I did – at an early stage on the journey. Then, it's new and exciting to all. Nights out after big games bring the group closer together. Losses don't cut so deep, especially since your lives are not as interlinked as they'll soon become. As a young couple, perhaps still living in different parts of the country, working in different jobs and having different social circles, the burden is not so heavy on either person, nor is the need for support so great. But as you mature and evolve in relationships, the more you learn to rely on each other.

I started going out with my wife Jennifer in 2003, when I was 20 years old. I knew her long before that as she is the sister of one of my best friends, Stephen. Jen has been with me through every All-Ireland final loss, every bad injury, every crisis in confidence. There's nothing we haven't shared with each other. Ours has been an equal partnership in life as a couple just as it is now in parenting and in business.

Throughout my footballing career, I was definitely the public face of that partnership but her unwavering support – often unseen and from the background – was just as much responsible for anything I achieved as any footballing ability, especially in the second half of my career as we started a family and business together. It was also the period of my life when I played by far my best football. That was no coincidence.

Like all equal partnerships, there was nothing submissive about Jenny's role in my footballing life. She didn't look at me gooey-eyed, thinking everything I did was right or great. Whenever she felt I was wrong or off in my reading of a situation, she would quickly let her feelings be known. That's the difference between a mother's love – unconditional and heavily biased – and the cold, objective eye of a loyal partner! When it came to football and me, Jen was a realist. She grew up in a football-mad house with her brothers Stephen and David Drake, who would both play for Mayo, and her father Noel who played football for Longford and Ballagh'. She was all too aware of the bullshit that goes with being a footballer and would have no trouble calling me out if she saw my ego get the better of me.

With that baseline established early in our relationship, it made normally difficult conversations a great deal easier. I could discuss my game with her and be assured of honesty in her views. She was there the first time I ran after doing my cruciate, literally doing the session with me, running alongside me. During my time as captain, I always ran ideas by Jen before introducing them to the players and management. Even after our first child Charlotte was born in late 2014, when Jen had to devote less time to her footballing husband and more to our young family, she still played an active role in my game preparation. In 2016, I remember her coming on a bog walk with my mate John Ginty and me to help with meditation and breathing exercises. She was a part of everything.

In 2019, as we all travelled together to New York for a weekend that was both a championship game and a transatlantic celebration of all things Mayo, Jen and the kids were stopped at emigration in Dublin for not having completed an ESTA form correctly. She was forced to travel a day later by herself, with two small children. Even when she got there, she couldn't attend the game as Charlotte was unwell.

In many ways, that incident sums up life as a supportive partner. We are all in it together until your wife gets stopped at the airport and you keep going with the team. Instances like that made the decision for me to retire – one we made together – all the easier.

It was only after retiring, however, that I truly appreciated the sacrifice that she and all the other partners made. When I say partners, I include every person who plays a supportive role in a player's sporting journey. I think of parents who themselves sacrifice so much to help their children achieve. It was only when I was suddenly available for every chore, every family appointment, every sleepless night, every drop-off and pick-up that I fully understood the depth of their invisible roles.

I can't speak for every player but I'm certain what was true for me with Jennifer was true for most of my teammates and peers in Mayo and teams across the country.

When the team runs out through the tunnel, it is only the players who get to wear the jersey. Only we get to stand in the arena and drink in a packed Croke Park, 82,000 people, noise that never fails to cause your heart to race. Only we get to experience the feeling of making a net rattle or a ball fly over a crossbar to win a game. Those who live with us, love us and support us, sit in stands and at home on couches, often afraid for us. Afraid we will get hurt, taken off or abused by the fella next to them in the stand. Winning matters to them also but not nearly as much as we, the players, often think. Which is a good thing. They are the life waiting for us beyond the line. They have their own careers, hopes and goals they wish to achieve. I count myself blessed that I didn't just find a supporter in Jennifer. I found a partner, one who was willing to often put me and my football first. To me, that is the real meaning of sacrifice.

*****

If Jennifer was the woman who kept me grounded outside the dressing room, another – psychologist Niamh Fitzpatrick – played a huge part in keeping my head together inside it. In all my time playing senior football for Mayo, I had seen many people come through the door with the express goal of helping us to improve our performances. Some were genuinely brilliant, others quite obviously charlatans just along for the ride. Niamh wasn't just in the former category. She was the best external influence I've seen. As a player, I learned so much from her. As a coach, I've learned even more.

Stephen Rochford was appointed Mayo manager in the winter of 2015, following the difficult and controversial departure of joint managers Pat Holmes and Noel Connelly. Whenever a new boss comes in there is tension in a group, with players sussing out the new guy and the new guy assessing the squad he must work with. At that point, we considered ourselves one of the top three teams in the country and our results showed that. For Rochy, it must have been an intimidating dressing room to walk into – a first-time intercounty manager – and, given the manner of his predecessors' departure, first impressions on both sides were important.

He immediately struck the right note with the make-up of his backroom team. Donie Buckley stayed on as coach, Peter Burke remained as goalkeeping coach and Armagh legend Tony McEntee and former Kiltane and Mayo player Sean Carey also joined the set-up. With Barry Solan and Conor Finn as our strength and conditioning coaches, we reached the All-Ireland final in Rochy's first season, coming within a whisker of beating Dublin in the drawn and replayed finals. With any doubts about Stephen's abilities as a manager put to bed, we came into the 2017 championship feeling fitter than we ever had as a team. Then, after beating Sligo, Galway knocked us out of the Connacht Championship for the second year running. Any loss to Galway is difficult, that one particularly so. We thought we had done the work, but something was missing.

Shortly before that Galway game, Stephen had introduced Niamh to the team. As a group we began sizing her up immediately. Unaware of her reputation, I, for one, was guilty of some reservations.

What's her motivation?
Will she 'get' us?
Will she 'get' me?

She immediately dispelled any doubts. Her first act was to have one-on-one sessions with each player with Stephen participating as manager. I had early reason to be grateful for Niamh's involvement. Stephen substituted me against Galway just as I felt I was hitting my stride. With Niamh's help, an honest and frank conversation followed, one that paved the way for a much healthier relationship throughout that summer. Everything we learned about Niamh told us she did not need our validation as a squad, nor did she have interest in any residual glory that might fall her way should we make history and win an All-Ireland with her help. She was there to help the team get the very best out of themselves. In her typically disarming way, she unearthed our insecurities as a playing group and went to work on them. She did the same for the management. Performance was the key, not results.

Niamh empowered players, making each of us outline what we had to do every day to help the team perform. These weren't empty promises either, said out loud for approval. She held us accountable. Her dedication to the message of performance over all else did, I believe, see us perform better than any Mayo team I was part of since 2003.

We hit a sweet spot over four games that, I felt, was as good as we ever played as a team. The spell began with a quarter-final replay against Roscommon on a Bank Holiday Monday in Croke Park where we dismantled our Connacht rivals even without our best player Lee Keegan. Over the course of two semi-finals versus Kerry, when Stephen was brave enough not once, but twice, to pick Aidan O'Shea at full-back to handle Kieran Donaghy, we saw further evidence that players and management were benefitting from Niamh's belief in us.

Stephen showed serious balls in not bowing to the media and supporter pressure to return Aidan to his usual role around the middle. He and his backroom team held their

A SPECIAL MOMENT:
Bringing my son Ollie onto
the pitch after the 2019
National League final victory
was one of my proudest
moments as a Mayo
footballer.

Photo: Inpho/James Crombie

THINK MORE, RUN LESS: Think yourself out of a hard situation. No matter the size, speed or physicality of an opponent, Chris Barrett always thought his way through.

Photo: Piaras Ó Mídheach/Sportsfile

SAFE HANDS: Games are won by fine margins. This save by Robbie was as important as Ciarán Treacy's goal in the 2019 National League final victory against Kerry.

Photo: Ramsey Cardy/Sportsfile

A FAMILY AFFAIR: National League victory in 2019 celebrated with David, Charlotte and Ollie.

BEST KITMAN GOING: Liam Ludden (right), as always, looking after the boys.

ALL-STARS: Enjoying a night at the All-Stars with Jennifer.

THE BALLAGH' BOYS: All-Star Awards 2017 with David Drake and Barry Solan.

PHILLY: Jennifer and me at an Eagles game on the All-Star trip to Philadelphia with Boyler and his wife Laura.

LAST NIGHT OUT: Myself and Jen on our last night out with the team in 2019.

LAST HOME MATCH: My last game for Mayo at MacHale Park.

Photo: Mick Hunt

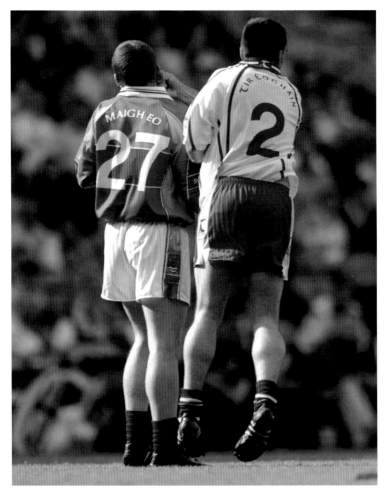

SAYING HELLO: My first introduction to senior championship football in Croke Park in 2004. The great Ryan McMenamin saying hello. *Photo: Brendan Moran/Sportsfile*

(Opposite)
HILL START: An epic start to an epic game. Mayo v Dublin 2006.

Photo: Ray Ryan/Sportsfile

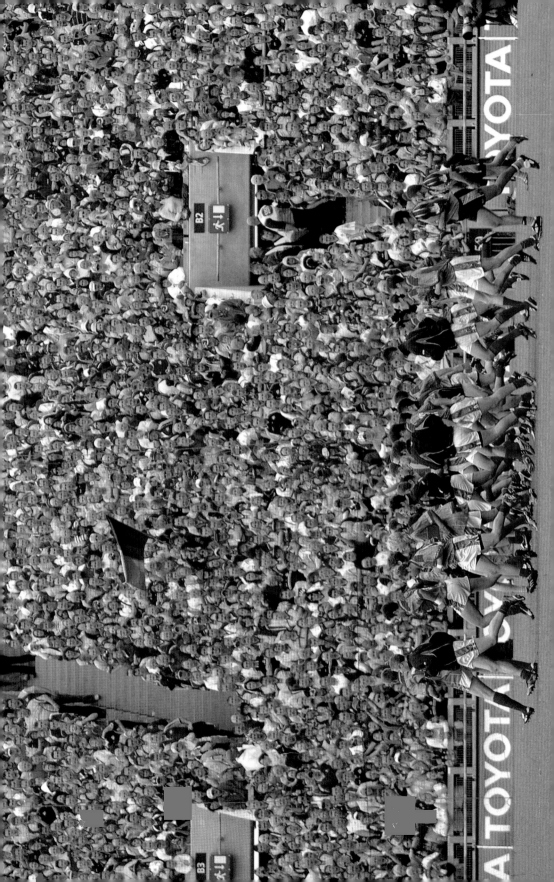

PEADAR'S BIG MOMENT: Celebrating his match-winning point against Galway in the 2009 Connacht Senior Championship final.

Photo: Ray Ryan/Sportsfile

ENJOYING THE WIN: Clubmates and friends Cian Hanley (centre) and David Drake with the National League trophy in 2019.

FINAL WHISTLE: The defeat of the great Cork team in 2011 started our rollercoaster decade.

Photo: Ray McManus/Sportsfile

SOUTH AFRICA: Team trip to South Africa in 2017. A trip where we set our sights on another assault of the championship.

CAPE TOWN: Exploring Cape Town. Taking in the views at the top of Table Mountain with Aidan, Seamie, Lorna, David and Jennifer.

GOOD TIMES: Time well spent with Clarkie (centre) and Donie (left).

BIG OCCASION: Mayo v Kerry All-Ireland Senior Championship 2014 semi-final replay at the Gaelic Grounds in Limerick. What an occasion. *Photo: Diarmuid Greene/Sportsfile*

THE SUPPORTERS: We are all in this together (Limerick 2014).
Photo: Dáire Brennan/Sportsfile

AUGUST 2021: Diarmuid O'Connor keeps the ball in play in the build-up to a Mayo point during the 2021 GAA football All-Ireland Senior Championship semi-final between Dublin and Mayo at Croke Park.

Photo: Stephen McCarthy/Sportsfile

LIFE AS A MAYO FAN! Watching the 2021 semi-final v Dublin from the stands with Jennifer – the first match we attended together. *Photos: courtesy of RTÉ Sport*

nerve and, by sticking with Aidan at full-back, I believe they won us the game. I know Niamh emboldened them to stick to their guns come what may. That was her power.

The last of those four games saw us play what I believe was our best game of football of the decade, considering context and circumstance. History will rightly show a winning scoreline for a brilliant Dublin side but the game itself was the best example we had of the team giving our all from captain to kitman. It wasn't enough. The result went against us but, honestly, the performance was as good as we could give. Niamh drove that.

She drove it by believing in people while never forcing her beliefs on them. She listened and in doing so enabled you to come up with the solutions. She guided you and asked difficult questions but when you left a meeting with her you had a plan to fix any problem. Niamh was the perfect go-between for players and management. The players felt they were listened to, and the management had space and time to think about big decisions without worrying about the psychological state of the players.

When people ask me how important psychology is to a modern-day playing group, my answer is always the same: it is as important as the physical aspect of training and is certainly more important now than it ever was in the past. If you take the Mayo squad of 2017 as an example, we had fathers, expectant fathers, students, entrepreneurs, employed, unemployed, single lads, others just getting engaged and some getting married. Each personality and individual situation bring with them their own baggage. How can a manager or coach be expected to deal with, and positively affect, the psychology of all these unique emotional animals when they themselves are under intense scrutiny from supporters, press and other vested interests? They can't, pure and simple. Niamh, especially, recognised this.

There are other elements she considered that had never required attention from management groups up to that point. Being an athlete today, whatever the size of your profile, involves scrutiny like never before. When I first started out in 2003, there were a few local papers that gave a damn about you from Christmas to July. After that, the national press may have paid attention to the team if it reached Croke Park. Elite level sport nowadays is completely different. Social media has given every supporter a voice. Every game matters and everything you do publicly is documented. It is so important to have someone in the backroom team looking out for players, particularly the younger ones, and guide them through this process.

Niamh's gift was her ability to deal with each player individually and make them feel important and empowered. She believed that the best way for teams to perform was for each member of the group to be happy, not afraid, and to be comfortable going into battle knowing that you have done everything in your power to be ready. She was a huge believer in the importance of support networks, especially of partners. She even maintained contact with them, offering advice on how to best cope or help in different situations.

She basically worked to cover every base. She improved everyone in the dressing room from Stephen Rochford to the water boys. Her awareness of the pressures we were under, from within and outside the group, enabled her to relate to us on a level that I hadn't previously experienced. There was something intensely genuine about her. She was human.

Typical of a footballer consumed by his own journey, I wasn't immediately aware of the connection between Niamh and Mayo when we met that first night in Breaffy House. Earlier that same evening, unbeknownst to our group, she had met with the crew of the RNLI Achill lifeboat who had taken the body of her sister, Captain Dara Fitzpatrick, from the water after the Rescue 116 helicopter crash off the Mayo coast had claimed her life, along with the lives of her three crewmates, in a brutal tragedy that dominated news bulletins throughout March 2017. It was Niamh's first opportunity to meet the crew since she had lost her sister. Because of this, she is connected to Mayo for reasons much greater than a bunch of footballers.

Knowing her as I now do, I can only imagine what an intensely emotional few hours that meeting in Achill must've been for her. Still, there she stood in front of us not long after, asking each one of us if we were willing to abandon ego and embrace the idea of team for the greater good? We looked at her not as someone who had just suffered this unspeakable tragedy, but as someone we hoped could help us win. In that context, football seems insignificant, but maybe, just maybe, we both needed each other.

★★★★★

There are other, less obvious, characters who populate your sporting life who contribute more than they'll likely ever know. Back in 2006, a young man walked into the Mayo dressing room as humble and unassuming then as he is today. Liam Ludden's dedication to Mayo football is one of the great untold stories. He became the kitman under Mickey Moran and John Morrison, no easy task given John's love of pranks. He passed early tests with flying colours, and he was an instant hit with the players. The level of detail he put into that job, the hours he spent on the pitch chasing footballs during individual kicking practice and the care he showed to players and the environment in which we worked were a constant reminder of how lucky we were to play for Mayo. I always saw Liam as the link between our great supporters and the team. Why does Liam Ludden turn up night after night, year after year? There is no material reward for him. There is no limelight. I believe he chose to do it because he saw his role as that of helping us players. And he certainly helped. His presence and personality were reassuring to us. He had no skin in the game. He was there because he wanted to help, because he loved Mayo football. Because, if he weren't inside the wire with us, he would've been outside screaming his head off in support. He was another piece in the jigsaw that made the journey great. If he weren't there, the puzzle would have been incomplete.

NINETEEN

Success Leaves Clues

'The fight is won or lost far away from witnesses, behind the lines, in the gym, and out on the road, long before I dance under the lights.'

– Muhammad Ali

THE individual honour of winning an All-Star is not something I was particularly focused on as a player, especially early in my career. Making the team, then staying on it, were the primary goals. I never set myself a target of picking up an All-Star. I was aware of the All-Stars certainly but always figured if I was on the team and playing well, individual awards would look after themselves.

I got my first nomination in 2009, a year which saw us beat Galway in a thrilling Connacht final before falling to Meath in Croke Park. It was another disappointing year for the team but a pleasing one for me on a personal level. Johno had picked me at wing-back and although it was not my preferred position, I played well all year. The nomination gave me great confidence. I was in my mid-20s. It was time for me to push on and become an established player. Although I didn't win the All-Star, being shortlisted brought positive attention on me and I welcomed it.

My second nomination came in 2011 as an inside forward after the team earned great respect for beating defending champions Cork and performing well against Kerry. I was quite nervous about the prospect of actually winning the award. I recall an enlightening conversation with our manager James Horan in the build-up to the awards night which made me think differently about the entire concept. He had called me to wish me luck and in conversation I downplayed my chances to him, stressing that while I felt honoured to be nominated, winning an All-Star wasn't that important in the bigger picture. I may not have believed what I was saying but was guarding against disappointment. James strongly disagreed, reminding me that Mayo had not won an All-Star since 2006. It would matter greatly to the team if I won one. It would signify progress and lay down a marker for us to realise that we deserved to be at the top table. Those words rang in my ears later that night as I collected my first All-Star and watched Cillian win Young Footballer of the Year. James was right: those moments did matter. Greatly.

There were other benefits to the All-Star scene which would serve a much bigger purpose for me and, by extension, the team. Back to my nomination in 2009. Although not selected for the team, I received a very late call-up to the All-Star tour to Kuala Lumpur the following year. All-Star tours are biannual so the '09 and '10 teams would travel together to play each other in an exhibition match. The GAA rep explained that Cork's Graham Canty had to pull out, so the spot was mine if I wanted it. At first, I suspected a prank call from one of my buddies. I was given until the end of the call to make up my mind as the trip was leaving four days later. It was an easy decision to make. I was on the plane.

The tour was enjoyable for all the reasons you'd expect. As the only Mayo man, it was brilliant to be able to socialise and train with players from other counties, some familiar to me but most strangers apart from our battles on the pitch. That tour had a much more profound effect on me than I could've imagined and it wasn't because of the scenery.

You've read it all before: the stories of the last lads to leave the training ground and the first to arrive. We had those boys in Mayo too, but what I saw on that All-Star trip was different: there was no tokenism. Nothing was done for the sake of it. It was player-led. It was unified. Hell, these boys were on a well-earned holiday after a long season and would have been forgiven for doing nothing at all!

One set of players stood out to me more than any other. From 2007 on, the best three teams in the country were Kerry, Tyrone and Cork. In 2010, the Rebel County got their reward for years of hard work. I have always felt that Cork team changed the game in terms of combining athleticism and footballing ability. They had a great mix of natural footballers like Paddy Kelly and Donncha O'Connor and outstanding athletes like Pearse O'Neill, John Miskella and Paudie Kissane. That trip to Kuala Lumpur was only a few months after their All-Ireland triumph. Heavy lies the crown as the saying goes but those boys wore it easily. It was a pleasure to be in their company and to observe their habits. Watching Kissane and O'Neill work out was a sight to behold. Their sessions were impressive enough, but it was their attitude, their encouragement of each other, and the quality of what they were doing that stood out. I thought I trained hard. That trip made it clear to me I was falling short.

The same went for Nicholas Murphy and Alan Quirke in terms of the guidance they gave the younger Cork players. Nothing too public or sanctimonious, nothing forced, just simple gestures and actions I might otherwise have missed had I not been so hungry to improve myself. Cork manager Conor Counihan was on that trip too but not once did I observe him in the gym cracking the whip or out on the training pitches nagging his players. It was clear as day to me that his senior players were leading by example.

Had I been surrounded by other Mayo players on that trip, much of what I observed would have passed me by. Instead, I had no choice but to step away from my comfort zone and drink in as much of the experience as I could. Mayo football, my career – together we were at a crossroads.

We had a new manager. We had a young crop of potentially brilliant players coming through. We had just suffered the worst four-year spell in the county in quarter of a century of football. Change was needed and it was already happening in Dublin under Pat Gilroy and in Donegal under Jim McGuinness. Looking back, one of the most remarkable postscripts to that tour was that Cork did not go on and win another couple of All-Irelands. As I saw it, this failure was not down to complacency but to the foresight of Gilroy, McGuinness and later Jim Gavin to observe, assess and execute new systems to match the likes of Cork, Kerry and Tyrone and eventually beat them.

★★★★★

Lest I lead you to believe the only lessons I learned from my maiden All-Star trip were from the gym and the playing pitches, that was not the case thankfully. Being in such an informal and social environment with so many lads I had played against so often was an incredible opportunity for me. Most of us, just like the Cork boys, were in 'pre' pre-season, but when it came to kicking back and relaxing nobody took themselves too seriously. Certainly, regarding my presence on the trip, I needed a thick skin, especially as I was a late call-up for an All-Ireland winning captain from an All-Star team picked over a year earlier. Late one night, maybe even early one morning, Bernard Brogan asked a question he said had been bothering him for days. With a table of people for an audience, he piped up:

"Andy... tell me this", his Dublin accent more pronounced given the ungodly hour, "Mayo lost to Sligo and Longford this year... what the f**k are you doing on this trip!"

Bernard's verbal shot to the kidneys was well meaning and delivered with customary humour. I laughed my head off too. At that moment, he was dead right to ask the question.

★★★★★

I came home a changed man. Up to that point, I always liked a beer on a night out but that changed. Sure, on an occasion like a stag or a wedding I might relax and have a few but outside of that I cut out alcohol. I don't think I ate a crisp for ten years, save for an annual Christmas binge. I reviewed my diet. John Morrison was right. I was carrying a little too much timber. Watching the Cork boys especially made me realise one fundamental thing: I was not going to play out the middle of the pitch ever again, not as a wing-back and not as a wing-forward. I hadn't the size or the aerobic capacity to compete with athletes like Miskella, O'Neill and Kissane. I had to reinvent myself as an inside forward. I knew what I was good at. I had game intelligence. I prided myself on making smart runs and outwitting defenders. I also saw a gap in the Mayo team in those positions. Cillian was only emerging. Conor Mort was in and out of form. Jason Doc was breaking through but was not a go-to guy yet. We had a new management team who would bring new ideas. I had to get to work.

One of the first things I did was reach out to Maurice Sheridan about my kicking. Maurice was one of the stars of the 1996 and 1997 teams and a deep thinker on the art of kicking from hand and ground. That winter after Kuala Lumpur, I spent a lot of time working on my shooting based on Maurice's instructions. The guidance he gave me in the winter of 2010 served me throughout the next decade.

That realisation that my future lay closer to goal coincided with James' arrival and the introduction of his own backroom team with Ed Coughlan coming in as skills coach and Liam Moffatt as strength and conditioning coach. I could see from our early meetings that these boys meant business, and this saw me double down on my renewed focus to change my attitude, my body and my skill set. Kuala Lumpur not only showed me how the winners conducted their business, but it also forced me to acknowledge my limits and concentrate on my strengths. I couldn't grow six inches. I was never going to cover every blade of grass on the pitch, but I could train to run faster over shorter distances. I could change my body shape. I could work on my shooting off either foot. I could develop an understanding with Jason Doc and Cillian. I could control the controllables. I just needed to identify what they were and commit.

Sport and life are funny. If Graham Canty hadn't got injured, my phone would never have rung. How different the next nine years of my life would have been! A year after coming back from Kuala Lumpur, I won my first All-Star.

★★★★★

If I was learning lessons from Cork on the field, there was plenty to learn off it too. As the 2011 season drew to a close, I was selected to join the International Rules squad. This was another prospect I had not previously dwelt on too much. But when the invitation came, I jumped at the chance to train and play with the game's best, not only to win that coveted cap for representing your country against Australia but to further broaden my thinking. I had a good first year with James Horan. I had met a lot of the targets I had set for myself since the All-Star trip. I wanted more.

During the fourth squad session, held on the day before the All-Ireland final, Ireland head coach Kieran McGeeney set up a drill which saw me contest a collision with Meath's 6' 3", 16-stone full-back Kevin Reilly. The basic idea was for me to carry the ball into Kevin's tackle, free my hands and pop the pass off my shoulder to a supporting runner.

In Gaelic football, this is routine stuff a good attacking player can do in his sleep. In International Rules, however, the play is complicated by the fact that the opposing player can effectively rugby tackle you to the ground. I remember standing there asking myself why the hell would I ever physically engage a monster like O'Reilly? My game is all about escape and evasion not carrying the ball into heavy contact. The whistle goes and I do as I'm told. O'Reilly smashes me and as he does my left leg gets trapped underneath me. You can hear the crack of the bone breaking all over Parnell Park.

It wasn't a dirty hit by O'Reilly, I hasten to add. He had executed a perfect tackle. If anything, my body positioning had been poor as I entered the tackle.

I am eventually stretchered off and, with the support of team selector Michael Kennedy, brought straight to Santry Sports Clinic for an x-ray. My left fibula is broken. Sitting there for the next four hours, the text messages start rolling in from teammates and friends. I let James Horan and all my family know. Jennifer eventually arrives, naturally upset for me. Later that evening after being discharged, as we make our way awkwardly into the car in the underground car park, three players from the International Rules squad arrive.

Michael Murphy, Karl Lacey and Neil McGee had finished training and before turning their cars north-west for the long drive to Donegal or perhaps going across the city to Kilmacud to enjoy the annual seven-a-side tournament, they made the choice to come see me first. This was 2011, smack bang in the middle of the Jimmy McGuinness revolution. To the outside world, McGuinness took a team of no-hopers and won an All-Ireland with them, inspiring a tactical revolution across the game in the process. I saw it differently. In 2007, Donegal won a National League title. Many of the 2012 squad had won multiple Sigerson Cups with IT Sligo. Colm McFadden, a man the same age as me, had been one of the top prospects in the game as an underage player and it was only a matter of time before he realised his potential as a senior. The talent was definitely there but they needed an architect to best enable their obvious abilities. It was no small task, but McGuinness did it.

Part of what he 'did' was bring a team spirit and a unity that had been lacking in Donegal for too long. On that day in Santry, I got a glimpse of that unity. Murphy, Lacey and McGee made the selfless choice and drove out of their way to check on a teammate who had just got injured. The Kilmacud Sevens was in full swing across the city. All-Ireland final weekend – there were plenty of other places for them to be. It meant a lot that they chose to come see me.

Within a group, ethos or culture have sadly all too often been manipulated by PR-obsessed advisors. In my opinion, these small, invisible gestures should remain unseen by the public, so that they are not corrupted and used to force respect or earn cheap plaudits. I thought about the Donegal

boys a lot after that. I wondered how much of that impromptu visit was down to a renewed sense of unity they
felt under McGuinness. I came to learn that they were willing to do anything for a teammate on the field. I believe the
same could be said for teammates off it. A year later, they
won their All-Ireland at the expense of Mayo. It hurt like
hell, but I wasn't surprised. In Donegal, I recognised a
team that understood that the little things matter.

★★★★★

Another All-Star tour, another valuable lesson. In 2012
we head to New York and I'm hobbling around the streets
of Manhattan looking for a pay-as-you-go gym to get a session done. I'm recovering from the anterior cruciate ligament injury I picked up during the All-Ireland quarter-
final versus Down earlier in the summer. I eventually find
one and get myself moving in the activation area. A few
minutes later I hear an Irish voice behind me.
  "Well!"
  "How's the knee?"
  "Who designed the programme?"
It's the great Henry Shefflin, midway through his own
session. Fresh from winning the 2012 Hurler of the Year
award, he was invited on the football tour as a rep from the
GAA and the GPA. Far from resting on his recent corona-
tion as Hurler of the Year, he's working out, looking for the
extra bit.
  I had only spoken to him once before. Not long after
suffering my cruciate injury, I called him for some advice
on the surgery itself and how his own recovery had gone.
He had previously torn his ACL and came back to be the
best hurler in the country, so I figured, who better to ring?
  Still, standing in front of him in the gym that day, I was
more than a little starstruck. We chatted for a while. He
was full of questions about my injury and how the rehab
was going, essentially comparing notes. He was so interested
in how I was getting on that I barely got to ask him anything!
We finished up the chat and went back to our respective
sessions. Even as I continued working out, I was struck by

him even being in the gym, far away from the hotel and prying eyes, getting his session done, not ceding an inch to his rivals. I was fascinated too by his level of genuine interest in me and his willingness to share his experiences to help me, a virtual stranger, in my process of rehabilitation.

I get back to the hotel and I'm buzzing. I tell Jennifer who I met at the gym – I'd say she was hoping to hear it was someone a little more exotic than King Henry – and resolve that the encounter will serve as a lesson that if Henry Shefflin is doing it when no one is looking there could be no excuses for me.

*****

Six years later, David Clarke, Colm Boyle and I are sitting in Dublin Airport on our way to Philadelphia on another All-Star trip. James Horan had been confirmed for his second spell with Mayo and the three of us – all veterans now – have committed to going back to play in 2019. For the first time in my career, I've contemplated retirement and with that playing in my mind, I know I need to expel any doubts. I chat to the boys and ask them for assistance during the trip. We agree to enjoy ourselves but also to use the week as a springboard for our training. On the first evening there, we check in and get settled before meeting up – with our partners Paula, Laura and Jennifer – for dinner and a few drinks. Of course, we stay out a little too late and I wake up at 8am to a load of missed calls from Clarkie and Boyler. I'd agreed to meet them at 7.30am in the gym.

I get to it. Clarkie and Boyler are worse for wear just like me but are already halfway through their session.

"You're some animals," I say to them.

"It's alright for you," Clarkie retorts, "you don't have (Michael) Schlingermann snapping at your ankles for your place like I do! What's more, you need to get your act together. James McCarthy and all the Dubs have already been and gone."

It's 8am on the first morning of an All-Star tour and the Dubs, fresh from their four-in-a-row, have their session done. Message received. At that moment, I realised that to have any chance of competing in 2019, I needed to stop doubting and get moving. These guys won an All-Ireland a couple of months ago and have already moved on. Enough said.

The term 'process' is often used when a team like Dublin comes around which, it has to be acknowledged, is not that often. These guys are four All-Irelands in and they are living the process, not talking about it or cashing in on it. Led by James McCarthy, who was recovering from a knee injury, Con O'Callaghan, Paul Mannion and Brian Howard hit the gym every morning of that trip. Like Cork in 2010, they are not resting on their medals. They are engaging in their processes, certain that back in Ireland their teammates are doing the same.

We learned this in Mayo over the decade. All-Star trips, Sigersons, International Rules series – all of them allowed others and me to inhale as many lessons as we could and bring them back home to the gyms and pitches of Mayo.

Sometimes the battle is won far away from the battlefield.

TWENTY

Learning From Others

'The first stage of learning is silence, the second stage is listening.'

– James Kerr, Legacy

MOTIVATION is a funny thing. As a better-than-average underage footballer, my desire to play for Mayo was born out of two things. Firstly, I genuinely loved the game. Secondly, and far more viscerally, it came from envy. Only a year out of minor, two friends and clubmates, Stephen Drake (who would later become my brother-in-law) and Sean Mangan were selected to play for the Mayo U21s. My memory of this was intense jealousy. Adamant that I wanted to emulate them, I set to work. The central thesis of my master plan was to cut weight and train twice a day for a year. Food-wise, this saw me eat nothing but chicken breasts and rice, topped off with a little sweet-and-sour sauce, practically every single day. My father, who was the cook in our house, thought I had lost my mind. He may have been right, but the plan worked.

I performed well for Ballagh' and in January 2003, I took a call from John Maughan inviting me into the Mayo senior squad. That call remains one of the highlights of my career.

The lessons came early. A few months before I joined the panel we had played Kiltimagh in a club game and, being the cheeky little shit I was, I may have reminded goalkeeper Peter Burke of a mistake or two he'd made. Maughan called a drill which saw groups break into four and sure enough I found myself with Fergal Kelly, Kenny Mortimer and my old friend Peter. The drill was intense but passed without incident until the final ball when I was lined up by Burkey. He absolutely nailed me. In my moment of pain, I knew what was happening and had got what I deserved. In between drills, I took a stroll down the pitch away from the group in an attempt to compose myself, even dry a tear. John, who had seen the hit, said nothing but I knew all eyes were on me. I drew breath and went again. To get respect I had to give it. Thanks to Peter, my lesson was learned.

*****

They say travel broadens the mind and although Sligo was not a great distance from my home town of Ballaghaderreen, moving there to attend college for four years was an intensely formative experience for me. I must admit, most of what I learned was on the football pitches and not in the lecture halls but education is education, and what my college years taught me served me well across every facet of my life, from sport to business and to family. Gaelic football can be a parochial bubble. First, you grow in the comfort zone of your local club. Then, if you're good enough and hungry enough, you'll progress to an underage set-up in your county. There, you'll find allies in clubmates and lads you know from different teams down through the years. Mayo may be a big county, but football is a unifying language spoken by pretty much everybody. It is a bubble. Once you're in it and accepted, you feel safe.

That's one of the things that makes college great. Ireland may be a small place but the diversity in attitudes, humour, language and even culture is surprising once you notice it. Being lucky enough to be exposed to it enabled me to broaden my thinking, not just about my football but about the direction of my life in general. I realised I wanted to be successful on and off the pitch. Much of this was influenced by the characters with whom I surrounded myself, some by accident, some by design.

In IT Sligo, I was lucky to have trusted allies in Keith Higgins and Alan Costello. Two great footballers and a pair of boys who knew how to enjoy themselves. Their social appetites made it easier for all of us to get to know people. Neither took themselves too seriously. Given that I tended to tense up when it came to football, having those guys around provided a balance in my life that stood to me.

I studied for a business degree, but football was a huge part of my life there. Like many who came before and after, those years allowed me to mature from boy to man, to make mistakes and to figure out what worked best for my personality. The players around me played a huge role in that education.

Sigerson football is the rarest of beasts. A competition a step below intercounty where team spirit and enjoying yourself are as important as any medal. You will have lads of all abilities training, rubbing shoulders with All-Ireland winners. Whatever your reputation as a footballer, no player is immune from being taken down a notch or two if their heads are getting too big. If you were struggling in other areas of your life – studies, relationships, family – a Sigerson squad was a safe harbour where you could be yourself.

There was some crew of footballers in Sligo at the time. Kevin Cassidy, Christy Toye, Karl Lacey, Paul Durcan and Eamon and Neil McGee, all from Donegal. The brilliant Paul Finlay from Monaghan. Many of them were just as good on the dance floor as they were on the field and that only added to the sense of craic about the team. Still, there was an extremely serious element to it. One victory in particular stands out for me – the Sigerson we won in 2005. It was the culmination of a lot of hard work from the team and me personally and was a great confidence-builder when it came to establishing my reputation within Mayo.

The final against Queens was emblematic of the unity of purpose within the squad. Just 12 minutes in, Jamie Murphy of Galway got sent off harshly. It was bitterly cold in Dundalk and the game was as dour as they come but we ground it out, finding a way to win against the odds. We were a special group. We had characters involved who simply made going to training a joy. Colm Cafferkey from Mayo and Dominic McGlinchey from the Robert Emmets club in Donegal were two very special teammates. They went out of their way to make that year memorable. McGlinchey was a pure performer. He had his own one-man band and many people in college thought he was mad. If you needed anything at any time of night, he was the man. The bus on game day was nuts, shaking from side to side as we entered the grounds, music blaring and a mad Donegal man singing. Our manager Kieran Gallagher, a Swinford man, had the awareness to see the worth of a man like McGlinchey. Kieran recognised how important he was to the team.

Before our semi-final against University College Cork (UCC), the 30-man panel was named. McGlinchey knew he wouldn't get a jersey. As the game unfolded, we were winning comfortably. Kieran Gallagher started ringing the changes and called Leitrim's Adrian O'Flynn to go on. O'Flynn looks around and spots McGlinchey. Adrian and I are studying the same course as Dominic so he knows how much Sigerson means to him. He quietly asks Kieran if Dominic can go on instead of him. Kieran agrees, understanding the gesture. Adrian takes off his jersey and throws it at McGlinchey who moments later runs on the field to make his Sigerson debut for IT Sligo. I've never seen a prouder man.

I don't think something like that could happen even at club level. What Adrian and Kieran did that day didn't demean the competition or the opposition – Dominic was a fine footballer in his own right. Instead, I believe their gesture defined Sigerson. We all badly wanted to win but we were only able to win because of the likes of McGlinchey and the X-factor he brought to the squad. As soon as we saw him coming on, every one of us understood why.

He walked tall that night, McGlinchey. The next morning, he gave one of his greatest ever performances entertaining the team before the final, playing a memorable role in our victory.

★★★★★

For all the stars on those IT Sligo teams, few shone brighter than Paul 'Jap' Finlay. The man had a left foot to die for and practically had a cult following his dismantling of All-Ireland champions Armagh in the summer of 2004. His range of passing and point-kicking was nothing short of phenomenal. Everyone saw his talent. What few people saw was how hard he worked behind the scenes.

Like a lot of college teams, it was never the easiest to get all our boys out training. There were a lot of competing interests especially if the Sigerson was still a way off, so there were some wet, windy evenings when you might have only a dozen lads out. Lads like Seánie McDermott and me always had to show up to have any hope of making the team. We were always guaranteed Paul Finlay would be there too, working on his stamina and perfecting his kicking, often in the most atrocious conditions. It was some inspiration to me to see such an established footballer put so much into his own game and into the team. How could I skip training if 'Jap' was going to be there? His attitude spoke volumes to me: no matter what level you've reached, there's always room for more.

He was another reason Sigerson was so special. You'd go training just to actually train with him. It was like having a free pass to greatness. The dread you'd feel looking out the window of the house at the thought of training that evening would quickly be offset by the realisation that Paul would be there. Therefore, so should you.

★★★★★

I learned plenty off the pitch too. I was mad about my football but found it difficult to reconcile an active social life in college with playing serious ball. Drink hurt my body too much. I gained weight easily, and I just couldn't socialise the way others could even if I wanted to. John Maughan called me up to the Mayo squad for the first time in 2003 and I knew my dancing days were numbered, especially as, when it came to the crew in Sligo, it was all or nothing! You could go out with the McGee brothers in Sligo on a Sunday night and end up in Tralee. The boys would appear the next day at training right as rain. I couldn't do both. I wasn't built that way. I knew if I were to progress as a footballer, I would have to forego that side of my life which, as a father now of two small kids, doesn't seem like that much of a sacrifice, but back then, when the party was happening all around me, it was a tough call to make. It takes a brave man to say no to Eamon McGee.

It wasn't clean living all the time either. I'd pick my moments. Every now and then, especially after a Donegal/Mayo league match when both sets of players would meet up in Sligo, I'd let the guard down and enjoy it. My body never thanked me for it though. Once I made my mind up that I couldn't do it, it made it easier to enjoy being around the lads. I learned to enjoy myself without it. Plus, somebody needed to mind those headers.

★★★★★

I was blessed to experience college football in two distinctly different environments. A year after finishing in Sligo, I completed a Masters in the University of Ulster, Jordanstown. My time there came smack in the middle of Tyrone's three All-Ireland successes. It was an unbelievable experience to be so intimately exposed to how passionate Ulster people are about football. It was genuinely mind-blowing. I always believed us to be football-mad in Mayo, but this was different. The game is a way of life up there. In the towns and parishes life revolves around the GAA club. Volunteers of all ages are involved. The club is not about one team, it's about everybody. It's about the game.

As I lived among them and called many of them my friends, the successes Armagh and Tyrone had recently enjoyed made perfect sense. The GAA was built from the dirt up. Not only were they brilliant footballers, but the GAA just meant more. It's difficult to understand without having seen it. I recall taking trips out to the Na Fianna club in Tyrone with Peter Donnelly and just chatting to people around the club. Their love for football was infectious and, I could tell, unconditional. Tyrone winning meant a lot, but it wasn't the basis for their passion. That would endure regardless.

I learned so much too from their ambivalence towards other teams. They couldn't give a rats about the reputation of traditional powerhouses like Kerry, Meath or Dublin. It was as if they too understood that the relationship they had with football was special. It was an eye-opener for me. College gave me that. It was a privilege to see.

★★★★★

One of the victims of the new age of Gaelic football has been the Sigerson Cup and all it represents. An increasingly congested fixture list has seen the competition become the runt of the litter in terms of priority. Pre-season intercounty leagues and U20s leave little room for college football to breathe. Many intercounty managers view the endeavour as a hindrance to their own personal needs, namely preparing their side for a National League which has become more and more important to teams as the provincial championships lose relevance. They are missing a huge trick. The benefits of Sigerson football to a player are many and varied and denying those players the opportunity to play is short-sighted and detrimental to their sporting and social development. Surely coaches must realise that a happy player is a better player?

The essence of the competition is great players playing with good ones and loving it. The scholarship system has been a brilliant way of helping top-level county footballers to play football and study. This needs to be supported if we want our players to continue playing while having healthy professional and personal lives. Look across the colleges and universities and you'll find coaches and managers of the highest standard linked to those educational institutions for decades, stretching all the way back to their own college days. There's a reason for this. My experiences in Sligo and Jordanstown are more the norm than the exception. Had we not won Sigerson Cups, I'm almost certain my time there would have been no less memorable or formative. Denying young footballers those opportunities to effectively grow up will negatively affect our games by either driving young ambitious people from them or producing less well-rounded players who will pass through their college years wrapped in cotton wool, oblivious to the real world around them. How is that healthy?

Third-level institutions will always exist. Footballers will always go to college and should be encouraged to enjoy every aspect of that experience to ensure they develop as players and, more importantly, as people. I understand that as I step into coaching I'll surely face the headache of a player being unavailable to me because of Sigerson commitments. I hope I do because that means the competition is living on.

Too often in sport we obsess over protecting personal legacy. In the case of the Sigerson, we should all be out to conserve something much bigger than us.

TWENTY-ONE

Learn What Works

*'Behaviour that get rewarded is
behaviour that gets repeated.'*

– Achra Avi

THROUGHOUT this book, I have looked outward at the people and experiences that made me the footballer and, by extension, the man I have become. That process of learning is not over for me. I may have retired from intercounty football in 2019 but my apprenticeship as a coach began the very next season with my home club Ballaghaderreen and the Mayo U20s. I was proud of the ceiling I reached as a player, but my race was well and truly run. The lessons continue, however.

One reason coaching appeals to me is because of how much I learned on my own journey. Leaving humility to one side momentarily, I readily acknowledge that I had an admirable playing career, one that may have exceeded my expectations as an 18-year-old left off a county minor team but a career that became more and more inevitable the longer I stayed at it, always seeking improvements and never standing still. There were obvious reasons for my desire to learn. I was not a Ciarán McDonald, an Aidan O'Shea or a Bernard Brogan. I was not a player defined by any one stand-out characteristic such as size, athleticism or a genius left foot. At my most basic, stripped-back level, I had many qualities, but I was disposable. That's where the real hard work came in. Ciarán, Aidan and Bernard are the exceptions. What I discovered throughout my playing career is that 90 per cent of footballers are like me, foot soldiers who need to consistently find ways to improve to compete and excel at the highest level.

Not relying on a trademark quality had its perks. It made me realise I needed to do a lot of things well and if they stopped working, I needed the balls to reassess and the intelligence to identify where I could adapt and evolve. That saw me change a lot as a player. If I didn't, I was dead.

I saw infinitely more gifted footballers than me struggle by virtue of the fact they were just that – 'more gifted'. If age or injury deprived them of their trademark step or the electric yard of pace that defined them, they were often unable to figure out a different way to play. I could never say that that inability to evolve was down to laziness or complacency because it's rational that if something works for you time and time again, there will likely be an unwillingness to tinker or consider contingencies for the day it stops working. I feel it's pervasive in our management styles too. Plan A is working so no need for a Plan B. The greater the stakes, we tighten up and become too rigid. What happens when your natural ability is compromised? What happens when, five minutes in, your master plan goes up in smoke?

I always needed a Plan B. Some would say a C and a D as well. I guess if any one characteristic defined my playing career, it was reinvention. Necessity drove it. Some changes worked and stayed with me till the very end. Others I tried before realising they weren't suited to me. Coming into 2014, I figured I needed size and strength to live with the new breed of emerging footballer. I devoured weights and increased my body weight to about 90kg. I stuck with it for two seasons before accepting it was unsustainable given my natural body shape. It was also a change that conflicted with the type of footballer I wanted to be – quick, instinctive and accurate. It proved a valuable lesson that just because you have the guts to change doesn't mean you have to blindly stick to it.

There was another, more profound, consequence from the realisation. In Gaelic football, too much of our training is still tailored toward the group and not the individual. What's good for, say, Chris Barrett in terms of nutrition and conditioning may not be good for me. Different body types require different training plans. Different players need to develop different skills. I took it upon myself to do my own research and with the help of Barry Solan in particular, I customised my training to maximise my talents.

Diet played a huge part. Footballers are generally taught that a high-carb diet best suits the demands of the game. Maybe it was the fact that I was approaching my mid-30s, but this no longer suited me. It may have been my metabolism, but I felt sluggish, even bloated, at times. I understood the science, yet my body was simply not where it needed to be for me to make an impact. Another element of my being older was that I felt less inclined to comply with nutritionists and coaches who looked more at the group and less at the individual. I don't mean this in a disruptive way, but I figured who knows my body better than me?

So, I decided to take control of those things I could control without deviating from the grander plan of the team. I was at a stage in my career that if it didn't work, maybe it would be curtains. The high-fat diet saw me eat more red meat, cheese and avocado. I lost weight but gained energy and focus. I was lighter on my feet. Crucially, my head was clearer.

It saved me as a player, prolonging my career by four seasons and resulting in me playing my best football. One of the hardest lessons to learn was figuring out what worked for me. You can't force these things. At any other time in my career, I wouldn't have risked going it alone for fear of upsetting the status quo within the group but the one-size-fits-all approach did not work. It took until I was 31. I had nothing to lose.

I was lucky too successive managers saw that I needed a different approach. Both the Holmes/Connelly and Stephen

Rochford coaching tickets understood that if I were to be of value in front of goal, I couldn't be running the length of the field tackling opposition players. That may sound selfish, but it was a physical impossibility. Playing me in the team meant more of a covering role for Kevin McLoughlin and Jason Doherty – they essentially became my protectors – which allowed me to concentrate on making runs, creating and scoring. It seems obvious but teams and managers, in particular, can be resistant to treating one player differently – not more favourably, I hasten to add – than another.

As a coach, it's a trap I hope never to fall into. I saw talents like Kevin O'Neill and Ciarán McDonald have disrupted playing careers because the structures within which they were asked to train and play were too rigid. It's undoubtedly a common failing in football but I believe we fall foul of this in Mayo more often than we should.

Players too can be stubborn but what works for one may not work for another. If it's true for individuals, it's even more true for a team of 30 players. Accommodating the different needs of players should not be deemed a weakness but a strength. Advances in sports technology have seen us become obsessed with metrics. A player may score high on his lateral leap but if he can't score in front of the goal, what are we achieving?

Getting the best out of a team of players is a coach's job. That requires more than just the implementation of a game plan. It necessitates reading the room. If there was somebody better than me at what I did, I wouldn't have been picked. I was lucky to have managers later in my career who saw what I could contribute and, crucially, how.

★★★★★

Over the last two decades, football has seen some great disrupters emerge. First Armagh, then Tyrone and later Donegal. Kerry, Dublin and, to a lesser extent, Cork, had tradition on their side but were no less innovative when it came to ways of evolving. Their evolution was never just tactical. It happened behind the scenes as clubs and county boards reviewed strategies and implemented change. Mickey

Harte or Jim McGuinness wouldn't have achieved what they did if effective support networks, both internally and externally, were not in place. Their success did not occur overnight. Change takes courage and putting your faith in the hands of one man, as in the case of Tyrone and Donegal, can leave many proud people open to ridicule when it falls flat.

To my mind, we have been lucky in Mayo to have had such a conveyor belt of players emerging over the last 30 years. Our underage structures were probably not much more advanced than other counties, but the tradition and quality of club football especially has inspired a steady stream of players who have taken their places among the very best in the game. Behind the scenes too we have always had a network of brilliant, inspirational people who have poured their lives into Mayo football. Some great work has been done. Yet, we can always do more.

One area where I feel we have been reluctant to change is in our attitude to tactics, particularly in one-off big games. We have always been a little bit behind the best teams. We play catch-up instead of frontrunner. Much of our success has been defined by outstanding play rather than a cohesive plan.

It has brought us so far but not far enough. We have won so many big games playing the way we do, perhaps it's difficult for us to adapt in win-or-die scenarios.

I believe some of it comes from a pride in how we see ourselves as footballers.

We like to think we play a certain way: the right way. We love our 'keepers to be commanding and good shot-stoppers not libero-style sweepers. We like our full-backs to be strong under the high ball, our centre-back to be a stopper, our wing-backs to attack and score, our midfielders to float through the air and fetch high balls and our forwards to be more honest than flashy. We want them to work as hard as our defence without the ball and still have the energy and skill to score. This creates a solid foundation but can become an obvious style for the better teams to combat. When we look at the changes Jim McGuinness brought to the game, or even the basketball-influenced tactics introduced by Dublin after 2014, would the Mayo footballing public be happy with those transition of styles? Would the players have been willing to adapt their games Sunday after Sunday?

I don't know the answer, but what I do know is that while we were always united in our goal, we somehow always came up short in our quest to get there. We keep producing players of the highest quality but the need to experiment with tactics has never been as evident. We see it in other sports, and even in business, all the time that sometimes you stumble on the best tactical innovations through trial and error. I know as a young player that I felt the weight of the supporters on my back. I was afraid to fail, to make a show of myself in front of the Mayo crowd. It wasn't until I got older and likely more selfish that I began to try little things, little strategies, many of which failed but some of which became trademark moves that helped me get the better of opponents who really should have been superior to me. I feel our development of strategies and getting players adaptable to new ways of thinking needs to start at a younger age.

All our clubs and coaches within the county have the best in mind for our players. However, to get us comfortable changing a strategy and trying something new, even on the eve of an All-Ireland final, should not be the nuclear event it sometimes has proven to be. In Mayo, change is often something to which we are resistant, and it can flow from the crowd into the subconscious of management and players. Even when we fail, we want to do it the 'right way'.

Since the start of the last decade, we have certainly improved our attitude towards change. Like most teams, we had adapted our style of play by crowding our defence to counteract the high-running teams like Cork and Kerry. While Donegal in particular chose mass defence, we played the entire league in 2011 with a seventh defender. It was a ploy that had worked brilliantly for James Horan and Ballintubber during their march to a county title in 2010. It was a plan we worked hard on and one which we would have undoubtedly employed throughout our championship campaign had it not backfired – almost spectacularly –

against London in Ruislip. Not scared to change, James, a first-year manager, dropped his trusted strategy. It was one he realised did not suit our team or our pressing game. In the same season, he converted veteran attacker Trevor Mortimer into a wing-back, a move that revitalised Trevor and improved the team.

Stephen Rochford, too, was not afraid to innovate. I have incredible respect for him having the courage of his convictions in not one but two huge games for Mayo. His decision to replace David Clarke with Robbie Hennelly before the 2016 All-Ireland final replay was held up by almost everybody outside of Dublin as the reason we lost that final. Stephen got hammered by the press and by his home support. I can only imagine the strain all that noise caused him, but he never regretted making the call. On reflection, I know and admire why he did it. I was too caught up in my own game to let the team announcement affect me too much. As I said previously, players are selfish like that but when I look back and try to break down why we hadn't won after so many close calls, I can see why Stephen did what he did. He rolled the dice. It was a bold change of strategy designed to disrupt Dublin's tactical press on our kickouts. Robbie was a proven top-class keeper who offered something different to Clarkie. The fact that he changed the goalie caused such drama, I believe, because we don't like change. We don't like risk. Stephen saw it as another way to win. How many times had we been there before and left with nothing? He wasn't going to die wondering.

A year later we returned to Croke Park and, undeterred by past failures, Stephen shocked everyone by picking Aidan at full-back on Kieran Donaghy. The first day, the experiment almost came unstuck. Stephen took savage abuse in the media once again. I'm sure his nerve was tested but, to our great relief as a team, he doubled down on his gamble and went with Aidan again at full-back in the replay. His decision played a huge part in the winning of the game.

As a footballing county, we can't just rely on our 'Mayoness' to win games. We are entitled to nothing. Although Dublin have dominated the last decade of football, the evolution of coaching around the country has seen many other counties develop strategies to play different ways on given days. We have survived at the top table for so long that we have never been broken enough to need fixing but we should be brave enough to dare.

TWENTY-TWO

The Easiest 'Hard' Decision Ever Made

'Success is peace of mind in knowing you did your best.'

– John Wooden

T HE end is never easy. Everybody always says they want to leave on their own terms. Few are afforded that luxury. Impatient managers, unresponsive physiques, unrelenting personal lives: they all play a part. What does it mean anyway? Walking away at the absolute peak of your powers is not as straightforward as it sounds. It can seem foolish, especially in the sporting context where there is always a desire for more. If you win something, you want to taste that feeling and win again. If you come close and lose, you want to push harder and correct it. Walking away is an inexact science. I feel lucky that I got to choose but it still hurt like hell.

Why does it hurt so much? Surely, discovering a life beyond football is plenty of reward for stepping away? Surely, reclaiming control over your daily choices – as a father, husband, business owner – is enough of an incentive to leave with no regrets but, even with all of that, making the decision to call time on something in which you are so embedded is not without its moments of doubt. It's not just because it instantly means intercounty football is gone. Nor is it leaving a group of people to whom you have committed your adult life. It's the sudden, final surrender of a dream. An entire sporting life revolving around a single focus – winning an All-Ireland for Mayo. When it's done, however it's done, it's done for good.

To be clear, when I started out, winning All-Irelands was not the definition of success. Making the team was, but as time passed my expectations evolved. Losing All-Irelands in 2004 and 2006 hurt, sure, but as I reflect now, we were not good enough to win in those years. Being there was an achievement. Those were formative experiences not least because I experienced the coaching and management styles of John Maughan, Mickey Moran and the late John Morrison but also because they gave me a taste of what the big leagues felt like. I was 20 and 22 years of age for those two finals. You couldn't but be profoundly affected by the sense of excitement around the county and the sense of occasion of the days themselves. The 2006 semi-final victory over Dublin lit up that championship summer and for a long time was talked about as the game of that decade. Had my career not had the second act it did, that day may well have been its apex.

Although John O'Mahony's second coming as manager did not live up to his or the county's expectations, it was a privilege to play under him. His parting words were nothing if not prophetic. Standing in the middle of a broken dressing room in Longford in 2010, he didn't shirk from accepting blame for our demise. Another man may have pointed to our failures as footballers. Instead, in typical Johno fashion, he looked forward not back: "You have a great future in front of you, but you're not just ready... yet."

By accident or design, he was proved right. I was there, on or close to the team, for almost eight seasons at that stage. After any defining loss, a purge takes place. I was confident whoever followed Johno would see my value and potential for growth as a player, but for any footballer your late 20s are a vulnerable time, especially when the pressure is on a new manager to look to the future and not to the past. I was adamant that I would be part of the former and not the latter. Thankfully, James Horan thought so too. Another manager may have had other ideas. Doctors differ, patients die. If it had been over for me then, I'm not sure how my sporting epitaph would've read: *Andy Moran – good, but not great?*

What followed – nine championship seasons that became the second half of my career – was the equivalent of a second sporting life. We went from unpredictable underdogs to a team nobody ever wanted to play. To be part of that revolution as a player and captain was both a privilege and a huge responsibility, one that weighed heavily at times. As years pass, you may gain wisdom which makes some things easier but you also lose innocence which makes other aspects much, much harder. Your life, too, inevitably becomes much more complicated if you're lucky.

As an up-and-coming footballer, being identified as such is an undoubted source of pride. Becoming 'Andy Moran the footballer' was something that went with the territory of playing for a county like Mayo. In some respects, life gets easier. People know you and there are some social, educational and professional perks which complement your 'status' as 'someone'. But this development can also be damaging. You can lose something of yourself. You compromise friendships and personal relationships because of football. Your mindset in the build-up to games becomes as delicate as that of a new-born.

Stay clear of Andy – he has a match this weekend.

A couple of times a summer, this might not matter so much but as our reputation as a football force grew so did the need for exceptional treatment from those people in your life who rely on you for anything from the practical to the emotional.

Your loved ones become prisoners to your moods and motives. In my case, for 17 summers, and I'm not the easiest man. For those 17 summers, I needed others to sacrifice themselves to allow me to pursue my own personal glory. Some of these sacrifices were small, others ridiculously large. Sure, I appreciate that those people who supported me did so willingly. They took pride in my achievements and those of the team, but every summer came at a price. That's why when the time is right, you gotta pay up.

It seems ludicrous to say that for only one of those 17 summers we got it almost right. That is to say, we got it righter than any other of the 16. I was there. It still wasn't quite enough but for a six-week spell in 2017, we hit a sweet spot unlike any other I experienced with a Mayo team. From the introduction of psychologist Niamh Fitzpatrick to dying with our boots on against Dublin in the All-Ireland final, we maxed out on every possible facet of our game. Our mental and physical fitness, our team morale, our tactical awareness: we were purring. Every detail mattered that summer. Alas, it wasn't to be. Losing to the last meaningful kick of an epic All-Ireland final to Dublin was a cruel blow to a group who literally left everything on Croke Park in pursuit of glory, but it was also just not enough. We gave it everything. They were somehow better. It was an extraordinary effort to be a part of. You could play 20 years and never experience it again. I should know, I played long enough.

As I sat in the Citywest Hotel the evening after that game, it was the first time I felt a defeat as fatal. Jennifer and I cried that night and even though she was too small to understand, baby Charlotte seemed to comprehend there was something different about this loss. That day, a part of me left the stage. Not intentionally but as the first thoughts of retirement danced around my tormented mind, I had subconsciously accepted the end was coming even if I still wasn't ready.

The next few months were indicative of everything life can throw at you. In November, I won Footballer of the Year and my second All-Star. Two months later, our second child Ollie was born. One day I was walking out of Castlebar hospital, the proudest father alive, counting my blessings that everybody was right as rain. Five weeks later, I was back there to bid farewell to my father Vincent who finally succumbed to Parkinson's disease and dementia. Before the 2018 season had even begun, I already had the toughest winter of my life.

Still, with the help of my two families – the first and most important being marshalled by Jennifer – I soldiered on, managing some decent performances along the way. A tired loss on the road to Kildare once again felt like the end of an era, causing me to take stock and assess another year. Ollie was not sleeping, which meant our own lack of sleep as a couple ensured nerves were often frayed on both sides of the parenting partnership. With the balancing act of sport and real life becoming harder, you'd expect any strong woman to tell you one thing: "It's time to stop being so selfish and put your family first." Instead, Jennifer – easily the one most affected by my many absences – urged me to go again. Her selfless attitude was simple: "You can't leave like this."

As she saw it, ending my career with my least enjoyable season in the green and red was not the way either of us wanted to go but, as the autumn turned to winter, there was another factor. James Horan was set to return as manager for his second spell. Curiosity was something that always coursed through me as a player. I still saw an All-Ireland in the team and knowing James would return with renewed vigour, I made myself available to come back for at least one more year in 2019 although, privately, between Jenny and me, we knew it would be my last.

Everyone takes a different path to these decisions. For me, it was seeing first-hand the toll football took on my family life that put the final nail in the coffin. In 2018, after Ollie was born and my father passed, a season-long moment of clarity emerged through the fog of no sleep that came with Ollie and the grief I felt about my father. I saw what Jennifer was dealing with at home trying to raise our family as I continued my quest. I felt that season on my 34-year-old body, but it also weighed heavily on my mind.

My mindset returning in 2019 was to enjoy every moment possible and to contribute whatever way I could. I never regretted going back for that one last season. We beat Kerry to win the National League in Croke Park, a moment I shared on the pitch afterwards with Ollie and Charlotte. Later that summer came one of my favourite Mayo memories when we defeated Donegal in a Super 8s decider in a

Castlebar deluge. There was something about that night – the crowd, the tension, duelling it out with a team with which we had built a rivalry over the previous years – that will stay with me forever.

My final game, coming on as a substitute against Dublin in the semi-final at Croke Park, was not the stirring contest a man would wish to exit the stage on but the nature of how the game unfolded gave me some closure at least.

Facing a second-half blitz that ended the match as a contest, I spent the last 20 minutes understanding what it meant to be fully 'present'. I became very aware of my surroundings: Hill 16 serenading their Dublin heroes, Mayo fans still roaring us on despite the scoreline. I looked over to where Dad used to sit in the disability area between the Cusack and Davin stands. More than 15 years of family memories came flooding back. In some respects, I wish that glorious defeat of Donegal in the rain had been my last time pulling on a Mayo jersey but, as I reflect on it now, I understand that's not how life works and those final minutes in Croke Park provided me with all the closure I needed.

There was, as there often is in these emotional times, a moment of absurd comedy. The clock ticking down, Mayo won a free close to the Dublin goal. Sensing that tapping it over may be a tad selfish as my last act as a Mayo footballer, I decided to play it short to Fergal Boland to try to work a goal that would least give the scoreline some respectability. Fergie took my pass, and, in keeping with the forwards' code of looking after number one, promptly tapped the ball over the bar for his own score! Further proof that, as an attacker, you should always go with your gut! I was just about to eat the head off Fergie when I had a flashback to me doing the exact same thing at the end of the 2004 final loss to Kerry. Twenty-years-young with my red boots on, I wanted to score in an All-Ireland final. My journey was just about to end; Fergie's was just beginning.

Those moments only add to an almost infinite collection of memories I will forever treasure. I quickly realised how little bandwidth the victories take up in your heart and how important the non-football stuff had grown to be as my career progressed. What stuck out more than anything were the stories from trips away, bus journeys, team holidays, individual moments in matches and atmosphere from certain games. I had been playing to win the whole time, sure, but the more I played the less it became about the actual winning. I had decided to leave but I was going with a lifetime of memories.

I understood that once I left, there would be no going back. The decision was terminal. In one moment, you sever the connection you had with a group of players for over a decade. There would be no more deep and meaningful conversations with any of them until they, too, retired. I knew this to be particularly true given my propensity for asking questions. I couldn't do small talk. I'd always want to know what's going on. I was and remain obsessed with football. Walking away wasn't going to change that.

I'm an impatient man too. Jennifer and I had made our decision which I knew was irreversible. Not willing to wait until the dead of winter, I called James Horan the week of the All-Ireland final and informed him. He thanked me and wished me well. Once the commotion of my announcement died down, my connection to a team where I had grown up and become a man was gone.

There are many factors which made my departure much more palatable than it might otherwise have been. Staying that extra year allowed me that sense of closure I might otherwise have craved. Open and honest discussions with Jennifer about what was best for us as a family removed any sense of suddenness. Understanding my life beyond football allowed the transition to be much smoother than it might have been. Crucially, I got busy quickly. We grew our business from one to three gyms. I began coaching with my club Ballaghaderreen. Most importantly, I was ready to be available to my family rather than they always being there for me.

I realise how fortunate I was to step away how and when I did. Not every player will have that luxury but understanding there is a life to be lived beyond football is a something that can be developed in every player.

Playing for Mayo was the privilege of a lifetime. The pleasure was all mine.

TWENTY-THREE

Regrets

'Regrets, I've had a few, but then again, too few to mention.'

– Frank Sinatra

WHAT is it to regret? The things that make any of us who we are can be very complicated, built from many experiences and events. We constantly talk about the past being the past. Not to look back in anger. That we have 'no regrets'. It's quite a definitive, binary statement. I like to think of myself as a positive person but while I don't dwell on mistakes, I use 'the past' as a canvas for learning and reflection as I've grown as a person and as a sportsman. In a single game of football, you will do some things you technically 'regret' or wish to correct. The perfect game has never been played. As a younger footballer, I found it tough to reconcile the losses with the learning; the same way it's hard to objectively assess a failed relationship or professional setback as having a higher purpose. Age, perspective, love and loss undoubtedly help.

When it comes to Gaelic football, the natural assumption is that the Mayo story is one riddled with regret. No All-Ireland since 1951. We have lost ten finals in 31 years, the longest unbroken streak in history. The losses, as you would expect, have ticked every box in terms of trauma and emotion. We have bottled it. We have been hard done by. We have been unlucky. Pick your game, overlay any given narrative and you'll have your story. In the end, people will always assume there will be regret. In the most clinical terms, they would be right.

A missed goal chance in '89. A bouncing ball and a brawl in '96. A brace of own goals in '16. These are moments we all wish went our way. They didn't but ultimately, we rolled the dice. It didn't land on the numbers we wanted. It doesn't mean we can't reflect on them and, crucially, learn from them.

Of course, I regret tearing my cruciate in 2012 but that was not a choice or a bad decision. It was bad luck. One of those things. It cost me playing in an All-Ireland against Donegal. On an even more selfish level, I was captain and so I missed out on potentially being the first Mayo man to climb the steps of the Hogan Stand to lift Sam since Seán Flanagan in 1951. For me, that final will always be the one that got away. It was our one final where neither team was experienced in the art of winning All-Irelands. Cork, Meath, Kerry and Dublin – our conquerors before and since – all of them knew 'how to win', whether by habit or tradition. In 2012, it was an anomaly. Two young managers, both in their sophomore seasons, both revolutionising the respective cultures of their counties. Whichever team won would make history. There was no obvious favourite. For all those reasons, I felt it was a huge opportunity, maybe our best of the last decade. We started badly and the rest is history. A great Donegal team were deserving winners.

Missing that final was a regret, sure, but that injury proved a crossroads in my career. It amplified many of the corrections I was already implementing in my game. The recovery, though physically and emotionally brutal, changed me as a person. It likely brought me closer to my wife Jennifer. It informed my thinking about injuries and coaching and how we treat players who need a more nuanced approach in their preparation. Would I have played the football I did from 2013 to 2019? Maybe. That's not important. I can't change it, but I can learn from it.

When you are in the moment, a prisoner to some recent misfortune – an ill-advised pass, a badly executed shot or a rush of blood to the head – regret is, of course, inevitable. It can eat you up and sow insidious seeds of doubt. I may have made some bad decisions in big games but, as the old Wayne Gretzky quote goes, you miss 100 per cent of the shots you don't take. I'm a firm believer in that. What I would regret is passing the responsibility.

You never want to make a bad decision but making the decision is sometimes the hardest part. Wrong decisions are a necessary part of personal development. You can't live in a vacuum with no external factors influencing your life, especially if you want to excel and be successful. The butterfly effect of seemingly insignificant moments ripples throughout all our daily lives. Nowhere is this truer than in the world of sport.

*****

I regret not trusting myself earlier in my career. I regret the time given to self-doubt, to a fixation on results rather than performance. I associated my self-worth with results far too often in my younger days. If I achieved my goals, I was on a high. If I did not, I was devastated. The bigger the game, this became particularly detrimental. As a player – likely as a team – I was so focused on winning All-Irelands that the weight of the objective became too big a cross to bear and impeded the performance.

It got better for me. The nerves remained but a simple shift in my thought process alleviated some of the more potent demons. Almost counterintuitively, I started to imagine everything that could go wrong and rationalised my reactions to assuage my fears:

My direct marker beats me out for the first few balls.
He runs me up the field and gets a score.
My lack of pace is shown up.
I miss the first shot.
Maybe the first three shots.
I can't win the ball inside.
I get taken off early.

I thought through each scenario. I realised that, regardless of the outcome, the bigger things in my life wouldn't change. This realisation was compounded by the arrival of our first child Charlotte in 2014. Any anger or anxiety I felt about football dissolved much quicker than it previously would have. I still loved the game. I still loved to train and I was still trying to win no matter what but, crucially, when I left the dressing room and went home, there was something far bigger waiting for me, something much greater than anything we could achieve as a team. It was a great leveller.

If a performance coach tried to teach me that when I was 23, I wouldn't have had the perspective or emotional intelligence to compute it. It's a shame. Years beset by self-doubt may have been easier. Just another thing you can't force or contrive but something I don't want my kids or any footballers I coach to regret.

★★★★★

The first captain I played under for Mayo was Fergal Costello. He was Mayo to the core, honest as the day is long, aggressive and boy could he play. He was an army man and seemed born for the role of team captain. It was a privilege to play under him and since that time I dreamed that I might one day do the same and captain Mayo. It was an honour James Horan was to bestow upon me in 2012, one I took enormous pride in receiving. It meant a lot to me as I knew it did to my family and my club Ballaghaderreen. At the age of 29, everything was in place. It was the right time in my life, and I was ready to lead. Unfortunately, I tore my anterior cruciate ligament against Down in the quarter-final, my season over and my captaincy cut short. I returned to action the following May, but my form was patchy, in large part due to my body not being right. I did enough to get my place in the team but not enough to perform to my true potential. We lost the final to Dublin and I knew I had a huge off-season ahead of me in terms of getting myself right.

During our team holiday in Dubai, James Horan asked me for a coffee. By then, I had already made up my mind:

I loved being captain, but I needed to concentrate more on myself to get physically and mentally ready to play and perform. To do this, I needed time away from the training field to focus on strength and conditioning work. I knew the right thing to do was to step down as captain.

During our coffee, James asks me to be captain again for the upcoming season. I can't say why for sure – ego maybe – but, of course, I say yes. That is one decision I had control over that I regret. To me, a captain must lead by example on the training field. It is one of his fundamental duties. My body simply did not allow me to do this. Not wanting to let the team and James down, I neglected the individual work I should've been doing to further rehab my body and trained as if I were the man I had been before the injury. It eventually caught up with me. On the flight to New York, I feel my back lock up. When we arrive and shake out, I immediately go for a walk. My hamstring is on fire. The sensation doesn't go away. My training after the New York game deteriorated and I got dropped for the first time since 2004. Worse, it was against Roscommon. I struggled for form for the rest of the season. By the end of 2014, my body was in far worse shape than it had been 12 months earlier when James asked me for the coffee, and I hadn't been able to say no to him. Emotion, pride, ego: they all played their part. The braver decision was to say no and explain why.

At least I learned. In October 2014, I visited Eanna Falvey in the Santry Sports Clinic. He administered a nerve fusion block injection into my back. Eanna, along with Mayo's new strength and conditioning coach Barry Solan, developed a six-month return-to-play protocol for me. At the end of March 2015, I returned to football. I was ready to compete.

★★★★★

Ballaghaderreen is on the doorstep of Mayo, an off-ramp into the heart of the west. I often visualised what the town would be like were we to win just once. Knowing every inch of the road, I pictured where the bonfires would be. I could see the kids waving flags outside the houses. I recognised the faces of the men and women, understanding what winning would mean to them. I imagined the square in town as a sea of green and red. I dreamed of bringing Sam home to the town where I grew up. The field where I learned to kick a ball. The house where I was a baby. I didn't just picture this once or twice, I imagined it a lot. I had a front-row seat as Johno – my teacher and mentor – won with Galway. I saw how his successes brought joy to the town and pride to many of us, his students. I saw how we celebrated Seamus Cunniffe, Darragh Dunne and Cian Hanley in 2013 when they won an All-Ireland minor title with Mayo. I was one of the many who welcomed back teammates and friends Mike Solan and John Ginty after they managed Mayo to All-Ireland U21 victory in 2016, with Ballagh' players Seamus, Shairoze Akram and Ryan Lynch in the squad. I saw the excitement on the people's faces. I realise how much it meant.

County championship wins with Ballagh' in 2008 and 2012 further whetted my appetite for ultimate glory with Mayo. Those victories came after decades of trying, fluctuating fortunes and many missed chances.

I wanted desperately for this to be part of my story with Mayo. I wanted to be part of history. I thought of all the great supporters who passed away while we were trying, how poignant and fitting it would have been for them to see us win in their lifetime. The older I got, the more I understood the deeper meaning of our journey to thousands of Mayo people overseas. The team I was fortunate enough to play on worked as a connection between home and an exiled people. What would an All-Ireland mean to them? I thought about all this many, many times. I visualised us winning and I, too, allowed myself to dream. I never felt it added pressure. If anything, it drove me harder.

Naturally, not realising that dream is a regret. The closer you get to something the harder it is to accept defeat. Retirement put a full stop on any hope I had of being part of that history. As I reflected upon my career for this book, I constantly asked the question why: why not us? To me, there is no one answer. No one moment. No bad decision or overhit pass. There are tiny moments, of course, and those tiny moments accumulate into something bigger. Even so, to lose by a single point so often is enough for any man to question his faith. What if I had done this or that? What if I had turned left instead of right? It's a natural part of the process of grief, I guess. Everything gets easier with time.

I wonder about the burden of history. Did it cause us to tighten up and to be less cavalier in our approach to finals? To be less inclined to take risks? I say all this acknowledging that we were almost there so often in my time, and in the two decades before, the summit in sight. It was no fluke. Often, the routes my teams took to get there were dramatic and decidedly off-piste, but I never regret those. Those digressions from the normal path made us who we were as a team. Poor form could be corrected in an instant. A dismal season turned around with one big win. We confounded our critics many, many times. We never set out to sow such confusion and doubt, but we knew we had real talent and determination. It always felt like we could turn a year around any time. Crucially, so did the opposition.

Still, not winning hurts. It rankles and will until we do, but I don't regret giving 17 seasons to trying. Whether that's this year or next, I will not be playing. It's a small matter only important to me.

I'll be the one lighting the bonfire on the way into Ballagh', my children wearing my old jerseys and waving their Mayo flags. It will mean as much to me as anyone, more maybe, because I gave so much of my life to realising that dream. Real regret is not shooting your shot. I sure as hell shot mine.

TWENTY-FOUR

Games

I SPENT 17 seasons playing for Mayo, but I never stopped being a fan. Amid all the worry, anxiety, adrenalin and commitment that went with being a part of a county set-up, I retained a boyish innocence whenever I had to watch a game from the sidelines or cheer on one of our underage teams. As a player, selfishness can be a quality that drives you to get the best out of yourself therefore benefiting the group, but as a fan, when I reflect on some of my favourite games, including ones I played in and some I didn't, it's like being a kid all over again. We love Mayo football because of what it means to us beyond the pitch. It is part of our identity as people, tattooed onto our souls.

The quest for glory continues but I believe it is because of that great longing that we have been involved in so many incredible games since I started in 2003.

The following battles are my selection of favourite games – some I played in, others I did not. Some we won, others we lost. All of them have one common, defining characteristic: Mayo gave it everything and in doing so left our faithful fans in no doubt that whatever the result, no stone had been left unturned.

I hope you enjoy reading about them as much as I enjoyed writing about them.

Maigh Eo abú.

2004 All-Ireland Quarter-Final v Tyrone

After Mickey Harte led Tyrone to an incredible first All-Ireland in 2003, it was clear to everybody that with the players they had at their disposal and Harte's managerial mastery, there was much more to come from this team. That they would win three All-Irelands inside six seasons tells us everything we need to know about them. Conor Gormley, Sean Cavanagh, Brian Dooher, Stephen O'Neill and the brilliant Peter Canavan were among the best footballers ever to play the game. So, when we met them in the All-Ireland quarter-final in 2004, they were red-hot favourites to do away with us and take another step towards retaining their title.

Mayo, on the other hand, were rebuilding under John Maughan. We had plenty of new blood breaking through from decent minor teams with James Gill, Conor Mortimer and Alan Dillon all bringing a freshness that offered renewed hope for the future. It was my first year on the squad too and I quickly learned how good John was at taking young, hungry footballers and moulding them a certain way.

He had a few old dogs as well like Gary Ruane, Fergal Costello and Jimmy Nallen who brought a steel and a cuteness to things that made us the perfect team to catch Tyrone out. An amazing training camp in the Catskill mountains after our championship opener in New York had us in incredible shape for the summer ahead and John had another ace up his sleeve in the inimitable Ciarán McDonald who rejoined the panel shortly after.

Watching McDonald in full flight against Galway and Roscommon was a sight to behold, especially for me in my first year on the squad. He gave us unreal confidence orchestrating things from centre-forward, leading young forwards who looked up to him like the rockstar footballer he was.

We prepared brilliantly for that Tyrone game. A series of in-house matches with our U21s had the entire squad buzzing. For Tyrone, John and his coach Liam McHale developed a game plan specifically to combat Tyrone's Sean Cavanagh, fast becoming one of the country's most dominant footballers. Cavanagh, a natural midfielder, was doing most of his damage from wing-forward, often exposing a mismatch between himself and a more stereotypical opposing half-back. John and Liam picked Ronan McGarrity, an athletic, physically imposing midfielder, to man-mark Cavanagh. It was not an obvious thing to do but it worked brilliantly. With Cavanagh neutralised, it allowed David Brady to dominate the middle. Incredibly, David, who was not known as a scorer, added three points in an outstanding individual performance.

Once dominance of the middle third was established, Ciarán Mc and James Gill could link the play with our young, dynamic forward-line. Alan Dillon and Conor Mort may have only looked like boys back then but against the toughest defenders in the game, they played like fearless men. As footballers, their talent was never in doubt. On that famous day they arrived on the biggest stage, kicking nine points between them.

There was another piece of managerial brilliance from John that further emphasised why, as a young player, you'd follow him anywhere. Peter Canavan had been struggling with injuries all year and Mickey Harte had held him mostly on the bench, springing him to lift the team and the crowd as a game required it. John identified this, impressing upon us that when Canavan came on, Tyrone would be desperate and need the energy the arrival of Peter the Great would give them. As a team, we were to use his introduction as a trigger to increase our intensity levels for the next five minutes and go flat out, as hard as we could, all over the field. John had called it right: we stepped up and suppressed the Tyrone wave. Their crowd quietened, we went on to cause a huge shock, eliminating the defending champions and announcing ourselves to the summer.

On a personal note, I made my Croke Park debut as a senior that day, a second-half substitute. The difference in intensity between my previous appearances in Connacht against New York, Galway and Roscommon was literally as subtle as a punch in the face. I came on to be marked by Ryan McMenamin who greeted me as you'd might expect. The physical confrontation was immediate: first, a full-on body check. Next a hand in the face – captured brilliantly in a photograph, by the way. Not a glove had been laid on me when I was introduced as a sub in the provincial games. Ryan's unique welcome was an initiation for me. I welcomed it, understanding that this was the big leagues. I had my taster and I wanted more.

2006 All-Ireland Semi-Final v Dublin

This was less of a game of football and more a moment in time. For all GAA fans, Mayo v Dublin on that warm August Sunday became an unforgettable totem of the magic of sport. Many neutral observers tuned in expecting to see one thing only to witness ten games within one. Those lucky enough to be there can testify to an occasion with an atmosphere unlike any other. There were reasons for that, of course, and I will get to them in a bit.

It was not just about the game and its circumstances that made that day so special but the bigger picture around it. It was 2006, peak Celtic Tiger. You can be guaranteed many Mayo and Dublin fans had the Monday off, eyeing up the Sunday night out as much as the game itself. There was a change afoot in the attitude to Gaelic games, particularly football. The games had become more popular, sexier even, attracting a following that was less the traditional father-and-son dynamic and more the young professionals with money in their pockets and a cause to support. Dublin, to their credit, had done much to boost this new wave of popularity. Driven by their manager Paul 'Pillar' Caffrey, they packed out Croke Park Sunday after Sunday. Hill 16 was a huge factor. Caffrey embraced the noise of the Hill, and in contrast to the humble, no-nonsense approach we were more accustomed to in the west, Caffrey enabled his players by making the partisan Dublin support part of the team's identity. This included a slow march down to Hill 16 before every game, players' arms linked. This was new and brash and there was nothing humble or particularly Irish about it. In truth, it was very in keeping with the times. Whatever the external attitudes towards the act, it was working for Dublin.

Though we may not have been linking arms and walking methodically towards our home support, there were some obvious changes in the Mayo set-up too. Mickey Moran and John Morrison had replaced John Maughan as the management ticket. Both men were innovators and they challenged us as players in new and brilliant ways. Mayo always seemed to regard innovators with suspicion, especially ones from outside the county. Mickey and John perhaps knew their window for success with us as a group was short and set about making an impact quickly. Ciarán McDonald was once again central to the team and given that we also had a returning Kevin O'Neill, for the first time in many a year we had a team built around creative talent and not just athletic ability or big men. McDonald was box office. Watching him negotiate his way around the team hotel, an environment that should be a safe space for a player, you could see it was a jungle for him. He's a naturally shy guy yet everyone from Mayo or elsewhere wanted a piece of him.

There were residual benefits to the rebranding of Gaelic football which even reached the lesser names like me. We all got Nike boot deals that summer, a small but significant thing for a young footballer. It all added to the sense that we were part of something bigger. The Dubs in Croker on a hot summer Sunday would reveal whether we deserved to be there or not.

We came into the game as Connacht champions, but all eyes were on Dublin. This was their time. Kerry had already qualified for the final. The purists wanted a Dublin v Kerry final to revive the classic rivalry of the 1970s and '80s. It was building beautifully for the emerging new age of Gaelic football. Incidentally, it was the first meeting of Mayo and Dublin in championship football in 21 years. Little did we know then how a fierce new rivalry would unfold. This was the first chapter.

The short journey to the pitch that day was like driving through a carnival. Croke Park was rocking, Hill 16 bursting with colour. I remember us sprinting across for our team photo and being blown away by the atmosphere. The noise was spine-tingling. Earlier that week at training we had joked about hijacking the Hill by running down there for our warm-up. That was it. It was a joke. Just as we were about to break from the photo, our captain David Heaney said, "f**k it. Let's do it."

And so, we ran down to Hill 16. The place went wild. We couldn't hear ourselves. There was no plan, yet we were somehow all on the same page. Our management team had no clue what was going on. It was crazy and for a player it was exhilarating.

The madness intensified once Dublin entered the pitch. Immediately, we could tell they were rattled. To be fair, what team wouldn't be? You prepare for one thing, and you are greeted by something unexpected and different. If they ceded the Hill end to us, they'd have looked unforgivably weak to their own support. The only thing they could do was accept the challenge and engage us. Sixty players from Mayo and Dublin warming up in a 60 x 100-yard space. Managers hitting digs on each other, backroom staff laid out by flying footballs. It was chaos. And it was brilliant. The game hadn't even started but the battle had begun.

The game, when it eventually got going, had everything. Perhaps unsurprisingly, we started brilliantly, racing into a 0-5 to 0-1 lead after 20 minutes. Dublin reeled us in, and the lead went back and forth. Dublin's Ciarán Whelan famously escaped with a yellow card for a dangerously high tackle on Ronan McGarrity. Thanks to a pair of quality points from Kevin O'Neill and Conor Mort, we somehow went in a point up. Kevin came on for Mickey Conroy minutes before the break. Then 33, Kevin hadn't played half the football for Mayo he should have due to injury and working abroad, allied to Mayo's hesitancy in trusting a maverick. He was a player of incredible creativity and intelligence, blessed with a soccer player's vision and the sweetest of left feet. His score right before half-time was a classic example of what he brought to the team. Winning a dirty ball he had no right to, he sold an outrageous dummy-solo before bisecting the posts.

In keeping with the craziness of the game, we found ourselves 2-11 to 0-10 down after 46 minutes. We looked cooked. A minute later, after Ger Brady had reduced the deficit to six points, RTÉ commentator Ger Canning told the audience, "Mayo fans not giving up on this game…" Usually, this is said as a team's fans have already given up! The muted reaction to Brady's point was indicative of the dire situation in which we had found ourselves.

As a sub watching from the sideline, I was as engrossed as everybody else. I recall warming up alongside James Gill and telling him I saw a huge opportunity to exploit Dublin along the flanks. The more dominant they became, the more they were packing the middle of the field, resulting in space I felt we had to attack. Jogging back up the sideline, I made for John Morrison and told him straight, "Stick me on and I'll get you a goal." It wasn't like me to say something like that, but I just thought, "f**k it, what have we got to lose?" There was also an energy about the day that felt unnatural. Anything was possible.

I came on at centre-back for James Nallen. We were barely hanging on but as I felt my way into the game, I could see what I had noticed from the sideline unfolding in front of me. Ciarán McDonald won a ball about 55 yards out and had five Dublin defenders around him. I made an initial burst up the wing but it was impossible for him to see me. Dublin's Shane Ryan tracked me but after putting in a huge 50 minutes of football himself, he was beaten. I kept going. Ciarán played a pass into Kevin O'Neill who, stepping onto his killer left boot, spotted my run. He didn't so much kick as caress a pass into my path. I didn't have to break stride. Taking the contact from Shane Ryan, I spun onto my left and buried it under Hill 16.

My celebration was a mixture of joy and comedy as I wheeled away with a huge smile on my face pointing at John Morrison, a little tribute to the faith he had just shown in me. Suddenly, we went from being five down and drifting to two down and rising.

The next 15 minutes were manic. Dublin had been obsessed with matchups all day but as the game got looser and looser, matchups mattered less. We found space and capitalised. Their panic was palpable. Although we never pulled away, I remember feeling we had control. We just needed to plant the dagger.

And plant it we did.

Keith Higgins, who had endured a torrid afternoon from Bernard Brogan, bursts up the field in the 68th minute, carrying deep into Dublin territory. As Keith runs out of road, Kevin O'Neill reads the play and moves to him, offering support. Ciarán Mc, watching, holds his run and stays away until Kevin has the ball. One maestro feeds another. Ciarán swings his glorious left peg and splits the posts. The Hill is silenced. Mayo supporters go wild. Not done, Dublin regroup and win a 45 to the right of the Mayo goal. Mark Vaughan strikes it well, but David Clarke rises above the crossbar to claw it away. Again, Dublin regain possession and Jason Sherlock shoots only to see Keith Higgins execute a heroic block at full stretch. The ball is cleared. Dublin are on their knees and we somehow see the game out. What a win.

What was an incredible day turned into an unforgettable night. We travelled back to Mayo and rather embarrassingly I was carried shoulder high into the bars. They blocked the roads around the town. Bonfires were lit. Sure, I get it, we had won nothing but days like those are so rare in our sporting lives. The ecstasy we felt as a team and county is something I will never forget. The same goes for everyone there and watching across the world. Sometimes, you just have to let go and enjoy what is rare and wonderful. That was one of those days.

Whenever I recall that day, I think of my friend John Morrison. John was different. A thinker and a mentor who saw things like few others. His sense of humour was only matched by his knowledge of the game. A true original, he passed away in 2019. A year earlier, he was still sending me notes on how to improve myself. He was a man who loved life and left an unforgettable mark on me and all who knew him.

2009 Connacht Final v Galway, 1-14 – 2-12

The Mayo/Galway rivalry is a special one. Connacht being a small province, the tie is usually an annual occurrence with each clash bringing a fresh take on a story as old as time. As a kid growing up in the north-east of the county, I never felt the same intensity about the rivalry as many other Mayo people did. My antipathy was reserved for my Roscommon neighbours who were always on hand to remind me and others from Ballagh' about our outlier status on the border between the two counties. Moreso, when my teacher and coach John O'Mahony guided Galway to victory as manager in 1998, I was naturally happy for him and, by extension, the team.

My perspective on the Mayo-Galway rivalry changed as a player, however. From representing Mayo at underage level all the way through to my last senior involvement against them in a crucial Super 8s game in Limerick in 2019, my appreciation of what made Mayo versus Galway so special was acutely enhanced by every encounter. The adage of the formbook going out the window was, and remains, never truer than when applied to this rivalry. As we consistently proved ourselves one of the best three teams in the country over the last decade, Galway were always there ready to knock us off our perch. Likewise, as they won All-Irelands at the turn of the century, we gladly bided our time and no matter our own state of dysfunction or disarray found a way to ground them. Whatever the rivalry is, it's healthy.

On this July Sunday in 2009, both teams were in a curious place of confusion. We'd both had relatively recent underage successes. The tradition and recent history were there but as current challengers to Cork, Kerry and Tyrone we were both adrift from the pack. It never took from the games though. The stakes were always high, not least because Johno was in his third season back with Mayo and returning to his old base Pearse Stadium for a date with destiny.

Three seasons on since losing to Kerry in the 2006 final we had flattered to deceive. Ciarán Mc and Kevin O'Neill had gone and while Dillo and Conor and Trevor Mort had led the line, we needed a win of substance to define us as a team. The Galway game always offered you that opportunity. It could make you or break you.

Salthill is a wind tunnel even on the finest of days and it proved no different this time out. With that in mind, Johno opted for two big men inside – Barry Moran and our rookie Aidan O'Shea – with Aidan Kilcoyne working off them. This provided the first big story of the tie. Conor Mort, our talismanic scorer-in-chief, was not selected. The Galway game was always of particular significance to 'The Mort', being from the village of Shrule on the Mayo/Galway border. Conor had gone to school in the legendary north Galway academy of St Jarlath's College, Tuam.

However controversial, Johno's plan initially worked. We scored 1-9 with the breeze, all from play, and went in at half-time five points up.

Still, we knew it wasn't enough, especially as Galway possessed three deadly forwards in the iconic Padraic Joyce, his cousin Nicky and the brilliant Michael Meehan. Johno brought Conor in at half-time but as a team we played far too defensively and invited Galway back into the game. We only managed 1-3 in the second half, 1-2 coming from Conor, his goal ushering in one of the most memorable Gaelic football celebrations of all time. After palming the ball to the net, he pulled his jersey over his head to reveal a message, 'RIP MICHEAL JACKSON', scrawled on his t-shirt, in memory of the King of Pop who had passed away just days before. It was a bizarre moment in keeping with his personality but one of which I was completely unaware until after the game.

Despite Galway dominating us throughout the second half, we entered injury time Conor's goal to the good. Un-forgivably, we turned over the ball with Dillo and Conor naively trying to kill off the game on the sideline. No sooner had it happened than Galway moved the ball directly down to the deadly Meehan. Despite Ger Caff trying everything to stop him, legally and illegally, Meehan couldn't be halted. He buried his shot past Kenneth O'Malley. Honestly, it was the punishment we deserved.

As the stadium erupted O'Malley readied his kickout. As often happens after big moments like Michael's goal, things get chaotic. Playing in the half-back line, I see Nicky Joyce drift out to pick me up for the restart. Nicky is the best player on the pitch that day and although he's a deadly finisher, I fancy myself to win any break that comes in our direction. I signal at Kenneth to kick long our side and hope for the best. Sure enough, the breaking ball drops right in front of me. I win it and play a one-two with Ronan McGarrity before being dragged down by Joe Bergin about 55 yards out. We know it's the final play. That dead time between the ref's whistle and the restart is so often misused. Galway, like us, are out on their feet and trying to grab a breath. As Conor trots out to take the ball from me, I catch Peadar Gardiner's eye. No words are needed as he breaks from my shoulder and makes a run inside the Galway 45. Ignoring Conor, I kick a pass into Peadar's stride, and he pings a screamer from 40 yards into the breeze. Just as the Galway crowd had gone nuts moments before, it is Mayo's turn to go wild. Moments later we are Connacht champions again, our first provincial win since 2006 and the first for Kenneth O'Malley, Ger Cafferkey, Donal Vaughan and Seamus and Aidan O'Shea. Trevor Mortimer lifts the Nestor Cup to the joy of all our travelling fans. Mayo have beaten Galway, and all is right with the world.

There was a brilliant atmosphere among the players after the game. We felt Johno needed it just as much as we did and the dramatic nature of the victory only added to the sense of relief and euphoria. The craic was amplified by the Conor Mort goal celebration. Every highlight reel of the game that evening featured his testimonial to Jackson. It was something nobody expected to see at a Connacht final and further added to the lore of the Mayo/Galway fixture.

The significance of that win didn't fully hit home until much later. It's only in hindsight you see how important that clutch point from Peadar really was. Johno's reign would ultimately end in disappointment the following summer, but the nucleus of our team had been set and we had survived a formative encounter. On the other hand, the Galway team from that day began to fracture and the county entered a period of transition. Galway failed to beat us again until 2016. It was a famous win against a famous rival.

2011 All-Ireland Quarter-Final v Cork

To the untrained eye, I don't think two teams looked more diametrically opposed in their trajectories than Cork and Mayo when we met in the 2011 All-Ireland quarter-final. Cork were reigning All-Ireland champions and had just won their third National League title on the trot. They won one of those leagues at our expense in 2010 when they handed us a heavy beating. They may have lost the Munster final to Kerry in 2011 but had bounced back with a trouncing of a good Down team. Cork were a team in their pomp.

Mayo, on the other hand… well, we were trying to figure ourselves out. As Cork were busy putting together a historically good summer in 2010, we were busy losing to Sligo and Longford. A lot of the progress achieved under Johno was quickly forgotten as we left Pearse Park with our heads hung low. Mayo supporters may be loyal but, like family, they will quickly tell you when they feel let down. That was one of those nights. A low ebb consistently cited by many as a tipping-point for Mayo football.

It was low. I was there. I felt the pain of that loss acutely but also felt and still feel that one disastrous summer was not representative of the hard work we had done under Johno. We needed more time, but I felt we were getting there.

Still, a fresh approach was needed, and James Horan most certainly brought that. A rookie intercounty manager, he surrounded himself with talented individuals like skills coach Ed Coughlan, physio Liam Moffatt and psychologist Kieran Shannon, the latter working externally. James' first winter was an extremely positive one. You could sense the group was coming together and players felt enabled and trusted to take responsibility for themselves. Then we went to Ruislip and nearly followed up the 2010 losses to Sligo and Longford with a first-ever loss to London. As a team we may have felt progress but from the outside it must have looked like we had a long way to go.

We won a poor Connacht Championship, our victory against Roscommon notable only for the immense kicking display of a young Cillian O'Connor. Cork in Croke Park, with their outrageous size and athleticism, would be galaxies beyond London in terms of ability. Still confident in the direction we were headed, however, we felt an upset coming. All eyes were on them. A respectable performance would suffice for us to point at progress, publicly at least. Thankfully, James had no interest in that.

He saw Cork as vulnerable, his thesis based upon three key messages he relayed to the team in a meeting the week before the game. Firstly, he made the case for how incredibly difficult it was for teams to defend their All-Ireland titles. The deeper a team went into a championship, the more vulnerable to defeat they were. Dynasties were rare. This was before the later iteration of Dublin, which will forever be the exception not the rule. Nobody had retained their crown since 1990, 22 seasons previous. James was tapping into a flaw in most teams who have won and might relax. Make them tired. Make them want to take a break. Convince them they have won one and that's enough for today.

Secondly, he spoke about this group's history with Cork. In 2006, we beat them in an All-Ireland U21 final. The nucleus of both teams five years later came from that final. Sure, they had beaten us in a recent league final. We chose to ignore that though, concentrating instead on the positives. We had beaten them in the 2011 league. A small but significant point. They held no fear for us. We needed to exploit the muscle memory of beating Cork, this version of Cork in particular.

Lastly, and most emphatically, James argued that their legs were gone. He looked at their strengths and convinced us that those very strengths would prove their undoing. 2010 was their apex, the culmination of years of hard work and graft to build a team so reliant on physical domination of opponents that if you stayed with them, sowed the seeds of doubt in their heads by not going away when they expected you to, they would crumble. James used the Munster final against Kerry as an example. Live with them. Weather their storm. Make them doubt; then go in for the kill.

Objectively speaking, you could argue the counterpoint to every one of James' messages but what I loved about it as a player was the simplicity and the positivity. James had altered our expectations by focusing on 'what can be done' rather than 'what can't be done'. It was a subtle if extremely simple adjustment of mindset that served us greatly in those early seasons under him. Every player could understand the logic of Cork not wanting a battle if we wouldn't just go away. We had all been there at the most basic of levels. Some days, no matter what you've achieved, if you're nagged and annoyed enough, you succumb if only to give yourself a break. This is what we wanted to do to Cork: convince them that they'd earned their break.

Still, expectations outside the team were low, epitomised by a crowd of only 28,000 in Croke Park for the game. In a strange way, that suited us. The game started at a frantic pace as we expected it would. We conceded a penalty after just four minutes which Donncha O'Connor converted. Sixteen minutes in and we were six points down. This obviously was not the plan but we steadied ourselves, pegging back a couple of points before a moment of genius from Kevin McLoughlin. Taking the ball on the Cork 45, he tore their defence to shreds before unleashing an unstoppable shot past Alan Quirke. Suddenly, we sensed the game was on. Moments later, Kevin's goal was cancelled out by a Paul Kerrigan flick to the net. Another day and Mayo would crumble from here but James Horan's words were ringing in our ears: "live with them".

I kick a good score. We steady ourselves. After two bad turnovers, Aidan O'Shea responds by timing a crucial covering shoulder on Paul Kerrigan that leaves the Cork man flailing. Another big 'small' moment and the crowd responds. We are going to make mistakes, but we know it is the next play that matters every time.

We go in at the break two points down. Given our response to the two goal concessions, it feels like a lead. As we make for the tunnel the Mayo crowd are on their feet applauding us. Many make for the tunnel just to roar us in. We get inside and collectively we feel the same thing. The game is there for us just like we thought it would be.

The second-half performance was one of the best team displays I was ever part of with Mayo. Aidan and Seamus O'Shea began to dominate the middle third. Our defence kept Cork, the defending All-Ireland champions, to a single point for the entire half. A single point. That Cork score came in the 52nd minute and was scored by John Miskella who was playing at centre half-back. The introduction of veterans Ronan McGarrity and Peadar Gardiner added steel and energy when we needed it. Once we had a lead on Cork, we felt the life drain from them. If we were game but naive early in the first half, we grew cuter as the game went on. Every turnover felt like a score. Although the stadium was less than half empty, the noise amplified with every point we kicked. As we believed, so did our support.

With ten minutes to go, we only led by three but, based upon our psychological preparation, it felt like ten. They were chasing shadows. Our hope – that they would wilt under our constant pressure – was borne out. This was a great Cork team that met a Mayo side that had them figured out. It was no accident.

It was a landmark day. Our first big win under James. Our first big win in Croke Park in five seasons. I received man of the match that day, but you could've picked any one of 15 lads in green and red. That victory proved to us that something was working. That if we focused on who we were rather than who we weren't, we could compete. The few thousand Mayo fans there witnessed the first steps of what became an epic journey. To the outside world, this was just an upset. To us, we had got a taste of who we wanted to be.

2012 All-Ireland Semi-Final v Dublin

As if we were making a habit of it, in 2012 we once again found ourselves in the path of the defending All-Ireland champions. Dublin's victory in 2011 was signalled as the dawn of a new era for a coming team. The symbolism of Stephen Cluxton striking the winning free into Hill 16 against their great rivals Kerry only added to the sense that this was not a one-off. Media, fans, everybody loves a story and though Dublin as a county was hardly worthy of too much sympathy in terms of lack of success, 16 years between titles represented a mini-famine for them. Their relief was compounded by the fact that they had built a reputation for themselves as a brash, confident set of players under Paul 'Pillar' Caffrey (see Dublin v Mayo, 2006) only for that to be deconstructed and rebuilt under new boss Pat Gilroy. This new version of Dublin was a lot more palatable to the neutral. Like the country, they may have gotten carried away with themselves during the Celtic Tiger era with their march to the Hill but now, like the country, they had emerged, contrite and humble. That was the narrative – we always need a narrative – put out there following their win, not by Dublin themselves but by the media. The flipside was that everyone outside of Kerry was happy to see them beaten. The lesser of two evils, I guess.

What was indisputable was the quality of players Dublin had, even then. The Brogan brothers, Diarmuid Connolly, Ciarán Kilkenny, Michael Darragh MacAuley and Paul Flynn, all of them elite footballers. In Cluxton, they had a master conductor. The pieces of the puzzle had come together for Dublin in 2011: the following summer they were looking to double down.

We didn't fear them. An inconsistent league campaign had seen us perform well against Kerry and abysmally against Donegal (the famous "double day/double spill" game). Our stand-out performance came against the Dubs in a tie rescheduled after the original fixture had fallen foul to freezing fog in February. Six weeks later we wiped them in Castlebar, winning 0-20 to 0-8. The key to that victory was disrupting their kickout. Cluxton was their metronome, and we knew if we could interfere with his rhythm, we could attack their game plan. It was one of those games where everything clicked – Alan Dillon, Mickey C and Conor Mort all scoring for fun. We understood it was 'only the league' but we stored it away, hoping we'd see them again come summer.

We had a less than emphatic provincial campaign, easing by Leitrim before limping past Sligo. Croke Park had started to become a positive factor for us as a group. We put in a big performance against Down in the quarter-final, a game in which I ruptured my cruciate ligament, ending my season.

How we handled that injury was indicative of how we were coming together as a group. I was captain and now I was out. No big deal. Clarkie took over the armband. I was kept within the group. My injury was a setback – especially for me – but there was a grander purpose. We moved on.

Despite our encouraging showing in 2011 we were still very much the underdogs for the Dublin game. Deservedly so. They were defending champions and unlike Cork the year before, the sense was that this Dublin team was only starting. Their legs would not give in. Their support would not abandon them. They may not have been marching arms-linked towards the Hill anymore, but they weren't giving it up either.

We prepared well. Kieran Shannon once again put together a package of mental triggers to ready us for battle. One setback beforehand was the loss of Colm Boyle from the starting XV due to a stomach virus. We quickly went two points down but scored three on the trot to settle ourselves. Mickey C was giving Michael Fitzsimons a roasting, a matchup we had worked on in advance. Twenty-seven minutes in, Bernard Brogan takes a pass from his brother Alan and pulls the trigger. Ger Caff is there to execute an incredible block and preserve our two-point lead. Caff and Kevin Keane were majestic all afternoon in the full-back line. That was only one moment of many they produced to keep us alive.

One critical area of Dublin's game we had identified beforehand was their use of the half-back line. Unlike other teams, including Mayo, they liked their line to sit on their own 45 to protect their defence from counter-attacks. The idea was to invite the opposition onto them, allowing them to engage and turn over before launching an offensive of their own. With Jason Doc, Dillo and Kevin McLoughlin in our half-forward line, we were primed for this. All three had the ability to operate in the space between both 45-metre lines, popping passes into Cillian, Mickey C and Enda Varley. All three were exceptional kickers from distance too. They contributed six points from play that day between the three of them. The ability of our forward-line to interchange also kept Dublin guessing.

Alan's greatest skill was his ability to move ghost like around the field. Jason Doc was as good as an inside forward as he was as a working half-forward. His score on 33 minutes which saw him collect the ball way out, 45 yards from goal at an angle, only to turn and kick a bomb was a brilliant example of his quality.

A phenomenal team effort sees us go in six points up. James Horan's message at half-time is simple: Dublin will respond. Be proactive. Keep going like the break never came. Don't allow them rhythm or momentum.

The next 20 minutes after the restart are extraordinarily physical but we heed James' words and don't let up. A perfect example of what was working so well for us comes on 48 minutes. Alan, calmly in possession 70 yards out, picks out a 40-yard pass to Richie Feeney who promptly turns and kicks a screamer, putting us 14-7 up. From the kickout we press up on Dublin, depriving Cluxton the oxygen he needs to find his man. He shanks his kick straight to Kevin Mc who feeds Cillian. He bombs one from 45. The stadium is rocking. Losing to Longford in front of a few thousand fans suddenly seems like a lifetime ago. Two minutes later, Dillo is at it again, jinking up the field, playing a one-two with Donie before popping over another. It was a sensational few minutes of football. Twenty minutes to go and we lead by ten.

Perhaps understandably given the effort, we start to wilt. Everything becomes a struggle for us. Dublin bring Kevin McManamon on but the key change comes when Michael Darragh MacAuley moves to midfield. He begins to dominate our kickout and this gives them a platform for attack. They chip away at the scoreboard and before long it's 17-14. A long ball from Ciarán Kilkenny finds their best finisher Bernard Brogan one-on-one with David Clarke. College mates from Maynooth, Clarkie knows Brogan's form better than almost any other 'keeper. He spreads big and pulls off an incredible save under a disbelieving Hill 16. Paul Flynn knocks over the rebound to cut the lead to two but it feels like a big let-off.

In the next phase of play, we create a goal chance starting with a typical Colm Boyle turnover. Two phases later, Jason

Doherty releases Jason Gibbons through the middle. He feeds Cillian who slices a goal chance wide. It's the most un-Cillian thing to do. Moments later, Mickey C, who has been brilliant all day, mis-connects with the ball as he attempts to handpass a point after a wonderful move involving Donie, Cillian and Keith. Can this be happening? Dublin are still in the game. Just like in 2006, it's going to the wire. Cillian and Bernard Brogan exchange pointed frees.

The next ball is vital. When we need it most, Barry Moran makes a play for the ages, plucking Clarkie's kickout from the Croke Park sky. Chris Barrett and Alan Dillon combine to create space for the onrushing Seamus O'Shea. Only on the pitch a few minutes, he obliges the Mayo following with a brilliant finish. It extends the gap to three. Dublin have one more chance to salvage a draw when Cluxton drops a 45 into the square. Amidst a plethora of bodies, Keith Higgins emerges like a survivor from the wreckage, clutching the ball. Joe McQuillan blows the full-time whistle, and the Mayo supporters go wild. We are once again back in the All-Ireland final.

Any game taken in isolation can seem more meaningful than it might actually have been, but this game... well, it confirmed for us everything we were starting to believe about ourselves as a team and a group. Unlike against Cork 12 months before, our support had started to believe it too. We had built it. They had come, and on one glorious Sunday afternoon, we had delivered.

2014 All-Ireland Semi-Final v Kerry (x2)

By the time the 2014 season rolled around, a first crossroads loomed for Mayo under James Horan. It was his fourth season with us. We had reached two All-Ireland finals in his first three years. We had gone from the confusion and disillusionment of the Longford dressing room to being one of the most consistent teams in the country, laden down with All-Stars. An All-Ireland still eluded us, however. We made phenomenal progress under James but we knew this was likely to be our last chance with him in charge. For any manager and team, four seasons knocking on the door takes its toll.

We had played in back-to-back finals, losing the 2013 decider by the tightest of margins. Everybody was keen to tell us we had just blown our best chance to win one. Deep down, we knew there was another big kick in us.

Typically, our league form was patchy. However, big performances against Kerry, Dublin and Cork gave us confidence that whatever came later in the summer, we'd be ready for it.

We picked up our fourth Connacht Championship in a row with an emphatic win over Galway in Castlebar. There was muscle memory in those victories. We were expected to win games in which we might have struggled previously. We wore the expectation comfortably.

Croke Park had become like a second home for us. As a team we loved playing there. The aberration that was the small crowd for the Cork quarter-final in 2011 was now forgotten. Everywhere we played after that our support followed us in droves. The idea of the 'long-suffering' Mayo fan was fading away. Sure, we were still chasing the ultimate prize, but we were competing, and the journey was a thrilling one.

After a comprehensive dismantling of Cork in the 2014 quarter-final, we faced Kerry as we attempted to reach our third final on the trot. Kerry had the best forward in the game that summer in James O'Donoghue. The word was that he was carrying this Kerry team on his back but a quick glance at his support cast – Declan O'Sullivan, Donnchadh Walsh, David Moran and Paul Geaney – was enough to tell even the most casual observer this was a dangerous Kerry team. Throw veterans Marc Ó Sé, Aidan O'Mahony, Bryan Sheehan, Kieran Donaghy and Colm 'Gooch' Cooper into the mix and Kerry are formidable opposition. Despite us being favourites, we know the task we face.

The game starts frantically before settling into a classic tale of cat and mouse. Strangely for us, we become more suffocated by our own tactic of swarming the space around James O'Donoghue. It backfires. Approaching half-time we are three down and struggling to find a rhythm. Then, out of nowhere, Lee gets sent off. It's one of those moments when, as a player or as a fan, your heart just sinks. We quickly go four down. Mercifully, the break comes. Everything looks against us. Our best player has been sent off. Cillian has missed a few chances. The Kerry bench is loaded. To all looking in, it seems inevitable that our journey will stop here.

We don't panic. As can sometimes happen with events like Lee's sending off, it forced us to stop overthinking things and to just simplify our approach. Kevin McLoughlin, a natural defender, switched back into Lee's position and we reverted to playing with five forwards while committing to keeping a better shape. Lee was emotional in the dressing room and though he didn't need to he gave us a few words heading out the door. Every player has been in that position so, as teammates, we felt nothing but a desire to do it for him as much as for ourselves and, of course, for James. Taking a beating off Kerry was not how we wanted him to leave us.

Tom Parsons came on at midfield to combat David Moran's growing influence. We traded scores early and quickly felt that we were playing better. Nobody epitomised this more emphatically than Colm Boyle. His second-half performance that day was nothing short of sensational. He hit everything that moved and, in Lee's absence, provided a huge attacking threat. His point on 41 minutes to cut the deficit to two was the catalyst for the madness to come. Five minutes later, Cillian kicks a screamer to equalise. The game suddenly bears no resemblance to the first half. The crowd responds to every play as if it's the deciding one. With 12 minutes to go, a brilliant run and pass from Seamus O'Shea sees Donal Vaughan split the Kerry defence. Donal is taken out just as he's about to shoot. Penalty Mayo. We go from four points and a man down to three points up.

Kerry introduce Kieran Donaghy just as Cillian strikes his penalty. Moments later, Cillian adds a brilliant point off his left to put us four up. He follows that with a bomb from 50 yards. The atmosphere at this point is off the charts.

On 66 minutes, Donaghy wins a catch. Out of favour and off the team all summer long, this is his first touch of the 2014 championship. The next six minutes see him turn the entire season on its head. His second touch is a majestic fetch over Ger Caff followed by a quick dish to James O'Donoghue who buries it. The rollercoaster continues. Kieran O'Leary levels things for the eighth time with moments left. The drama of that second half is incredible but only a sign of things to come.

The conversation between draw and replay was dominated by two things – the appeal against Lee's red card and the decision to stage the replay in Limerick, a Munster venue. Often, when there is so much noise about external issues that players can't affect, it makes preparation for a game a lot easier for a team. In the end, Lee's red card was rescinded, and the game was indeed played in Limerick despite discontent from many in Mayo about the decision.

The replay was one of the most incredible occasions I was ever at, either as a player or fan. The atmosphere was like nothing I'd ever experienced. As captain, I had the privilege of leading the team around in the pre-game parade. It was the only time in my playing career that neither team broke away before the end. It was as if both teams understood there was nothing normal about that Saturday afternoon. We were part of something special.

The game had everything. The first half was out of control. Physicality, pace, super performances by players on both sides, controversial decisions by the referee Cormac Reilly and a crowd engrossed in every play. Keith's battle with James O'Donoghue was epic. Aidan backed up his immense second-half display in the drawn game by causing havoc at midfield and full-forward. Twenty-one minutes in and we were two goals up. Minutes later, Donaghy – fast becoming a pantomime villain for Mayo fans and loving it – volleyed to the net from close range. The Gaelic Grounds was simmering.

Adding to the drama, Cillian and Aidan clashed heads just before half-time. Every moment seemed to carry added significance. We conceded a second penalty from an identical play that saw Donaghy win a catch before feeding the assassin O'Donoghue who gets pulled down. The same man stuck the penalty. By the time Aidan reappeared in the 48th minute, we were a point down after being four up. Minutes later, I scrambled our third goal. Another twist.

Kerry continue to exploit Donaghy's dominance at the edge of the square. He is like a man possessed. Everything sticks to him, and he feeds his supporting forwards, all of whom can finish. With eight minutes to go, another long ball causes more chaos in our defence. O'Donoghue is onto it like a flash and just as he's about to strike, Ger Caff slides in with a last-ditch tackle. The ref reads it as a foul and Kerry have their second penalty. O'Donoghue obliges again.

And so it goes, over and back until the death. Deep into injury time, we are a point down and desperate for an equaliser. Great work from Mickey C sees Donie Vaughan burst through the Kerry defence. For a moment, there is a goal on but with the game on the line, Donie fists the leveller.

Even then, there's more drama. We win a free on the 45-metre line out by the sideline. Robbie strikes it well, but it hangs a little too much and drops short. As it hits the ground, I grab the break but the ref blows the final whistle. Extra time, we go again.

The rest is a blur. We open well, kicking a couple of quick points but because of our intensive running game, we are spent. The rate of scoring understandably slows for both teams but, crucially, we fail to score for the next 18 minutes. With cramp, bruises, concussions and ultimately many regrets, the game was up and we knew it. Kerry won 3-16 to 3-13.

At that stage in my career, it was a loss unlike any other. The devastation was visceral and hit all of us without exception. James, as expected, stepped down in the dressing room. The build-up, the occasion, the drama and the physical effort: all of it culminated in an overwhelming sense of grief the likes of which I never felt before or since in a dressing room. As a footballer, you just never know if the team, or you the player, will be back again. Was this the end? We didn't know. At that moment in the bowels of the Gaelic Grounds, it felt like it.

It was another dramatic evening for our supporters too. Already aggrieved by having to travel to a Munster venue, some decisions that went against us that day that added to the profound sense of injustice – one which, in retrospect, I feel was more emotional that reality. The emotion we all felt was compounded by the Limerick factor and the sense that we, the team, had left the game behind us in Croke Park. Those supporters travelled to Limerick, many of them leaving Mayo and Dublin before noon and not getting home till after midnight. The journey home was long and tortuous. Like us, they had no idea if the journey was over or simply at a fork in the road. The only certainty was we had shared something much bigger than a game of football. Another chapter had been written.

2015 All Ireland Semi-Final v Dublin

The mind is its own place. I can't overstate how low I was leaving the Gaelic Grounds in 2014. James' departure left huge doubt in my head as to what the future held. The 2014 season had been a struggle for me. I couldn't get fit due to the back injury I had picked up in New York so, for a footballer the far side of 30, I wasn't sure departing Limerick what lay in store. New management would demand new things. An old, wounded animal like me might well be deemed surplus to requirements. Phrases like 'transition' and 'rebuild' are the enemy of the veteran footballer. The journey home from Limerick may have only been four hours but, in my mind, it felt like four weeks.

Winter rolled into spring and, of course, the emotional hangover gave way to a renewed sense of pragmatic optimism. Pat Holmes and Noel Connelly succeeded James and as if in the blink of an eye, we found ourselves back in Croke Park 12 months after losing to Kerry, facing Dublin in an All-Ireland semi-final. A decent league was followed by a blowout Connacht Championship and suddenly we were right back where we had left off. Subconsciously, the older I got the quicker I wanted to get to Croke Park. It had become a home from home. As a team, you want to get to that sweet spot of feeling most comfortable in the most hostile and exhilarating environments. By 2015, we were definitely there.

Dublin were still reeling from their shock defeat to Donegal in the 2014 semi-final. Having met in '12 and '13, there was recent history between the teams. Each league encounter had only enhanced the sense of a growing rivalry. The opening half of the game is a tense and cagey affair. We concede an early penalty which Diarmuid Connolly dispatches. Big hits from Donie Vaughan on Jack McCaffrey and Tom Parsons on Ciarán Kilkenny set an early physical tone. In an astute tactical move, Pat and Noel had identified that they needed to keep our best scorers close to goal. To do that, the defensive burden that comes with playing a team of Dublin's quality needed to be redistributed. They had picked my clubmate and brother-in-law David Drake at centre-forward. David is blessed with an incredible engine. His job that day was to track everything that passed the Dublin 45-metre line, leaving Cillian and Aidan to concentrate on the scoring end.

Although David had played a lot of football this was his first championship start for Mayo. It was huge moment for him but one he couldn't share with any of his family before the game. Coincidentally, he was coming into the team at my expense so the pair of us had to let on it was business as usual for the few days beforehand. His own Dad, Noel, took a phone call from someone watching at home to tell him David was starting. I'm sure it quickened his step into Croker!

From a defensive standpoint, the plan worked brilliantly. David's role offered protection for our midfielders and defence so they would not be caught with overlapping players. We conceded just one scorable free in the first half and that was in the fifth minute. The Dubs managed just 1-7 in the first 35 minutes. On the flipside we were struggling to score freely. The supply to our full-forward line wasn't good enough and the good ball Aidan was winning was going to waste through lack of support play.

At 50 minutes in a low-scoring game, we were a point down and well in the hunt. Before the game we had discussed keeping it tight until the hour mark before going for broke. That plan was working until Kevin McManamon came on for Dublin and scored a scrappy goal. Suddenly, they go five points up with 12 minutes to go. In a game with scores so scarce, it's a lead that looks uncatchable. The Hill is rocking now. Cillian is single-handedly keeping us in it with a majestic display of place-kicking. Even so, with nine minutes to go we are seven down to a ravenous Dublin team playing into a crazed Hill 16. The season is as good as done.

We chip away at the lead, scoring three points in a row. We put pressure on Stephen Cluxton's kickouts and we take energy from the fact that he's not finding his man. Even though they lead by four, we can smell their panic. Still, we need a goal. Some brilliant footwork by Cillian releases Colm Boyle who had started the move back on his own 21-yard line. Boyler gathers bravely and spins before being taken down to win us a penalty. The stadium, for so long lulled into an eerie silence by the tension, explodes.

Cillian O'Connor steps up. Still only 23-years-old, he has already kicked nine points, keeping us alive as Dublin tried to break clear. The nature of sport is such that if he misses the kick, Dublin win and Cillian will be the culprit despite his heroic display. Facing Cluxton, he buries it in the top left corner of the net. The Mayo support is going crazy and, on the field, we know Dublin are there for the taking.

Cluxton once again turns over the ball from the ensuing restart. Kevin McLoughlin wins it. He works it forward to Aidan who feeds Cillian. Off balance, he slips me a hand-pass and I kick the equaliser with 30 seconds of normal time left. Dublin are a boxer on the ropes now, praying for the bell. Again, Cluxton kicks long and again we win the break. I release Aidan through the middle. He feeds Alan Freeman but slightly over-hits the pass. Alan does brilliantly to recover it and we recycle, patiently waiting for a chance to strike. The game is out of the hands of managers and coaches now. Players, many of them brutally fatigued, sprint as if on thin ice, knowing one misjudged tackle or pass could lose their team the game.

Sensing that a winner is in us, we work the ball down the right-hand side. Mikey Sweeney, who has just come on as a sub, takes a pass and spots an opportunity to strike. Cutting onto his left foot, he shoots only to see his kick brilliantly blocked down. Dublin lift the siege. Cluxton gets a chance to breathe again and their defence reorganises. Slowing the game down, they retain the ball like a basketball team playing the clock, waiting for their chance to make their clutch play. They get their chance, winning a free in a similar position to where Cluxton kicked the famous winning score of the 2011 All-Ireland final.

Cluxton misses. A minute later, the game is over.

A famous 20-minute comeback from Mayo had given us another shot at beating Dublin. It was undeniably a chance missed, however. There was no one moment. Mikey Sweeney's blocked kick sticks out but that was just one play among half a dozen. If we had turned the other way, made a better pass or were a tad more patient, any one of those plays could have resulted in victory. Dublin won the replay and went on to capture their third title of the decade, the first of their six-in-a-row.

When you get those chances, you must take them. It's worth reflecting too on the effects of pressure on players, even great ones. Cluxton will deservedly go down as one of the greatest footballers of all time. For 20 minutes of that chaotic second half, he couldn't put a foot right. Every kick-out was turned over. As a team, we could see it and we pounced. It wasn't enough. It's worth remembering though when we chose to criticise individuals for specific plays, especially in the clutch, that even Cluxton has felt the pressure. Nobody is immune.

2016 All-Ireland Quarter-Final v Tyrone

After the acrimonious departure of co-managers Pat Holmes and Noel Connelly at the back end of the 2015 season, we were a team under pressure to deliver in 2016. The season proved particularly difficult early on. We lost to Galway in the Connacht Championship and justified criticism followed. Stephen Rochford, in his first year in charge, remained calm and though our performances were sub-par the mood within the camp remained one of positivity. We were a year on from losing to All-Ireland champions Dublin after a replay. We felt we were close. Our early championship displays indicated otherwise.

A favourable draw in the qualifiers saw us play and beat Fermanagh, Kildare and Westmeath. Even though we were heavily favoured to win those games, we were still well off our best, often suffering second-half slumps that saw weaker teams reel us in. Against Westmeath particularly, in Croke Park, a place we considered a second home, we struggled after a promising start.

That led us to a quarter-final against Tyrone, a team that never quite went away after winning three All-Irelands in six years the previous decade. Ever the innovator, Mickey Harte had found new ways to invigorate old stars – Justin McMahon and Sean Cavanagh were enjoying Indian summers after glittering careers in the red and white. Tyrone were flying high that year. We were struggling on one wing.

Part of what was inhibiting our performance was adapting to a new manager with progressive ideas about how he wanted us to play. As our game plan developed, so did our faith in him and his team that he was a risk-taker, someone who would roll the dice in big games and not worry about the consequences. Our first big test was against Tyrone in Croke Park. They were favourites. That suited us. With Tipperary shocking Galway to reach a semi-final on our side of the draw, the consensus was that our game was a de facto semi-final.

In Mayo, we had a reputation for playing fast, free-flowing football. We knew Tyrone would be ready for this especially as their preferred formation was to line up with midfielder Colm Cavanagh and centre-back Justin McMahon dropping back to protect their full-back line.

Eschewing our reputation for saying 'to hell with the opposition', Stephen pulled a master stroke by picking Alan Dillon as a floating centre-forward. Alan had a license to occupy the spaces left by Cavanagh. He would be Justin McMahon's responsibility. Dillo's ability to pick up ball and do damage from deep was the perfect antidote to Tyrone's defensive set-up. He ran the game like a quarterback for 35 minutes, so much so that McMahon, a key piece in the Tyrone jigsaw, was withdrawn before half-time. Tyrone could never have expected Alan's inclusion given he had featured very little all season. To hand him a starting role in such a big game took great courage from Stephen and huge balls from Alan to execute it so brilliantly.

He gave it everything and was replaced at half-time by Tom Parsons who brought huge energy and pace to our second-half offensive. It was seven points apiece at the break. Low-scoring and suffocatingly tight. With their game plan disrupted, we had them where we wanted them. Now came the part we had struggled with all season: the finish.

In the second half, our defence steps up. Bar one breach which led to an outrageous save from Clarkie on Conor McAliskey, we hold Tyrone to two brilliant points from Peter Harte from play and three converted frees.

The key battle, however, was between our own Lee Keegan and the great Sean Cavanagh. Cavanagh was approaching the end of his career and Lee was approaching his prime. As usual when Lee set foot in Croke Park a different animal emerged. He just meant business. He was everywhere that day, dominating the game and allowing Cavanagh no space. His defensive efforts were heroic enough but just as the game entered the clutch, he stepped up to hit two unbelievable scores to finish Tyrone off. This was a game where every score was incredibly hard earned. Trailing 0-11 to 0-10, Cillian feeds Lee on his left, running towards the Hill 16 goal. Without breaking stride, he shoots with the inside of his left foot. I have seen Lee take on this very shot a thousand times or more in training. More often than not, he misses. His whole reason for trying this kick is for moments like these. He nails it. Game level.

Minutes later, Cavanagh gets sent off for a second yellow following a high challenge on Aido. Lee, too, had been on a yellow. It was a highwire act for Lee and Cavanagh all afternoon. Confrontational and combative to the last, it went the wrong way for Sean ten minutes from the end. Lee, however, was not finished yet.

We exchange scores. It's 12 points apiece and the game is in the balance. As is his way, Lee, abandoning caution, finds himself ahead of the ball. He takes a pass from Seamus O'Shea with his back to goal and turning on to his preferred right side, swings over the winner. What a win, what a performance of character from a team struggling to find its form. A lot was on the line that day. A loss would've seriously undermined the team and its new management. The formbook was against us but as we often did before and since, we found a way.

2017 All Ireland Final v Dublin

There is a lot I miss about playing for Mayo. Some of it – the craic, the camaraderie, the sense of achievement – can manifest itself in different ways in retirement, as a coach, supporter or proud parent. There are other things, however, you will never get to feel again. Perhaps the most profound is the 20 minutes before an All-Ireland final, from running out the tunnel to standing for the national anthem. These are experiences unique to the player, ones you can never replicate. They exist way out there on their own. The noise, the atmosphere, the colour. Take everything you expect it is and multiply it times a hundred. It is an immense feeling. I was lucky enough to do it six times. The last, fittingly, was the most memorable.

The four games we played in August and September 2017 were the best I ever saw us produce as a team. From the quarter-final replay demolition of Roscommon through a pair of classic semi-finals with Kerry and on to a heroic effort against Dublin in the final – for six weeks we hit a stride I felt we never equalled. Physically, we were flying. Mentally, we were humming along. The mood in the camp was like nothing I'd ever experienced. To the outside world, we were as cavalier and unpredictable as ever – a typically bumpy ride through the qualifiers did little to debunk that theory – but, behind closed doors, we were buzzing.

It made the build-up to the final against Dublin even more special. There was a sense among us that we were primed to dethrone the champions. We worked hard on all our matchups in the build-up. We felt we saw weaknesses we could exploit in Dublin.

Leaving our training camp in Limerick the weekend before the game, I had absolutely no doubt we would beat them. We were fitter and stronger than I'd ever seen us as a team. We had ourselves ready. We had our homework done. Croke Park was our second home. There was no fear of what was to come, only excitement.

I always loved the thrill of those journeys up to Dublin the Saturday before. The second you'd stand on the bus, the craic would start. We knew each other so well. We'd actually feel sorry for the likes of Dublin not getting to experience those special weekends in the same way. As an older player, it was like stepping into a parallel universe for a couple of days. Away with your mates. Everything taken care of for you and, at the centre of it all, playing in front of 82,000 people in an All-Ireland final.

There were many things I loved about the day itself, but the parade was something special. The parade allowed you a breather. I'd always be buried after an intense warm-up. That long walk around Croke Park was my time to find my bearings and to catch my breath. My senses invariably became more heightened the closer it got to game time. Colour, noise, touch; all of them amplified. It made me hyperaware of my surroundings. I never felt more present in a moment than right before an All-Ireland final. I loved looking up to where I knew my family was sitting. I always scanned the crowd, soaking up the atmosphere and appreciating the colour and the noise. Playing Dublin especially, the atmosphere was incredible. No two sets of supporters brought more to an occasion than Dublin's and Mayo's. For ten minutes before battle, there was a certain kind of calm. Then came the chaos.

As referee Joe McQuillan threw in the ball to start the match, the anticipation in the ground for what's to come is palpable. Aido wins the throw-in as he has done all year but 90 seconds later Clarkie is picking the ball out of his net. The new kid on the block, Dublin's Con O'Callaghan, took possession on our 45. There seemed little danger as we had cover in Boyler and Donie Vaughan. Out of the blue, O'Callaghan neutralises both with a killer step and is in on goal. He rolls the ball into the bottom corner of the net as if he's playing a training game. The Hill erupts. It's a sensational start for Dublin.

As Con scored, I had the oddest thought. In the lead-up to the game, both of us had been mentioned as contenders for Footballer of the Year. It wasn't something that occupied too much bandwidth in my brain but in that moment after he scored, I can remember thinking, "well, that's that decided!". When you are a long way from the play, these random thoughts can sometimes occur. The upshot of Con's blistering start was that the award never crossed my mind again.

With Dublin getting a dream start, how do we react? An injury to Jack McCaffrey leads to a small break in play on four minutes. The ensuing hop-ball on our 20-metre line is contested by Aidan and Brian Fenton. Aido wins it, throws off Eoghan O'Gara and launches an attack. Kevin Mc finds me with a good, quick ball and we have our first point. We are off the mark. On 15 minutes, we've clawed back the deficit. We've settled. The game is pinging back and forth.

Our press on Cluxton's kickout is causing him to kick long which, in turn, is allowing our midfielders Seamus O'Shea and Tom Parsons to contest and win in the middle of the park. Superbly aided by Aidan and Donal Vaughan, the lads could physically and aerobically match Fenton, James McCarthy and Paul Flynn, the latter having come on for the injured Jack McCaffrey. Stephen and his management team had built our attacking strategy around not allowing Dublin to create a sweeper in front of their full-back line. With the four boys around the middle driving forward, the Dublin defence simply had to go and meet them. This gave us the platform and space up front to produce our highest-scoring performance in an All-Ireland final. In the first half, all four forwards who stayed high up the field (Kevin, Jason, Cillian and me) had scored from play. It was an outstanding first half from both teams at the peak of their powers. Boyler recovers brilliantly from a rocky start from Con's goal to kick an unbelievable score just before the break.

We go in at half-time one point to the good. The game is anybody's.

Dublin make the first tactical move, introducing Diarmuid Connolly and Kevin McManamon, two proven closers. Stephen reacts by moving Paddy Durcan from Paul Mannion on to McManamon. It backfires as Mannion, who had been quiet in the first half, comes alive. Of the first four scores of the second half, he kicks two and assists in the other two. The last of the four is scored by McManamon. Dublin's famed bench is making a difference.

We keep attacking. I put Jason through for a one-on-one with Cluxton. He saves brilliantly but Jason does well to secure the rebound and win a tap-over free. Minutes later, Mannion forces a superb save out of Clarkie. It's that type of game. Everything is happening. Every moment matters.

On 45 minutes, the game on a knife edge, John Small clatters into Boyler to receive his second yellow. Donie Vaughan has a rush of blood to the head and follows through into Small, leaving Joe McQuillan with no choice but to send him off too. It's just another huge incident in a game packed with them. It's that type of game.

Rattled by the nature of Donie's dismissal, we slip two points behind. It's a slender lead but this is usually the period of games when Dublin pull away. We need something. So often, the man who came from nowhere to provide that inspiration was Lee Keegan. On this day, he devoted his game to stopping Ciarán Kilkenny. Suddenly, he appears in attack, crashing the ball to the Dublin net in the 53rd minute following a move that began with our goalkeeper and ended with Lee taking a pop pass from me in the inside line after tracking the play the length of the field. That one play was the personification of the class of Lee Keegan. We lead by one.

Two incredible scores follow from Diarmuid Connolly and Kevin McLoughlin. Cillian puts Mayo a point up with a score from play and then makes the margin two with a free won by Lee. Dublin bring it back level and then go a point up when Rock opts to fist it over the bar with Mannion free for a tap-in to the net at the back post. Cillian hits an outrageous point to bring it level at 1-16 apiece. With 68 minutes on the clock, Keith Higgins does brilliantly to force a turnover on Bernard Brogan. We attack and Cillian wins a free deep in the left corner on the 20-metre line. Normal time is up, but there are six minutes of injury time to play. Cillian takes his time and strikes the ball well but hits the post on the high side. The Dubs react quicker and claim the rebound. The next few minutes are suffocating. Keith gets a huge block in on Brogan. Connolly takes a wild shot off his left. Each team now knows the next score will win it.

Off the next kickout, Dublin press hard. James McCarthy brilliantly fetches it. He feeds Connolly who runs directly at Chrissy Barrett. Chrissy had one of his best games for Mayo that day. Connolly is cute and forces the foul. It results in a free for Dublin, 40 metres out. All eyes are on Dean Rock. He pulls the trigger and breaks our hearts.

It might appear odd that this game ranks among my favourites. It was my last All-Ireland. It was an epic occasion. We were beaten by worthy champions. I feel it was the best performance of a Mayo team that produced so many great performances from 2011 to 2019. It wasn't enough.

2019 National League Final – Mayo v Kerry

The sceptics might say it was only the league. The cynics might have watched us celebrate on the field afterwards with our families and rolled their eyes, citing it as another example of 'why Mayo won't win an All-Ireland'. That day more than any other, we couldn't have cared less what they thought. The Mayo team that beat Kerry in Croke Park in the 2019 National League Final was a team exhaling deeply. A team that had been together for almost ten years infused with new blood. A team that had a new, old manager, back to finish what he had started in 2011. It was also a team without its talisman Cillian O'Connor who was out through injury. We hadn't won a league title in 18 years and, as we were so often reminded, no trophy in Croke Park in all that time either despite appearing in six All-Ireland and three league finals. I had appeared in eight of those nine defeats. We wanted this one badly.

James' return as manager rejuvenated the squad after a particularly tough campaign in 2018 that saw us exit in the qualifiers on a famous night in Newbridge. Perhaps understandably, many obituaries were written for us as a team that had been together for eight seasons, each season throwing up a new storyline or narrative. The loss to Kildare had a sense of finality about it. Undeniably, the team looked tired. What the obituaries missed was the supply of players we had coming through. Mattie Ruane, James Carr, Fionn McDonagh and Ryan O'Donoghue were all players of great promise. Diarmuid O'Connor was only approaching his prime and the age profiles of Aidan and Cillian were such that although the miles on the clock were many there was still much more to come. I may have been approaching the end, but most others had plenty left to give. James recognised this. I am sure that's why he came back.

As with other years, our league form was erratic but strong wins against Kerry away and Monaghan at home saw us qualify for the final. Once there, the polite thing to do was to just go and win it.

As league finals go, it was an incredible occasion. There were 45,000 people in Croker that day. Mayo fans, obviously feeling robbed of their August pilgrimages to Croke Park the previous season, sensed a little history. For a game so early in the season, it had a championship atmosphere about it. Kerry played their part too. They were a coming team. Much excitement surrounded the emergence of their two wunderkinds David Clifford and Sean O'Shea. These players would draw any neutral in. Another novel element was a final in Croke Park not involving the dominant Dubs. For all these reasons, it was a league final with an edge. The game didn't disappoint.

We started slow, and with Clifford and O'Shea firing for Kerry we trailed by four at the break. Adamant we weren't heading home empty-handed, we upped it a gear or two in the second half. Tellingly, it was three players from the new guard who drove the change. James Carr, the first player from the Ardagh club to play senior for Mayo, and making his league debut that day, kicked a couple of points shortly after the restart.

Mattie Ruane, too, played a blinder from midfield, kicking a goal and a point to announce his arrival on the senior scene. The real star, however, was Diarmuid O'Connor. He was pure box-office that day. His goal and a couple of points inspired us as a team. It was virtuoso stuff.

In the 71st minute, we led 2-11 to 2-9 when Stephen O'Brien came in along the end-line, popped the ball across to David Clifford who rose to get a hand to it and steer it towards the net. In a moment of poetic redemption, as the watching crowd expected only one outcome and the editors dusted off their 'More heartbreak for Mayo' headlines, Robbie Hennelly somehow denied Clifford at point-blank range. If any man deserved a moment in the Croke Park sun, it was Robbie. That save typified his resolve as a player and as a man.

The game wasn't done. Three more minutes of Kerry attacking and us repelling. A point would do a lot to kill it for us. We work a move up the middle of the pitch which sees me play young Ciarán Treacy in on goal. As he bears down on Kerry 'keeper Shane Ryan, every living Mayo man, woman and child must've been praying he'd fist the ball over the bar to re-establish our two-point cushion. Ciarán, clearly oblivious to the decades of discourse lamenting Mayo's lack of a killer edge, ignores the anxiety of his supporters (and teammates) and delivers a brilliant finish to the bottom corner of the net. The game is ours.

Yes, it's only the league but to hear the *Green and Red of Mayo* blare out of the PA at Croke Park was a special moment. To have so many Mayo fans present for it, the same ones who had traversed the country with us for so many seasons before, gave that day a sense of occasion we couldn't have expected. The manner in which the game ended – a young, innocent, fearless player, unburdened by all the negative muscle memory of previous losses, unwilling to play it safe – added further significance to the win as it provided hope that the future was bright for us. Hope that though the faces change, the journey continues unabated.

Yes, it was a day to remember. To share it with teammates and fans and family is something I will never forget. To have Jennifer, Charlotte and Ollie there after an incredibly difficult year felt profoundly poignant. Without them, there was no me.

On reflection, it's a bittersweet memory. That day gave an insight into what winning an All-Ireland might be like for Mayo. The joy on people's faces. The feeling of delivering on a lifetime of broken dreams and unfulfilled promises. It came too late for me but will serve as a taste of brighter days ahead for all those younger lads whose race is far from run.

Persist and Resist

AS THIS book was on the final leg of its journey to the printing press, Mayo did something which encapsulates so many of the reasons why I wanted to write it in the first place. Dublin, arguably the greatest Gaelic football team in history, were heavily fancied to beat Mayo in the 2021 All-Ireland semi-final and go on to challenge for a historic seventh championship title in a row. Mayo, by contrast, were limping rather than bouncing to Croke Park, missing our talisman Cillian O'Connor and reigning Young Footballer of the Year Oisín Mullin, both out with injury. Trailing 10-4 at half-time, there was a sullen air of inevitability about what was to come. Dublin built an empire on grinding teams into submission. As I sat in the Davin Stand with my wife Jennifer – our first ever Mayo game to attend together, incidentally – I worried for the second half and what effect a demoralising defeat would have on us as a team and on Gaelic football as Dublin's monopoly on titles looked set to continue undisturbed.

What happened next was the most Mayo thing imaginable. Trailing by five with under ten minutes to play, we unearthed that indefinable quality that has set us apart from so many other teams for so long. Diarmuid O'Connor (who else?) stretched out his leg to keep alive a lost cause and the team drew from a well of resilience many assumed to be empty. Rather than revert to self-pity for decisions that had gone against them, they instead pressed supposedly unbeatable opposition into pure panic.

This was a Mayo team led by new players like Ryan O'Donoghue and Padraig O'Hora, mimicking veterans Lee Keegan and Diarmuid O'Connor in their Herculean efforts to keep going, to never give up. We equalised with the last kick of the game and what a kick it was!

Robbie Hennelly, one of the most maligned men in Mayo football outside the dressing room, and one of the most valuable men inside it, stepped up to nail a 45 knowing that missing meant the end. After everything he had endured in Croke Park, especially against Dublin, the fact it was him meant something much more than victory. Much more than defeat. For his parents there watching. His fiancée Orla. This was a redemption few get to experience.

There was a fitting closing of a certain kind of circle too. One that few commentators spotted. In 2011, as the rain fell in Croke Park, a goalkeeper, Stephen Cluxton, kicked Dublin to win their first All-Ireland in 16 years. That kick heralded a run of eight All-Ireland wins in ten years.

Ten years later, another 'keeper, Robbie, effectively ended it with one ping of his right foot. He nailed a kick with an extreme degree of difficulty in the most incredible of circumstances in a game that will long be remembered for its significance.

For Robbie and for Mayo, this was absolution.

The momentum of the act and those preceding it meant that there could only be one winner in extra-time. We obliterated Dublin.

On a personal note, it meant so much to me that it was Mayo who stopped that incredible team. We – the players, supporters and media – may have considered it a rivalry but it was one that for eight seasons had only one victor. We understood that Dublin respected us but despite our best efforts in successive finals they always had our number. Then, on 14 August 2021, a Mayo team littered with rookies and an unproven bench defied the odds and brought to a dramatic halt the greatest unbeaten championship run in the history of Gaelic football, a phenomenal 45 matches.

The victory was typified by so many of the qualities I reference in this book. Tommy Conroy, a man we hope and believe will have a long and brilliant career for Mayo, was having a tough afternoon. Another player might have dropped his head and waited for his number to be called. Instead, he kept going, again and again. With the game on the line, he forgot his mistakes and stepped up to kick three of the most memorable points any Mayo man has ever managed in such intense circumstances. Lee Keegan, once again inspired by his favourite venue, gave a vintage performance many doubted was still in him. O'Hora, in his first full season starting for Mayo, grew into more and more of a leader with every passing play.

The stag, when pressed, became a lion.

As the dust settled on that victory, thoughts inevitably turned to another All-Ireland final, our eleventh in 32 years and our fourth time to reach a final in consecutive seasons during that same period.

While winning, ending the famine, breaking the drought, will always be the thing we ultimately fixate on, there was something about that Dublin victory that transcended all of that. It's as if it could not happen to another county – not the way it did anyway, with those little elements coming together: an injury-hit team, controversial refereeing decisions, Robbie's kick. These moments are bigger than titles. Of course, we want to win titles too but winning in the manner we did meant something much bigger than football. For all my years playing football for Mayo, and the incredible memories I brought with me, that night, sitting in the stands with Jennifer, was my proudest ever.

Players can be replaced but that feeling of who we are and what we represent can never be lost. On that one rainy night in Dublin, being from Mayo never meant more.

Unfortunately, we lost the final to Tyrone just a few weeks later. The search for ultimate glory continues. People sometimes ask after a final defeat 'what now for Mayo football?' What now? What it's always been: we get back up and we go again. That's what we have always done. Our spirit is strong and once that's there, hope will continue to spring eternal.

Would I Do It All Again?

'What is delayed is not denied.'

– Dawn Staley

I CAME to write this book in a curious way. When I retired in 2019, the last thing I wanted to do was put something out there about myself. I was not vain enough to think 400 pages about 'my story' would captivate anybody. I count myself lucky that I am a rather ordinary person. My upbringing in the west of Ireland was a typically happy one. My parents worked hard and sacrificed a lot to provide a good home for their kids. Like most children around me I was mad about sport, particularly Gaelic football and soccer. I grew up in a time when Mayo were contesting All-Irelands and the entire county was in thrall to their journey. I desperately wanted to be part of it. It was only then that things got interesting.

What got interesting were the people and it was the people who inspired this book. Many footballers go through a period after they retire when they struggle to fill the vacuum that top-level sport occupies. I was adamant not to be one of them and in the early days my strategy of immersing myself in family, business and coaching largely worked.

There was, however, an unforeseen event that put a halt to my gallop or rather put a halt to my gallop becoming a sustainable canter. The outbreak of Covid-19, and the subsequent lockdowns it inspired, accentuated the gap that retiring from football had left in my life. It saw my businesses temporarily close. There were no football teams to coach. It was a global crisis whose effects were felt in the most parochial of ways. Like many, I was left with a lot of time to think. A lot of time to reflect.

So, I started journalling as a way of documenting as many of the lessons I learned from playing football for Mayo as I could remember. The original purpose was to provide me with a black book I could reference as I began my own coaching career.

What did I learn from Johno?
What made Cillian so great?
What could I have done differently?
Why didn't we win?

Some parts were easier to remember than others, some questions harder to answer. The motivation for the reflection was the realisation that I was so privileged to be exposed to a lot of brilliant people trying to achieve extraordinary things. I feel my own dalliance with imposter syndrome. For so long this held me back in the sense that I often felt I didn't belong. However, it also acutely enhanced my ability to observe and learn from others. I'm inquisitive by nature. If I saw somebody doing something different, I wanted to know why and how it could help me.

I often wonder if I was a nuisance to managers and coaches – the annoying kid in the class always asking why. This was partly because I may not have been as naturally talented as many of my peers, so I had a greater need to understand the why of things.

That desire served me well. Whether reinventing myself as an inside forward or rehabilitating my body from successive injuries, wanting to know the mechanics of things provided me with a platform to figure things out. That platform may have been absent had the game come easier to me. It's one of the big reasons why I see a future for myself in coaching. If I can understand it, I can teach it.

★★★★★

This book was not written to ignore the fact I played in and lost so many finals during my career. If anything, it was written because of that: our run was a remarkable one. I was privileged to have played a role in many of those epic seasons and games. I take no joy in the losses, but I do take joy in being I part of something and contributing to a cause that meant so much to so many people around the county and the world. Each loss genuinely stung more than the previous, especially as an aging player when the realisation that the journey cannot continue forever becomes more and more apparent. There can be no denying, however, that there is something different about Mayo, especially the team of the last decade. Our ability to return time after time, setback after setback, proved to me that we are, in fact, made of different stuff.

Who knows? Had we won that All-Ireland in 2012, what would it have meant for the rest of the decade? You could argue 'who cares?', but had we won and gone away happy, there may have been no epic battles with Dublin, no memorable episodes with Kerry in Croker and Limerick. No crazy comebacks. To win just once, sure, but in not winning we wrote a story that may have been more memorable.

Mayo will win an All-Ireland. I am sure of that. What happens after will be just as important as the winning itself. We could get so consumed about the winning that we may ignore the follow-up. How do you tap into what we did since 2011 and replicate that resilience, that want to keep going, that pride of place and self? Our obsession with the curse and the famine and crossing the Shannon with Sam could see us gorge ourselves when we finally achieve it. How tolerable will we be to listen to? Will the humility on which we pride ourselves give way to a sudden obnoxiousness? Will we have the structures in place to continue to develop our youth and our coaches in the right way?

Is it the struggle that sustains us? Would we be just another county if the titles came slowly and steadily since 1951?

These are unanswerable questions, but still ones I contemplated when writing the book.

What is indisputable is that the foundations of football within the county need to be solid for future generations, regardless of whether we win Sam once or 30 times. Short-sightedness will only result in an erosion of whatever it is that makes us so special. Legacy protection by players, coaches and officials does nothing but stymie progress. The brand of Mayo football is an attractive one to be associated with for all the reasons spelled out in this book. It is imperative that all of us keep sight of what is most important when we seek to be involved. Winning an All-Ireland is not the be-all and end-all of everything.

★★★★★

As Stephen Cluxton kicked the winning free of the 2011 All-Ireland final against Kerry, there were few if any commentators predicting the dominance that was to define a decade. Dublin have arguably become the greatest football team in history. Their application and ethos would be the envy of any professional outfit never mind an amateur intercounty team. Undoubtedly, funding from the GAA has created an imbalance that needs to be redressed. As a player I never fixated on that as there was nothing we could do about it as a team. The only focus was the game. The only place you could beat them was on the field. Now that I'm done, I have a different perspective on the Dublin machine. Like any small business looking at a bigger and more successful competitor my intuition is to look and learn. What are they doing that we are not? Is it culture? Is it training and development? Is it coaching? Is it skills?

Are we studying the Dublin model to see what we can learn? We don't need to copy, but we do need to be informed. Have we exhausted all avenues to ensure we are maximising the goodwill of Mayo supporters in terms of marketing and promotion of the game? Are we trying to

develop a style of play which relies on us producing footballers as opposed to following trends which may prioritise
athletes over artists?

The danger with Mayo is we fall into a trap of shrugging
our shoulders, saying 'we are Mayo' and assuming we will
then find a way. It can't be let happen like that. What we
have achieved this last decade should be the catalyst for the
next generation to emerge and inspire, but nothing is guaranteed. That's why it is imperative that we plan now for the
rainy day even as we are one of the top counties in Gaelic
football.

There is enormous goodwill towards Mayo football. People at home and abroad wear their association with us as a
badge of honour. That goodwill is precious and is not just
predicated on results but in doing things the right way. We
should all do whatever it takes to keep the county where it
belongs – at the top table of Gaelic football.

★★★★★

It's all about the kids. Clubs, schools and families have
all played a phenomenal part in the development of our
youth. The simple act of bringing kids to games is so often
the start of a love affair that will last a lifetime. The GAA
pitch needs to be a safe place. A place where kids can go
and play and watch their heroes. We need to show children
the game, encourage them to imitate the characteristics of
their heroes, make the sport a joyful experience and be
their support when they need it. Positive role models can
play such a powerful part in our children's lives and those
role models are not just the players but volunteers whose
efforts are a study in what it means to be a leader in a community. Far from the lights of Croke Park, these women
and men work tirelessly, not seeking limelight or glory. They
do their work in darkness. Without them, there would be
no bright lights for our kids or our adult stars.

It was for them, too, that I wrote this book. So much
about what we read about Mayo is contributed by outsiders,
undoubtedly in good faith, but too often it concentrates on
the misery of our losing. Why is that? We win far more than

we lose. We often do so in a fashion that is admirable and an example to others. I wanted this book to be an homage to every player, volunteer and supporter who has contributed to that journey. For me, it's been a glorious ride.

The people I write about in this book are only some of the many who have helped me and are themselves products of families, clubs, schools and communities for whom Mayo football is almost everything. If you're reading this book, you're likely one of them. I want to say thanks to each and every one of you.

★★★★★

Our day will come, but the journey will go on forever. Will there be more pain along the way? I am sure of it.

Would I do it all again? I hope you knew the answer after reading the first page of the book. Let us always remember that we all want the same thing. We are in this together.

ACKNOWLEDGEMENTS

My family life, my career with Mayo and my work would all look incredibly different if it wasn't for the great people I have encountered along my journey. One of the motives for writing this book was to allow myself a platform for saying thanks to all those who played a part in positively influencing my life. It's said it takes a village to raise a child, in my case I feel it took an entire county.

My wife Jennifer and our two wonderful children, Charlotte and Ollie, have given everything in my life a deeper meaning. They have allowed me space to do the things I love, while always giving the support needed when things may not go as well as expected. I am truly in awe of the patience they have shown me throughout this footballing odyssey. As a father and husband, all I can do is promise to repay it.

My family, in particular my mother Philomena and my late father Vincent provided me with such a wonderful childhood. I was blessed to grow up having such exemplary role models. Their sacrifice allowed me to pursue my dreams from an early age. What is true of them is also true for so many other families in our community who drove my friends and me all around the country to play football as kids. When it came to support, we wanted for nothing. Noel and Marguerite Drake, who later became my father and mother-in-law, deserve special mention in this regard.

I will be forever indebted, too, to my club Ballaghaderreen GAA, and all the coaches who helped me along the way. What a journey it has been from my first day kicking a ball. The happiest days of my life were spent on that pitch. I hope I can give back to the club even a fraction of the joy it gave me. It is truly an exceptional place, and I look forward to the future together.

Playing football at the highest level is a selfish endeavour. For many years my friends tolerated my absence from some very special moments. I never took their understanding for granted. I am extremely grateful to have such a unique group who have been with me every step of the way. Their loyalty and honesty is something I will forever cherish.

So much of what made playing for Mayo so memorable to me was the supporters. The relationship between our players and those on the other side of the wire is a special one. I understand that your patience has been tested many, many times. I hope, too, that we, the players, have provided our fans with moments that will outlast any victory or defeat. Mayo is a unique place, and I always felt our players and supporters brought the best out of each other. Long may it continue.

To all the players I had the privilege to call teammates, I can only hope this book appropriately captures so much of what we went through together. I learned so much from each and every one of you. My senior career with Mayo ran from 2003 to 2019. I couldn't mention everyone in this book, but I feel truly blessed to have met so many great people and their families. Players, management, support teams – all of these characters contributed to the dressing room being such a happy place for me.

A special mention of thanks must go to David Drake and Evan Regan. David is a friend, clubmate and brother-in-law. David is a terrific footballer and my right-hand man. We did everything together during our time with Mayo. We shared everything, from the silent emotions following team selection on car journeys to the joy around famous victories. It was a magical time for me, and he was a huge part of that. We have stories to last us a lifetime, and it was special to share that with someone who is so close to me.

Evan joined the panel in 2012. We shared great times in the dressing room but it was when we both left the team at the end of the 2019 season that we helped each other through what is a difficult time for any sportsperson. Sharing memories and stories helped me bridge that gap from player to spectator. Hidden in the journey of playing a team sport is the creation of great friendships and loyalty. As I transitioned from playing, Evan was always there to listen. I hope I provided as much help to him.

Finally, this book would never have been completed without the dedication and talent of Colin. We forged a great relationship throughout our collaboration. Our shared passion for Mayo and football made this a joyful and therapeutic experience. Suffice to say, he got me. I thank Colin for his patience and friendship throughout this process; it was one I will remember forever.

– **Andy**